HOMES
OF
CRICKET

Picture Credits

All pictures are supplied by *Patrick Eagar* with the following exceptions:

All Sport/Adrian Murrell: 70-71
Basingstoke and North Hampshire C.C.: 93
BBC Hulton Picture Library: 137, 145, 180-81, 183, 193, 217
David Frith: 78-9, 107, 178
Hampshire C.C.C.: 80
Harrogate C.C.: 179
taken from *Homes of Sport: Cricket* by N. Yardley and J. Kilburn: 150-51, 157
Illustrated London News: 12, 21, 30, 72, 73, 91, 98-9, 164B, 177, 180
Ken Kelly: 139, 144
Kent C.C.C.: 45, 46-7, 54-5
Lancashire C.C.C.: 166-7
Luton Museum and Art Gallery: 212
Lytham Cricket and Sports Club: 170
MCC: 16
Photosource: 18-9, 22, 32-3, 117, 162-3T, 172, 173T, 184-5
George Plumptre: 90, 92, 101B, 123, 168
Bill Smith: 28-9, 41, 60-1, 109, 114-5, 124-5, 141, 142, 148, 199, 210L, 210-11, 216
E.E. Snow: 200-201
Somerset Cricket Museum: 103R
Southport and Birkdale C.C.: 169
Sport and General Press Agency: 10-11, 13, 34-5, 48-9, 113
Sussex C.C.C.: 64L, 64-5, 68
John Watson: 203
Victor Hopkins/*Western Mail:* 120-1
Worksop Cricket and Sports Club: 191

HOMES OF CRICKET

The First-Class Grounds of England and Wales

GEORGE PLUMPTRE
Consultant Editor: E.W. Swanton

Macdonald
Queen Anne Press

A *Queen Anne Press* BOOK.
© George Plumptre 1988
First published in Great Britain in 1988 by
Queen Anne Press, a division of
Macdonald & Co (Publishers) Ltd
3rd Floor
Greater London House
Hampstead Road
London
NW1 7QX

A member of Maxwell Pergamon Publishing
Corporation plc

British Library Cataloguing in Publication Data
Plumptre, George
    Homes of cricket: the first-class
    grounds of England.
    1. England. Cricket grounds
    I. Title
    796.35′8′06842

    ISBN 0-356-15671-0

Typeset by Butler and Tanner Limited, Frome
Reproduced, Printed and bound in Great Britain
by Hazell, Watson & Viney Ltd,
Member of BPCC plc, Aylesbury, Bucks

CONTENTS

Acknowledgements

Firstly, I must thank Jim Swanton, the book's Consultant Editor, for his advice and many personal memories about different grounds and Patrick Eagar, who took the great majority of the book's contemporary photographs. In addition I was given invaluable help about their own counties by the secretaries or managers at the seventeen first-class headquarters.

I also received help and advice from the following other people who, for simplicity's sake, I have listed alphabetically:

Colin Adamson, Brian Bearshaw, Alec Bedser, Caroline Fardell, Rose Fitzgibbon, Andrew Hignell, Derek Hodgson, Malcolm Lorimer, Mike Marshall, Tony Mitchener, Tom Osborn, Frank Peach, Bryan Perkins, Peter Quinn, Andrew Radd, Eric Snow, Richard Streeton, Colin Wiggans, John Woodcock and Peter Wynne-Thomas.

Finally I must thank Alan Samson and Richard Beswick of Queen Anne Press and my agent Vivienne Schuster.

INTRODUCTION

In retrospect 1987 was not perhaps the best of summers to embark upon a comprehensive tour of England's county grounds. Even by the standards we have got used to it was wet – very wet. On more occasions than I care to mention the covers were on as I arrived – sometimes temporarily, but as often as not for the rest of the day. The most uneconomic day was when I drove three and a half hours each way to Cheltenham for fifteen minutes' cricket.

Nonetheless, despite trying its best the weather by no means ruined the summer. Cricket has got used to its vagaries and as in most seasons, it was remarkable that so many hours of play were achieved. I say achieved, rather than just happened, for as I discovered no grounds are self-sufficient – far from it, they demand hours of attention throughout the year. Without doubt the groundsmen are the unsung heroes of English cricket.

In 1987 county championship matches were played on 54 grounds, to which I have added those of Oxford and Cambridge. They are a fascinating cross-section, ranging from the enormous, permanent Test Match centres to a large number of club grounds whose fixtures for a county visit look extremely temporary and which go 'en fête' for three days of the year. Large or small, however, they share the same commitment to staging the game – for players and spectators alike – to the best of their ability.

This is one of the most dramatic ways in which the grounds have changed in recent years – or, more accurately, since the 1960s. The post-war era saw a surge in cricket crowds, as many other sports enjoyed as well, and, for instance, Bradman's 1948 Australians played up and down the country on grounds bursting at the seams with spectators. By the early 1960s this support was fading fast; television, a more affluent society, changing interests – and many other factors – all had an influence.

The message to county cricket was that the crowds who were once prepared to turn up in their thousands for a three-day game, probably stand on open terraces, and enjoy a cheese sandwich and pint of bitter, or cup of tea as the extent of the refreshments offered, were no longer turning up. At the same time the other half of a frightening cleft-stick was developing; as support was waning so the staging of cricket and maintenance and management of grounds were getting rapidly more expensive.

So cricket entered the commercial age and county clubs started attracting a new kind of support; companies who would pay for a boundary advertising board, take an executive box for a day – or a season – pay to have their logo on the players' clothes, or hold meetings or conferences in a suitable room on the ground out of season. Membership of county clubs and the revenue it produces have remained as important as ever, with most counties offering a varied package of options to attract companies as well as private individuals. What has decreased in importance is the revenue from gate-money, as is shown by the random example of Edgbaston where, in 1986, out of Warwickshire's total income from cricket of over £500,000 (including the contribution from the TCCB), the income from gate-money for county championship matches was less than £10,000.

Now virtually all of the seventeen county headquarters boast some sort of commercial entertainment facilities, at some you are able to hold the reception after your daughter's marriage, in and out of season. Lesser ones import marquees booked by local companies. At the same time the average spectator has got more demanding so more general improvements in what is on offer during a day's cricket have had to be made. As a result the appearance of many grounds has changed in the last few years, with in some cases whole new buildings being erected, in others a less ambitious face-lift being carried out. Since the late-1970s the appearance of eleven county headquarters has been radically altered by the addition of a substantial new building on the boundary.

If the look of the grounds has changed so too has the way they are managed. What has not changed is their commitment to cricket and the manner in which they reflect the game's changing character up and down the country. This is why I have arranged the grounds in the pattern of a journey a visitor might take: starting in London, moving out to the home counties, along the south coast to the south-west, over the border into Wales, up through the west midlands to the north of England and back down to end up in the two University cities.

The grounds, and their surroundings, also reflect the different character of England's counties to a degree which I did not expect. A cricket ground in Glamorgan is a world apart from one in Kent or Lancashire, and it is this which gives the grounds some of their flavour. Even the local companies whose names are proclaimed on boundary boards give an idea about what goes on in a certain part of the country. This is reassuring, for it means that while the county clubs have had to adapt their grounds to attract a new kind of support and face the fact that crowds for county championship matches today are often numbered in hundreds rather than thousands, they have not done so in such a way that has made their grounds depressingly uniform. Far from it, they all have some idiosyncrasy or some particularly individual feature and even those who have only staged county games for a few years have usually witnessed a match which was memorable in some way or other. This is what, in their various descriptions, I have attempted to show.

MIDDLESEX

LORD'S

It is inevitable that a book on the county cricket grounds, which does not arrange itself alphabetically, should either begin or end at Lord's. Cricket may have been played in the southern counties before the foundation of MCC in 1787, but from the day that the Yorkshireman Thomas Lord moved his turf for the second time and, in 1815, the first match was played on the third and last ground to bear his name, Lord's rapidly became the undisputed centre of the organized game: so it has remained ever since.

The history of Lord's and the personalities who dominate it are as well-known to members of MCC and cricket enthusiasts as the stories from the Bible. For some they are more important. The decades of the nineteenth century saw MCC rise steadily and confidently in the style of the best Victorian success stories to a position of unchallenged supremacy in the cricket world. By the time they celebrated their centenary they ran it.

Highlights among the way were the staging at Lord's of leading annual fixtures: Gents v Players (first played in 1806), the University Match (first played in 1827) and Eton v Harrow (first played in 1805), all of which gave Lord's social as well as cricketing importance; the decision by Middlesex in the 1870s to accept MCC's offer for them to play their county matches at Lord's and, in 1884, the first Test Match on the ground.

The mixture of entrepreneurial spirit and enthusiasm for cricket which Thomas Lord demonstrated in most of his activities was continued by his successors. In the end the former got the better of Lord and his attempt to sell the ground's perimeter land for building was only forestalled by William Ward buying his lease for £5,000. Ward was a cricketer and banker whose respective skills enabled him to score 278 in 1820 – for many years the record score on the ground – and organize building a new pavilion after the original one was burnt down in 1825. He handed over the lease to James Dark and the partnership of Dark as proprietor and Benjamin Aislabie as Secretary of MCC brought healthy times to Lord's.

Thereafter the fortunes of the ground were more and more in the hands of the MCC men and it has been the outstanding officers of the club who have been responsible for its progress and development. If many of the Presidents were little more than aristocratic figureheads the Secretaries and Treasurers have been very different characters. Of the former group R. A. Fitzgerald achieved a decisive step towards entrenchment when, during his period of office from 1863–76 the freehold of the ground was secured by MCC. His successor, Henry Perkins, 'fierce as a bantam-cock' according to one contemporary, was in office when the ground of the Nursery End was secured at the end of the 1880s.

Among the Treasurers, the augustly named Sir Spencer Ponsonby-Fane, who held office from 1879 until 1915, initiated a line of considerable cricketing distinction: Lord Harris, Lord Hawke, Viscount Cobham (the ninth), H. S. Altham, Viscount Cobham (the tenth), G. O. Allen, J. G. W. Davies, D. G. Clark and, currently, G. H. G. Doggart.

Dry history and eminent MCC persons should not, however, distract us from Lord's 'bricks and mortar'. Although it may appear banal to say so, what sets Lord's apart is its sense of place as somewhere far more significant than just a cricket ground. Len Bates, the Warwickshire professional who was born in the Edgbaston pavilion, said about Lord's, 'That place breathes cricket – I daresay the pigeons lay eggs with seams on them'.

It is this overpowering sense of cricket and of the ethos of the game which does not fail to impress even the most casual observer. As for the visitor to an empty cathedral, when he is left alone to the lofty architecture and the tombs of great men, Lord's is somewhere to visit when no cricket is being played. At one level, the visitor is likely to see the various ground officials at their most friendly, unbothered by members of MCC who wish that the place was their exclusive domain and members of the public who wish that they were members of MCC. At another he is able to appreciate the permanence of Lord's and its buildings. Ever since the present pavilion was first built, in a matter of eight months between September 1889 and the MCC's annual dinner on the first Wednesday of May in 1890, the face of Lord's has changed continually.

The Lord's pavilion is the only cricket building which, inside and out, has the presence of a great house. Quite deservedly it is a listed building. The architect, F. T. Verity was a man of his times and the building's rich colour and bold, symmetrical facade is as assured a statement of Victorian confidence as a Brunel viaduct. At the same time it is given necessary liveliness by its decorations – from the various balcony balustrades to the MCC motifs which surmount the twin turrets. Inside the impression of size is, if anything, greater, the quantity of rooms on various floors and broad staircase all leading to the great Long Room.

Everywhere you go in the Lord's pavilion there are paintings, drawings and other items – all celebrating or recording the game of cricket. In recent years Lord's role as custodian of the game's heritage has grown steadily more relevant and important – some people would say, in direct relation to the decline of MCC's active power over the game. The ground now houses an unrivalled collection of cricket paintings and other works of art. Many are on display in the pavilion while others fill the Memorial Gallery just behind, opened by the Duke of Edinburgh in 1953. Adjoining here is the new Library, opened in 1985. Also in this building behind the pavilion, old traditions are perpetuated in the squash and real tennis courts.

The pavilion is the oldest of Lord's present buildings, but virtually all of the others have replaced older ones – in some cases there have been a succession on the site. The various changes have often been commented upon – politely or otherwise – as in correspondence between Rupert Hart-Davis and George Lyttelton in 1957.

[Hart-Davis] We didn't see the finish of the Lord's match, for we were only there on the Monday, but the sun shone incessantly, we saw Graveney bat and Trueman bowl, and Adam loved it all. To my horror I found that my favourite stand, the low white one between the Press Box and the Grandstand, has been removed, the Green Mound behind it levelled, and the whole space given over to concrete and a huge hideous two-tier cantilever stand, which clearly won't be ready this year ... Of the Lord's of my boyhood only the Pavilion, the Tavern and the Mound Stand remain.

[Lyttelton] I saw the beginning of that stand at Lord's months ago, and augured the worst. It should impress you to know that *my* Lord's memories go

back to *before* the Mound Stand ... The first Eton v Harrow I saw was from a box above the Grandstand in 1895; a waiter had an apoplectic fit just outside.

The north side of the ground is taken up with the Grandstand which replaced the one visited by George Lyttelton, built in the 1920s by Sir Herbert Baker, better

known for his imperial architecture, who also made the surprise presentation of Father Time.

Between Grandstand and pavilion is the object of Hart-Davis's dislike, the Warner Stand, opened in 1958 and named after 'Plum' Warner. As well as his deeds as a player for England and work as an officer of MCC, Warner played for Middlesex for over twenty years, from 1894–1920, for many of them as captain, and in

his final season helped them win the Championship at Lord's when he was chaired off the field by the exultant crowd amid scenes of near-hysteria.

The far end from the pavilion, the Nursery End is now the only part of the ground where the upper tiers

Spectators in the Long Room during the England v Australia 'Victory' Test, 1945

of seating, which curve round from either side, are uncovered. Next, in the corner opposite the Warner Stand, is the latest addition to Lord's, the new Mound Stand, opened in 1987. Its decorative skyline has greatly enlivened this part of the ground as well as performing the useful job of shutting out a large part of the dull-looking blocks of flats and hotel behind.

Stretching on round the rest of the south side is the new Tavern Stand. When the old tavern was done away with in 1967 many MCC members created a rumpus – as only they know how – but the authorities got their way, the tavern was moved to its present position and the new stand built, complete with executive suites – of which Lord's now boasts an impressive number here, in the Grandstand and Mound Stand. The small gap between the Tavern Stand and pavilion is filled by the pre-war 'Q' Stand.

Sir Herbert Baker appears to have had something of a monopoly on inter-war construction at Lord's; as well as the Grandstand he designed not only the 'Q' Stand but also one of the ground's most familiar features, the Grace Gates, which were put up in 1923. Opening onto St John's Wood Road, the Grace Gates are one of the many additions to Lord's away from the scene of play which so enrich the ground. Behind the pavilion is the

Harris Memorial Garden, also opened between the wars in memory of the fourth Lord Harris, pillar of MCC and English cricket in general for something like half a century. Beyond the Mound Stand at the Nursery End is the Indoor School, opened in 1977.

Such has been Lord's importance and prestige as home of MCC and scene of Tests and other leading matches, that its resident county, Middlesex, have often appeared little more than poor relations, tenants who are tolerated rather than embraced. These days it is rare that the county benefits from one of the capacity crowds which attend the great occasions and if anything, the attendances at Lord's for their round of championship matches are smaller than at many other county grounds.

Over the years, however, Middlesex have produced many of the players who have given more pleasure at Lord's than any others – not least the two famous batting partnerships of J. W. Hearne and Patsy Hendren, and Bill Edrich and Denis Compton. Hearne and Hendren, who both joined the Lord's groundstaff as teenagers, played for Middlesex from before the First World War until just short of the Second and during that time they scored tens of thousands of runs at Lord's. Only Jack Hobbs and Frank Woolley scored more runs than Patsy Hendren, while 'Young Jack' Hearne also

found time to take 2,000 wickets. Compton and Edrich batting together during the immediate post-war years was one of the great crowd-pulling highlights of cricket history. Although they played regularly for England it was for Middlesex and at Lord's that they amassed the great quantity of their runs, which, in 1947, gave them their record aggregates for a season of 3,816 and 3,539 respectively.

Other than 'Plum' Warner the Middlesex man who has contributed most to Lord's as player, administrator and supporter is 'Gubby' Allen. Like Warner he has been knighted for his services to cricket. He created a unique association with the ground as a player in 1929 when he became the first – and only – bowler to take all the wickets in an innings in a county match at Lord's, with 10 for 40 against Lancashire. Since then his involvement with the place has been unceasing – indeed, he almost lives there as his house in Grove End Road backs onto the Harris Garden and he has the unique privilege of a private garden gate into the ground.

1987 was eagerly anticipated by MCC and all at Lord's as one of the historic milestones in the ground's

history, for it marked the bicentenary of the club. For most of the year, however, the celebrations seemed doomed. Things got off to a bad start when MCC's Secretary, Jack Bailey resigned and in sympathy with him, the Treasurer David Clark also departed – all in a storm over MCC's control at Lord's and the powers of the TCCB.

This started up a hue and cry among the volatile MCC members – always highly sensitive, often to the point of suspicion, about their 'rights' – which rumbled on for months. Things got worse: the huge marquee erected for the Bicentenary Ball blew down just before the event; the Mound Stand was not ready on time and was still swarming with workmen on the day of the official 'opening' by Prince Philip; and the MCC President, Colin Cowdrey ended up in hospital in the middle of the summer for a major operation.

The cloud which overhung the club through the summer was substantially dispersed at the end of July when a vote of no confidence in the committee was rejected by a vote of 88% by the members. It was not, however, until the MCC's Bicentenary Match against a

Opposite *Geese cropping the wicket at Lord's in 1915*

Above *S. C. Griffith, then Secretary of MCC, personally demolishing the old Tavern Stand in 1967*

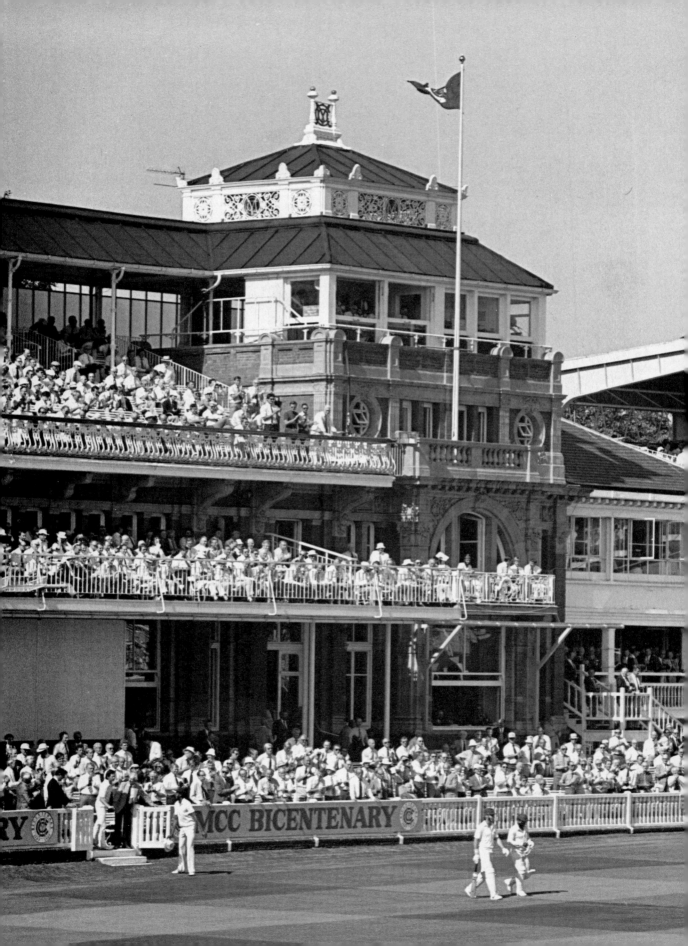

Rest of the World team in August, that a note of celebration truly emerged and the situation was redeemed at the eleventh hour. It was the sort of game which Lord's was designed to stage and for four days of blazing sunshine the players entertained as everyone hoped – but did not expect – that they would. On the fifth the weather asserted itself as it had done for most of the summer and the game was abandoned, but no one who attended or watched any of the four days of play could have been dissatisfied.

When I went on the first day the band of the Grenadier Guards played in the intervals, Gooch scored a hundred and all around was a festive atmosphere amongst the huge crowd such as is rarely experienced at a cricket match. At no other time has Lord's been more justified in its claim to be the home of cricket.

Opposite *A full pavilion for MCC's Bicentenary Match*

UXBRIDGE

When Middlesex visited Uxbridge to play Derbyshire, in 1980, it was only the third time since the Second World War that the county had ventured away from the hallowed turf of Lord's. That visit was through force of circumstance rather than choice, as Lord's was unavailable, being prepared for the Centenary Test.

From this tentative beginning Middlesex extended their visits to two games in 1981 and 1982 and, since 1983, there has developed an Uxbridge Week of two consecutive championship matches which, if it does not have a fixed place in the summer's calendar, has become a cricket occasion. Easily accessible just off the A40 Western Avenue the Uxbridge ground surprises a

Above *Uxbridge: Looking across the ground to the sports centre's club house and the cricket pavilion*

number of visitors with its rural appearance, thanks to the trees lining its south and west sides. As the ground enjoys an elevated position an impressive view extends in one direction over north-west London to Harrow on the Hill.

The ground is part of a sports complex which boasts tennis, bowls and a dry ski slope. The modern red-brick pavilion stands alongside a larger club house which, as well as its other facilities, has the dressing room for the visiting team, the pavilion itself housing Middlesex, although both sides use the balcony for watching the cricket. The ground is home to the Uxbridge club, who play in the Thames Valley league. It is maintained to an acknowledged high standard by Hillingdon borough council. From a player's point of view, one of the pleasures of visiting Uxbridge is the quality of the wicket.

When Middlesex visit temporary stands are erected and wooden seats brought in. In addition, a line of marquees are put up at one end, many of them taken by local companies whose sponsorship has been another bonus of the visits to Uxbridge.

The quality of the wickets and the ground's relatively small size often make for fast scoring at Uxbridge. In 1982 Leicestershire's Brian Davison cast a rare question-mark over Mike Brearley's captaincy when, taking advantage of Brearley's decision to put Leicestershire in, he scored a hundred before lunch. The year before, Mike Gatting made 169 – at the time the highest score of his career – against Surrey before taking the unusual step of running himself out off a no-ball.

The ground has by no means been a batsman's paradise, however, and on many occasions Middlesex's formidable spin attack has taken advantage of encouraging conditions. And in 1980 Middlesex's first visit was marked by Vincent van der Bijl taking 10 for 60 in the match, in a spell which typified the bowling which took him to the top of the national averages in his only full season in England.

Uxbridge is a pleasant interlude in the round of Middlesex's home matches at Lord's where playing in front of often only scattered spectators who make little impression upon the ground's great capacity can at times have a dampening effect upon both players' spirits and their performances. Like many smaller grounds it has carved a niche for itself through enterprise and good management.

An 18th-century view of Uxbridge

SURREY

THE OVAL

Writing about The Oval in the autumn of 1987 has an element of uncertainty. In recent years, not least as a result of the Bradford disaster, the need for renovation and modernization of much of the ground has become increasingly pressing. The first major stage was completed with the opening of the new buildings to the east of the pavilion in time for England's retention of the Ashes in 1985. This included nineteen hospitality boxes, an impressive dining-room and new seating. It cost £1 million.

Far more ambitious, however, was the plan to redevelop the old buildings to the west of the pavilion to include more boxes, new dressing-rooms for the players, bars and other catering facilities and, most importantly, an underground sports centre for the use of the local community as well as Surrey CCC, to be named after Ken Barrington. It is this which, at the time of writing, has come unstuck. With the help of Lambeth Council, the Sports Council, the Ken Barrington Trust and The Oval's landlords, the Duchy of Lancaster, Surrey have raised over £3 million of the £4½ million estimated total cost. But they are now faced with the strong possibility of the £1 million urban grant they were hoping for from the government being refused.

Fears about what this will mean were voiced by Raman Subba Row, chairman of Surrey's management.

Unless we can get a Government grant or an interest-free loan from another source, the development scheme is doomed and with it the future of cricket at The Oval. Parts of the ground, notably in the area of the West stand, are becoming derelict and outside the requirements of the safety regulations. Unless redevelopment takes place the Test and County Cricket Board will certainly withdraw Test status within two years and The Oval would cease to be viable as a County ground within three. This would mean Surrey becoming an itinerant club, playing perhaps at Guildford, Croydon, Woking and so on. Instead we envisaged a centre of sport and social amenity of tremendous value to the inner-city community.

To a certain extent this is the unpleasant reality of The Oval's long-standing dilemma: the fact that it is home of Surrey CCC and yet, in character and appearance firmly rooted in unprosperous South London, a world away from the security and prosperity of solicitor and stockbroker. In the past The Oval was the haunt of cockneys. Now it is still usually packed for Test Matches, a large proportion of the crowd coming from Kennington and neighbouring Brixton, but in 1986 less than 10,000 people paid to watch the county's twelve home county championship games. In the 1950s Surrey would have expected that many at each match.

There is little doubt that if The Oval had not been a Test Match ground, Surrey would have followed Essex's example and removed their headquarters out of London into the county's more representative heartland. The move has certainly been considered in the past. Lucky Middlesex have never had to worry about this, Lord's being primarily the responsibility of its owners, the MCC, not the county. But comparisons between The Oval and Lord's are quite meaningless and, anyway, in age and reputation, The Oval can more than hold its own as a Test Match ground, even if it comes second on grandeur and 'facilities'.

It is one of life's reassuring justices that while Lord's has always snatched the lion's share of prestige and accolade amongst the Test grounds, The Oval is the most senior by virtue of longevity. That is one of the corner-stones of its reputation. The second is the fact that, as a result of having traditionally been the stage for the final Test Match, ever since the first series in 1884, The Oval has witnessed matches decisive to the outcome of a Test Series no other Test ground can boast. Lord's may host its Test at the summer's sporting peak, around the same time as Royal Ascot, Wimbledon and the British Open. But it has never seen the Ashes decided.

One only has to think of the dates to conjure up the

Overleaf *Groundsmen at work on The Oval wicket in 1956*

years of England's triumphs in the Ashes at The Oval: 1926 and 1953 when, in both years their victories came after draws in all four preceding Tests and they regained the Ashes after fourteen and eighteen years respectively, and most recently, 1985. One should not forget 1902 when, although they lost the series, England won at The Oval one of the most thrilling Tests of all time. It was the occasion when Jessop scored a hundred in 85 minutes and Hirst and Rhodes scored the winning runs at the climax.

It was the members of the Montpelier Club, one of a number of enthusiastic Surrey clubs, who, threatened with the loss of their existing ground in 1845 took a lease on 'a Nursery and Garden ground in extent about ten acres, with buildings thereon, commonly known as The Oval'. Their landlords were the Duchy of Cornwall and in the same year the Montpelier members founded the Surrey club next door in the Horns tavern. Not long after, in 1854, the spectre of the developer who, to a greater or lesser degree, has threatened The Oval ever since such is the potential value of the site, reared his ugly head. Possible loss of the ground by Surrey was only averted by the intervention of the Prince Consort who was acting as self-appointed trustee for his youthful son the Prince of Wales, to whom the Duchy of Cornwall estates belonged.

Rather as at Lord's in its earliest days, The Oval was the scene of various attractions in attempts to extend the ground's appeal. More than one football cup final was staged and when, on one occasion, there was a suggestion for a greyhound track, *Punch* replied with a humorous protest, which needs little imagination to see W. G. Grace as the central figure. 'There was an Old Man with a beard/ Who said "I would never have feared/ That greyhounds would race/ In that sanctified place"/ And all right-minded cricketers cheered'.

Cricket survived and in 1880 The Oval pulled off its master-stroke, largely thanks to Surrey's energetic and imaginative secretary C. W. Alcock, when it staged the first Test Match against the visiting Australians. The Australians had already visited in 1878 and given English cricketers a warning by beating them at both Lord's and The Oval. No chances were taken for the first Test, limited only by the fact – according to one report – that a number of leading amateur players were already out of reach on the grouse moors, and as strong a side as possible was collected including three Graces, A. G. Steel, Hon. A. Lyttelton and Lord Harris as captain. W. G. led the way with 152 and England won by five wickets. It was Australia's victory on the ground two years later, in 1882, which inspired the saga of the Ashes.

Alcock's ingenuity was also intensely practical. After roughly 40,000 had attended the Test, he realized that improvements were urgently needed at The Oval. When he learnt that the authorities had decided to pipe underground the River Effra – one of London's many small rivers which used to follow its unhygienic course along the south side of The Oval – and needed somewhere to dump the huge amounts of spoil from their tunnel, he wasted no time in solving their problem by finding space for it at The Oval. Thereby the base of the ground's embankments was provided.

The successful negotiation of a new lease with the Duchy in 1896 was the cause for some celebration and as a result the present pavilion was built, replacing the old somewhat ramshackle affair which had just grown as further demands were made upon it. The tavern behind was built at the same time. The reputation of the recently completed pavilion at Old Trafford led the same architect to be employed at The Oval and there are obvious similarities in the two buildings: the twin turrets, the arrangement of the central block with ground floor, first floor with balcony, and upper section of tiered seating, the bold arched windows of the ground floor, and the side wings with their lesser roofs. The Oval lacks Old Trafford's copper lining to its domes, but has in return a far more satisfactorily positioned clock, in the centre of the roof rather than in one of the turrets. Both are eminently suitable pavilions for a Test Match ground.

Inside, The Oval pavilion is friendly and, since redecoration in the late-1970s, pretty spick-and-span. The main staircase is almost domestic compared to Lord's grand sweep and, with its 'Spy' cartoons could be in some cricket-lover's house, although one unfortunate member did plunge to his death after falling over the first-floor bannister. On the east side of the ground floor are offices and at the far end of the Long Room the members' writing room. Above the offices are the committee rooms and there is a direct passage to the 'banqueting facilities' in the Tavern behind.

Among the recent additions to The Oval is the Centenary Library opened in 1980 to mark the centenary of the first Test Match. In a rather incongruous fashion that is somehow typical of The Oval it is reached via one of the more scruffy areas of the pavilion's

Opposite top *The Oval's 19th-century pavilion from the back*

Opposite middle *The old pavilion being demolished in 1897*

Opposite bottom *The old pavilion interior*

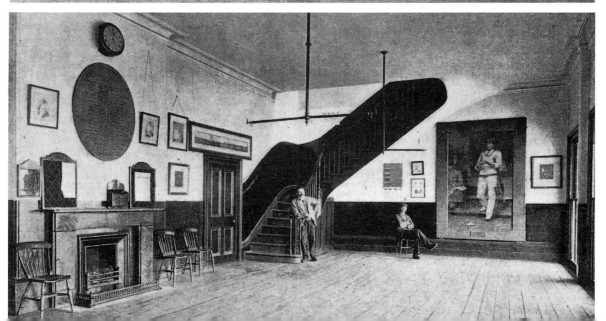

basements, but it is worth the journey. Modest in size, the books and other displays are presented quite immaculately.

Photographs abound in the members' bar but, quite rightly, the tone of the Long Room is retained by a series of portraits. I always respect somewhere with a proper portrait of Her Majesty and The Oval's, in pride of place over the central fireplace, is most elegant. At Lord's it is a measly photograph. Reassuringly around her are many of the people one would most wish to see at the headquarters of Surrey cricket, not least Jack Hobbs and Andrew Sandham.

Jack Hobbs's records speak for themselves, and descriptions of his gentlemanly character are legion. But I only realized to what extent he is revered at Surrey when being taken round the pavilion by Alec Bedser who was holding office as President of Surrey in 1987. When he joined the Surrey staff before the war the players had their quarters in the bottom of the pavilion where there are now physiotherapy rooms and the like. It did not bother them that conditions were overcrowded and primitive while upstairs probably one amateur had the solitary luxury of what is now the visiting team's dressing room. It was enough to know that one day he might walk out of the professional's gate at The Oval – as Jack Hobbs had done so many times.

For all professionals and, indeed most cricketers, Hobbs stood for everything they most admired and aspired to in the game. It is not surprising that when, in 1934, the new boundary wall was completed and the main entrance was adorned with a suitable pair of wrought-iron gates, unveiled by the President at the time, H. D. G. Leveson-Gower (himself a considerable figure in Surrey cricket), they were the Hobbs gates 'In honour of a Great Surrey and England Cricketer'.

Other than the pavilion and its buildings on either side, the only covered stands are at the far, Vauxhall Bridge end. In between wide open embankments sweep round, individual seats now where once much of the terracing was standing room only. Looking from the pavilion the ground is dominated by the group of gasholders beyond the north-east corner, as Kilburn and Yardley wrote, 'as famous in cricket scenery as the Worcester Cathedral, or the Canterbury tree, or even Father Time himself at Lord's'. Otherwise, tall blocks of London buildings line the curving roads which enclose the ground and give it – externally at least – its oval shape.

Opposite *The Hobbs Gates*

It is the gasholders which have given The Oval so much of its character in popular imagination, as a ground frequented by cheerful cockneys. It has never been either grand or intimidating and barracking has often been an indigenous feature. It is unlikely that a figure such as Albert Craig, 'the Surrey poet', would have been tolerated at Lord's. Craig, whose pretentions as a poet were definitely limited, was a familiar figure around the turn of the century, progressing round the ground with his odd assortment of scorecards, penny bags of sweets and hackneyed humour. In the sort of way that most Oval-lovers would approve, the ground usually gets its priorities right, like having the decent portrait of the Queen in the pavilion and, even though the public 'Gents' at the Vauxhall Bridge end leave much to be desired, I am reliably informed that the 'Ladies' adjacent to the pavilion end are unrivalled: palatial, spotless and comfortable, and on occasions decorated with flowers.

Surrey have enjoyed two great periods of dominance in the county championship; from the end of the 1880s until the turn of the century (nine victories in thirteen years) and the 1950s (seven consecutive victories). The first period belonged to the trilogy of fast bowlers, George Lohmann, Tom Richardson and Bill Lockwood and, foremost among the batsmen, Bobby Abel 'the Guv'nor', who, despite his diminutive size, scored 357 against Somerset at The Oval in 1899, when Surrey scored 811. Abel's score has only been beaten in county cricket by MacLaren's 424. In the 1950s it was the Bedser twins and Peter May, Laker, Lock and Loader, and Ken Barrington in his early years and the dynamic captain Stuart Surridge.

In between they have seen wonderful players and some great characters, but without the accompanying championship successes: Hayward, Hobbs and Sandham; Lord Dalmeny (later Earl of Rosebery) – not a great cricketer, but a good captain and most important to Surrey, for his influence with the Prince of Wales in 1905 which resulted in the club being able to adopt the badge of the Prince's feathers and 'I Serve' motto; Jardine, Fender and Holmes; Gover and Brown. In more recent years the stalwarts have been Edrich, Stewart, Pocock and Arnold – the last the club's present coach, while Stewart is the director of cricket.

Surrey's first period of supremacy also saw the beginnings of the reputation for run-scoring which dominated The Oval as a playing surface until the Second World War, when the ground's use as a prisoner-of-

Overleaf *England v Australia, 1985, in front of a full house at The Oval*

war camp and bomb damage made almost complete re-turfing inevitable. And it has seen run scoring such as no other English ground has experienced. In county cricket alone totals of 600 or more have been achieved on fifteen occasions (597 once, but near enough 600), and 120 individual double-hundreds have been scored. No other ground can boast anywhere near a hundred. Bobby Abel made nine 200s, and Hayward and Hobbs seven each.

This is no coincidence, for a succession of The Oval's groundsmen made it their dedicated task to prepare wickets that were as faultless for batting as any player could hope. The first was Sam Apted who served the club from 1887 until 1911. He was succeeded by Tom Martin, who in turn was succeeded in 1924 by the most famous of the three, his brother 'Bosser' Martin.

'Bosser' obviously knew his job for in 1935 he was called in by the Lord's authorities to deal with their plague of 'leather-jacket' beetles – or less colloquially *Tipula paludosa* – which he successfully did. But his vocation in life was the preparation of batting wickets at The Oval and for the Test of 1938 his ambitions achieved a somewhat ludicrous peak. With no limit to the game's duration, England scored 903 for seven, their innings dominated by Len Hutton batting for over thirteen hours to score 364. Bradman had to be helped off after he injured his ankle bowling, when he turned it over in the enormous hole dug by Bill O'Reilly and Hammond would only declare when he knew that Bradman would not be fit to bat. For 'Bosser' the game

was a disappointment because England had not scored 1,000 runs. His son became head-groundsman at Lord's.

Because of the war-damage to their ground Surrey could not celebrate their centenary until a year late, in 1946, by which time 40,000 new turves had been imported. They did so in the most nostalgic style, with a game against an 'Old England XI'. For one day a crowd of 15,000 including King George VI, were treated to a brief return by some of the great names from between the wars and earlier: Hobbs and Strudwick as umpires and a team of Holmes, Allom, Tate, Brooks, Sandham, Hendren, Jardine, Sutcliffe, Woolley, Knight and Freeman, captained by Fender.

Two years later another potentially nostalgic occasion was something of a personal anti-climax. Don

Bradman was given an uproarious reception by the crowd as he walked out from the pavilion to bat in his last Test in England in 1948, and then a round of three cheers from the England fielders as he arrived at the wicket. Only minutes later he was out second ball, bowled by Hollies.

Because of their local support, visits by the West Indies to The Oval in recent years have prompted some of the most ebullient and noisy scenes witnessed by the ground. And never have the trumpets blown louder, or the tin drums been beaten more incessantly than in

Guildford: Looking from the pavilion towards the marquees – a delightful county scene

1976, when the West Indies scored 687, I. V. A. Richards scored 291 to give him an aggregate of 829 in the series and M. A. Holding took 14 wickets. They were back again in 1984 to see their heroes inflict a five-nil series victory over England which had not been done since the series of 1920–21 in Australia.

This has been part of the changing face of The Oval which remains in character what it has always been, popular and certainly not posh. If it is no longer uncomfortable it is certainly not smart. It is intrinsically part of London's hubbub rather than an island of tranquillity as many urban cricket grounds are. And as Jim Kilburn commented, 'no cricketer plays at The Oval without a sense of place'. Without any question it deserves the stroke of generosity it appears to be presently in need of.

GUILDFORD

With The Oval as their headquarters Surrey have only ever played regularly elsewhere at Guildford, the county town – indeed, cathedral city. The first county game was in 1938 when the opponents were neighbouring Hampshire. The home team won by an innings and 71 runs and *Wisden* reported, 'The introduction of first-class cricket to the county town proved extremely popular and was a financial success'.

Financial success has usually been a hallmark of Surrey's visits to the city and a good reason for their continuation. Prosperous Guildford is a different story to inner-city south London. This is immediately evident in the car park behind the peppermint-green and white-striped marquees at the railway end of the ground. The array of large and expensive motor cars is frequently impressive.

For all this Guildford is an attractive ground, although not one of the quietest thanks to the continuous flow of traffic along one side – the main thoroughfare into the city centre from the A3 – and the more occasional clatter of trains across the red-brick bridge visible through a break in the trees at one end of the ground. Guildford is well screened by trees along this railway end and along the scoreboard side. Beyond here is Guildford's 'cathedral view' – though not quite in the Worcester class – however Guildford's relatively modern brick edifice looks rather monolithic set up on its hill.

At the opposite – city – end from the marquees is

A less familiar cathedral backdrop in evidence at Guildford

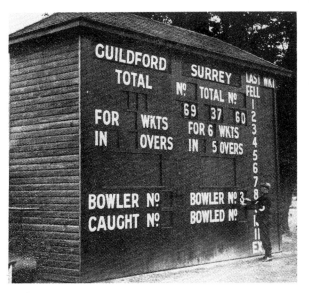

The old scoreboard at Guildford, built on the lines of the Sydney version and in its time as up to date as any

the pavilion, a modern building whose balcony affords a good view for the players, looking down the wicket. Set back from the ground on one side is Guildford's Roman Catholic church with its needle-like spire and just round the boundary on the opposite side is the refreshment marquee housing the public bar.

Along the busy road side of the ground is a row of rather elderly lime trees. On a sunny day they provide welcome shade for the wooden benches below – benches are the order of the day around most parts of the Guildford ground. There is little space between boundary and road, as there is on the far side, between the boundary and the trees, and Guildford's relatively small size has at times combined with an easy wicket to produce some impressive scoring.

In 1977 Gordon Greenidge scored 200 not out but Surrey managed nearly 300 in the fourth innings to win

quite comfortably. With Sussex, the second neighbouring county, Hampshire have been the most regular visitors. The following year Guildford witnessed its most mighty onslaught when Gloucestershire's Mike Procter rattled up 154, including eight sixes, in under two hours. In 1979 Surrey were given some unwelcome treatment by two erstwhile employees, Younis Ahmed scoring a hundred in his first season with Worcestershire after leaving Surrey and Jim Cumbes taking eight wickets to ensure Worcestershire's victory.

1982 saw the highest scoring match when between them, Surrey – who eventually won – and Glamorgan scored nearly 1400 runs. There were four individual hundreds as well as a number of other high scores and *Wisden* was moved to comment that, as well as Surrey's unfortunate captain, Roger Knight, finding that his car had taken a direct hit from one of the many sixes, 'several nearby houses lost some slates'.

Sussex were the visitors in 1987 and it was soon clear that the match drew a good deal of support from over the county boundary as well as for the home side. Jack Richards celebrated the occasion by claiming ten victims in the match. After a flurry of runs which gave him 56 in twenty minutes, Surrey's captain, Ian Greig, sent his old county in needing over 300 to win and had the satisfaction of bowling them out for less than 200 – largely thanks to some penetrating fast bowling by Tony Gray.

It would appear that Surrey's annual visit to Guildford has become a regular fixture in recent years. Even if it has not again been honoured with a visit from the Queen and the Duke of Edinburgh, as took place in 1957, when they met the Surrey and Hampshire sides, it is an enjoyable place to watch cricket, particularly on a sunny day, or if you are a guest of the Surrey committee, or one of the local companies who take the other marquees. If The Oval's uncertain future is not settled happily then Guildford will probably see considerably more of Surrey.

ESSEX

Chelmsford's weathervane

CHELMSFORD

In the old days it used to be said that, 'Essex is a flat county, bounded on one side by Southend pier and on the other by Johnny Douglas batting all day at Leyton'. This is no longer the case, for of the three first-class counties which extend into metropolitan London, Essex is the only one to have moved its base away from the city into the provinces. In the old days most of Essex was out on a limb in terms of the county circuit and it was logical that they should play predominantly in London, for convenience and to make the most of their support. Once this was no longer the case, Essex entered into a period of nomadic wandering between a series of grounds, none of which acted as headquarters, until finally in the mid-1960s they came to roost in the county town and Chelmsford became the county ground.

The county club had been founded at the Shire Hall in Chelmsford in 1876, but by the time first-class status was achieved in 1894 Essex cricket was firmly based in Leyton, at the ground bought from the Lyttelton estate for £12,000 in 1886. Here Essex remained until 1933, just one year after Holmes and Sutcliffe's record-breaking partnership of 555. The ground had been sold in 1922 and Essex continued as tenants for a further decade. Thereafter any number of grounds hosted county games, as Jim Kilburn eloquently described in *The World of Cricket* (1966): 'By ingenious improvisation and organization they transported not only players but also the trappings of presentation – scoreboard, printing-press, seating, secretarial offices and boundary boards. From seaside to inland centre, from public park to private club, the cavalcade moved down the lanes to the financial benefit of the county and for the wider spread of interest in the game.'

The continual wandering was not, however, quite as romantic as Kilburn suggests and it was a timely decision, not least for financial reasons, to make Chelmsford the county ground. One of the predominant features of modern county cricket has been the need for a secure headquarters where the necessary administration and financial organization can be carried out and which both players and members know to be the focus of the county's activities.

Today nearly a decade of breathtaking success has banished a century without victory in any competitions and Essex are riding high. It is to their credit that they have recovered from a state of impecuniousness so pressing that the pavilion at Chelmsford was only built thanks to the generosity of Warwickshire CCC who advanced an interest-free loan. The stream of victories – nine competitions in as many years since 1979 have given Essex the largest membership outside Yorkshire and Lancashire – 9,000 at the end of the 1987 season. Although it seems hardly possible for a county club, if the membership passes 9,500 it will be closed and a waiting list introduced, primarily because the seating at Chelmsford is only 7,000. Peter Edwards, the club's Secretary/Manager since 1979 has the confident air of a managing director whose company has consistently returned outstanding figures for the last few years. He has played a large part in the efficient management of the club's affairs. He is also the first person to acknowledge the enormous part played by Doug Insole, who appeared over 300 times for Essex, captaining them between 1950–60 and since his playing career a decisive influence on the club's fortunes.

If Chelmsford will never be a picturesque ground it is certainly one which caters for the modern game, with an atmosphere of confident prosperity. This mood is substantiated in real terms; since 1967 three-quarters of a million pounds have been spent on development. The pavilion itself was completed in 1970. The unremarkable wooden building, with a balcony for players and committee members, houses the dressing-rooms, club offices, and a long room and bar downstairs, all in more than adequate conditions.

Since 1970 the executive suite and Tom Pearce stand have been added and, behind the pavilion and press box, the indoor school, first used in 1977. Many old Essex hands feel it to have been no coincidence that two years later the breakthrough of a first title was achieved. Today the county is as watchful of its junior cricketers as any other – pointing to the home-grown talent which fills the current side. Although the day of the first female county cricketer may be a long way off, it is good that the county stresses that the indoor school is for boys and girls. In 1979 came the final symbolic break with the county's 'circus' days, when the impressive new scoreboard was erected on the city-centre side of the ground, ending the visits of the mobile scoreboard which had been such a well-known part of the Essex cavalcade.

For the visitor by car the best first view of the ground is from the roof of the multi-storey car park which lies across busy New Writtle Street and where it is advisable

to park – one of the few modern facilities Chelmsford is short of is space for cars. The bird's-eye view highlights the ground's small size – only Taunton and Southampton are smaller county grounds – and its uneven shape. It is perhaps because of its small size that one is always conscious of the noise of traffic and of the trains which pass frequently – admittedly at some distance from the pavilion end. The River Can flows along the New Writtle Street side, dividing the ground from the attractive lawns, flower beds and trees of Central Park next door. Beyond the pavilion and executive building are the floodlight towers and stands of Chelmsford City football ground, while overlooking the far left-hand corner of the ground is the grey-brick edifice of the County Hospital which has already been extensively run down and will shortly be sold off.

Access to the ground from here is at first boisterous as you pass through the flea-market in the bottom of the car park and thereafter can be distinctly confusing, as it is via a mini-labyrinth of paths leading under the

main road, over the river and – if you avoid branching off into the park or emerging mole-like on the pavement above – leads you eventually to the turnstiles at the River entrance.

Here one is greeted by what might surprise those visitors from outside the county who view Essex as dull and suburban – the extreme friendliness of the Chelmsford ground staff. Mention of researching a book on the county grounds drew me into immediate conversation filled with glowing references to the quality of Essex cricket and laughing requests for a mention, while the absence of my ticket was of no consequence and I was directed to the office of assistant-secretary Caroline Fardell, which was in the pavilion, with the welcoming introduction 'Caroline's a lovely girl – *and* she knows about cricket'.

Just inside the ground is the rather grandly named

River Restaurant and Britvic Picnic area, Britvic being a Chelmsford company and important supporter of county cricket. Altogether more imposing on this side of the ground is the new Tom Pearce stand, named after their former captain and president who has been as influential a figure as any in Essex cricket, and opened by the man himself in the spring of 1983.

Pearce played most of his cricket for Essex between the wars, when the county were able to draw upon – although, often not regularly enough – the talents of a number of spirited amateurs: not least the fast bowler Ken Farnes, killed on active service with the RAF in 1941 aged 30; Hubert Ashton – later Sir Hubert and MP for Chelmsford from 1950–64 – his brother Claude, like Farnes killed on active service with the RAF in 1942; and Leonard Crawley, one of a similarly gifted family of sportsmen.

Above *Essex players limbering up early in 1970, their pavilion under construction behind*

Overleaf *Leyton – with the Essex travelling scoreboard on the right – witnesses Essex v Pakistan, 1962*

Although only a minority of matches were played at Chelmsford at that time, Crawley was one of the main protagonists in a somewhat hysterical incident on the ground against Worcestershire in 1937, as is recorded in his *Wisden* obituary.

> The visiting captain, the Hon. C. J. Lyttelton, seeing him [Crawley] coming out to open and knowing that, given a chance, he would try to drive the first ball over the screen, instructed the bowler, Perks, to give him one slightly short of a length on the middle stump. Perks produced just the right ball and Crawley's bat struck it when its face was pointing straight upwards to the sky. The ball rose vertically to an astronomical height. A. P. Singleton in the gully put his hands in his pockets and said 'I'm not taking that'. Lyttelton looked round in desperation and finally said to Singleton, 'Sandy, you've got to take it', whereupon Singleton took his hands out of his pockets and held what in the circumstances was a fine catch.

Beyond the Pearce stand, as you progress towards the

Chelmsford, scene of many recent Essex successes, with the pavilion opposite and the Tom Pearce stand on the right

pavilion, is one of the smart blue-and-white striped entertainment marquees – taken by such firms as Hambro's Bank, for whom the journey from the City is an easy one – which, with the boxes of the Executive Suite, have been an important source of income for Essex in recent years.

In the pavilion most of the ground floor is taken up by the ubiquitous Long Room with, at the far end, a bar serving Tolly Cobbold, the local bitter. I quite agree with Tim Heald in his *The Character of Cricket* that the lights really do let the place down, even if they are in the club's colours but otherwise there is plenty of interest to browse through if you are not watching cricket through the tall windows: photographs, scorecards and a host of other cricketana.

A select handful of players are particularly prominent on the pavilion walls: Tom Pearce and Ken Farnes; A. C. 'Jack' Russell, the first man to score a century in each innings of a Test, which he did at Durban in 1923 and who died at Whipps Cross, a name that John Betjeman surely delighted in; M. S. 'Stan' Nichols who was, after Trevor Bailey, Essex's foremost all-rounder and who, in 1935, humiliated single-handed the great Yorkshire to defeat by an innings and 204 runs in a day and a half at Huddersfield, Nichols taking 11 for 54 in the match and scoring 146; P. A. Perrin, scorer of 343 in the lost cause at Chesterfield in 1904 and J. W. H. T.

Douglas, captain of Essex from 1911–28, cricketer, outstanding boxer and a pretty fair footballer, who once took an hour and a half to score eight runs and remarked about himself, 'An optimist is a man who batting with Johnny Douglas backs up for a run'. Douglas was drowned in 1930, trying to save his father after the steamship they were both travelling on collided with another in the Kattegatt Strait between Denmark and Sweden.

Most appealing, however, is Canon Frank Hay Gillingham, immortalized in an elegant 'Spy' cartoon, who was born in Tokyo in 1875 and died in Monte Carlo in 1953. He played his first cricket for Essex as a young curate in Leyton and *Wisden* wrote of him at this time, 'During this period he showed his love of the game when making his rounds of the parish by joining in street cricket with the local boys'. He went on to score 201 against Middlesex at Lord's and became Chaplain to King George VI.

Next to the pavilion is the press box, not one of Chelmsford's fortes as it is really a 'portakabin' but probably more comfortable than the tent they used to occupy on the far side of the ground next to the mobile scoreboard. Further on is the Executive Suite, marking the end of the members' enclosure which begins at the pavilion. Further round, on the far side of the ground, are more blue-and-white marquees.

On the day of my visit to Chelmsford for an early Benson and Hedges Cup match against Hampshire the rain had the best of things and the hosts and guests in the marquees and boxes accounted for the majority of the crowd. The stewards were more occupied answering questions such as 'where are Essex Computers?' than 'where can I find a scorecard?' One outfit that certainly drew some satisfaction from the conditions was Barclays Bank, for 'Barclays Bank covers Essex' was in evidence throughout most of the day, emblazoned across the covers in the middle. It was a day which revealed most clearly the importance of business entertainment and sponsorship and its increasing role in the modern county game; nowhere are they more conscious of it than at Chelmsford.

In the most subdued public areas of the ground the weather produced a mood of patient resignation rather than frustration. After the announcement of a 2 pm start – if there was no further rain – sandwiches were taken out for an early lunch, newspapers re-read or, as often as not crosswords done. It seems that the logical mind of a cricket buff who delights in facts and statistics is equally attracted to the challenges of crosswords. After a flurry of activity as 2 pm approached the crowd settled down, but not for long. There was time for a lively over from Foster and three balls from Page before the return of the rain and the players beat a hasty retreat

until late in the afternoon. The weather did little to dampen the spirits of the steward selling scorecards around the ground, whose calls of 'jolly old scorecards' could be heard from different points at regular intervals – at least until the abortive start. He also had time to give me his measured opinion of the transfer of the captaincy from Fletcher, who has been virtually deified in Chelmsford in recent years, to Gooch. 'Goochie's doing alright ... but he's not a Fletcher. Ah, Fletch, he was canny'. No doubt he was delighted by the announcement at the end of the 1987 season, that the veteran would return to the captaincy.

Certainly for the great majority of Essex members, if the players from the past have gilded reputations, it is these modern players who are the real heroes. Fletcher and Gooch, Ken McEwan, the South African who so delighted Chelmsford crowds for twelve seasons with his batting and who scored 218 there against Sussex in 1977 – one of only three double-hundreds ever scored at Chelmsford and the only one by an Essex man – and John Lever, the stalwart of the bowlers.

It is recent matches which are remembered, not least the Benson and Hedges Cup semi-final in 1979 when a crowd of 8,000 saw Essex beat Yorkshire and progress, at last, to their first final which they went on to win – the first trophy after 103 years and joined a few weeks later by the County Championship. In 1983 Surrey were skittled out for 14, the lowest score in the long and usually distinguished history of that county and later that year, the Championship was clinched during a match at the county ground, the only time it has been achieved at home in the four years Essex have won. When Surrey returned to Chelmsford in 1986 it was perhaps the thought of the ignominy of 1983 which led Surrey's captain, Pat Pocock, to cause a bit of a rumpus by storming into the press box on the first day and denouncing the wicket. If this was an isolated incident, it has often proved a difficult track to get a positive result on.

If the pace of development has slowed in recent years there is one outstanding project which would bring universal satisfaction, the improvement of the main entrance to the ground and its adornment with a suitably impressive set of gates. There will be no trouble paying for them as a sum was raised for them some years ago by the members and has probably been quietly earning interest in the meantime. Of course, the great dilemma will be the name. Originally it was to be the Members' Memorial Gates, but many feel something more personal to be better. Pearce has his stand, so who else: Douglas, Farnes, Insole, Bailey, Fletcher – it's a devilish choice.

COLCHESTER

When approaching a ground for a mid-week county championship day's cricket it is an encouraging sight that, half an hour before play is due to start, the spacious car park is nearly full and more vehicles are queuing along the road leading to the gates. This becomes not only encouraging but remarkable considering that the day I visited Colchester torrential overnight rain was followed by a dull, sultry day with a prospect of limited cricket, if any at all.

The above says a lot about Castle Park, Colchester where large crowds will turn out, but where the most susceptible of grounds to rain has all too often been plagued by bad weather. For a brief spell during the late-1960s and early-1970s the fixtures were moved to the town's second ground at the resident military garrison. The move was actually made in the middle of a match against Derbyshire in 1966, scheduled for Castle Park, when the first two days had been lost to rain and the last was played on the alternative ground. No doubt

the fact that Essex's secretary at the time, Major C. A. Brown, was a military man, had more than a little to do with the move.

In the end the county's move to the Garrison was short-lived and by the mid-1970s, after there had been no games at Colchester for a couple of years, the return to Castle Park was made, partly because attendances at the Garrison were disappointing and because the weather notwithstanding, Castle Park is the more attractive and better appointed of the two grounds. One visitor, Geoffrey Boycott, took full advantage of the temporary move to the military ground: in two consecutive years, 1970 and 1971 he scored 260 not out and 233.

A double-hundred in two successive visits is a rare achievement, but does not compare with the unique record which Arthur Fagg established in 1938. Playing for Kent at Castle Park, he scored 244 and 202 not out in the same match, the only instance in history of a batsman scoring a double-hundred in each innings.

Neville Cardus was obviously blessed with good weather on the visit to Castle Park which he recalled.

Lunch in a cool marquee was in itself enough to turn one back to schooldays; and there was veal and ham pie and ginger beer to wash it down, and an old lady with a kindly face asking you with a curtsy if you wanted any more.

On a fine day it is certainly an attractive setting for cricket. Along one side, behind the handsome modern pavilion which is set back from the boundary on one corner of the ground, the River Colne flows quietly past beneath weeping willows and footbridges giving access from the rest of the park on the far edge. On the opposite side of the main entrance from the pavilion the blue-and-white marquees, which are a distinctive sight at all Essex grounds, stretch along the boundary on the car park area of the ground, providing hospitality and enjoyment for sponsors and other companies whether there is cricket to watch or not.

Above *Looking across the ground to the pavilion of Castle Park, with the tower of the town hall in the distance*

The far side of the ground from the pavilion is lined by poplar trees and it is here, on one corner, that the famous navy-blue mobile scoreboard is drawn up. Further round is the public bar in a marquee – plain white and presumably not considered of sufficient status for the extra expense of blue-and-white – and returning towards the pavilion along the river side the rows of open, plastic seats are interrupted by a somewhat make-shift small stand, covered in with canvas.

The ground's draining problems derive from its proximity to the river and a high water-table. The flooding which used to occur has been dealt with but drainage is always poor and heavy rain almost immov-able. It is a disheartening sight to see groundsmen struggling against such odds to give the players and crowd some cricket.

What a shame it is that the weather has so often spoilt things at Castle Park for, now that the week's cricket is in August, good crowds of Essex supporters who have taken some holiday to watch their county and visiting holiday-makers are nearly always forthcoming. Also, since the county's return to the ground in 1975 their record has been formidable, with the great majority of the games there won and only a handful lost or drawn. No doubt the shrewd captaincy of Keith Fletcher on the occasions when play has been restricted by rain often played an important part.

Some of Essex's victories have been hard fought and none more so than that in the game against Glamorgan in 1981. After Glamorgan had established a first-innings lead this was soon demolished by hundreds from Essex's openers, Gooch and Hardie and a final score of 411 for nine declared. Glamorgan's reply to being set 325 in 323 minutes was dominated by one of the most exciting innings ever seen at Colchester from Javed Miandad, who scored 200 not out and only ran out of partners when his county were 14 runs short of victory.

No batsman can have enjoyed the Castle Park

Above *Castle Park, bounded on one side by the tree-lined River Colne*

Opposite *Southend, packed for a holiday fixture in the 1950s*

ground more than Ken McEwan, Essex's elegant and prolific South African. In four consecutive seasons, 1981–84, he scored five hundreds, reaching a peak in 1983 when he scored 181 against Gloucestershire and 189 against Worcestershire in the week. On both occasions Essex only needed to bat once.

Despite such deeds, the weather should – and does – have the last word at Castle Park and in 1975, during a match against Kent in the first week of June, it excelled itself as rain turned to snow and, as reported in the *Guardian,*

> The snow-flakes were so thick for a time that one correspondent reported he had lost his way between the pavilion and the press tent. The bar had not then been opened. By 3 pm the wicket, or was it the piste, was judged playable and by the end Kent had scored 132 for four off 58 overs in reply to the Essex total of 302. Nobody really complained when icy rain returned to cut off the final hour of play. All through, the conditions were so unpleasant that the luckiest fellows were those required to chase round the boundaries. The rest, whether batsmen or fielders, could only warm up by continual callisthenics.

SOUTHEND

There was a time when Essex used grounds at three of the county's seaside towns for county championship matches: Clacton, Westcliff and Southend. Today Southend is the only survivor and one hopes that it will continue to be used, for the connexion of Essex cricket with seaside resorts and holidays is a happy one.

Southchurch Park, which lies towards the eastern end of the town, set back from the sea front and promenade and surrounded by rows of typical seaside villas, is perhaps the most attractive ground on which the county play. The park's spaciousness, integral to the quality of the ground, is immediately recognizable from the fact that it has three cricket squares next to each other and room for two club games to be in progress at the same time. As a result, and most unusually, there are two pavilions. The central square is used exclusively by the county when they come in July, those on either side by two resident clubs. The pavilion used by the county is an elegant white wooden building with a central gable in its roof and a balcony supported by slender wooden pillars.

It is since 1977 that Southend has enjoyed its festival of two county championship matches and one Sunday league game in July. Up until then Chalkwell Park in neighbouring Westcliff had hosted the week and Southend had only been used occasionally. Owned and maintained by Southend council, the wicket is good and more often than not has produced a result – in roughly two-thirds of championship matches played there since 1977.

Whereas a number of counties regularly move from their headquarters to an outlying ground for one or two matches a season, Essex have spent part of their history 'on the road' and as a result are experts in the transportation of the necessary paraphernalia. During the cricket week the appearance of the park is transformed with tiered seating brought by the county and erected along one boundary and, on the other side, a row of marquees with the Mayor of Southend's prominent in the centre. On either side are sponsors and clubs. As well as loyal county supporters the crowds are always filled with holiday-makers, many of whom come to Southend every year for cricket week. The nearby boating lake is an ideal place for depositing children and ensuring parents a bit of peaceful spectating. The ground's size gives it a capacity of over 10,000 and on a fine day crowds of over 5,000 regularly attend the Sunday game.

Ken McEwan again features among the records at Southend for in 1977 he celebrated the return of Essex to Southchurch Park by joining the elite band of batsmen to score four hundreds in consecutive innings. His 106 not out against Gloucestershire followed a century in each innings against Warwickshire and 218 against Sussex, giving him an aggregate of 542 runs in ten days.

Some of the most memorable past games at Southend have been against visiting tourists – for many years Southchurch Park was the traditional ground used for these games, partly because of its size. In 1935 Essex was one of only two sides to beat the South Africans in the year the tourists won their first series in England. Not such a happy occasion for Essex supporters, but one which no one who was present will ever forget, was the visit of Bradman's Australians in 1948. On the first day the visitors ran up a total of 721 which remains the most runs scored in a day, Bradman himself contributing 187 not out in two hours and five minutes. The game had a number of intriguing sidelines. First, Keith Miller had wanted the match off as it was over the Whitsun holiday, but Bradman insisted that he play. When Miller came in to bat his captain had just put on 219 in 90 minutes with Brown, but far from the expected onslaught from the Australian all-rounder, in order to register his anger, Miller played no stroke to a straight ball and allowed Bailey to bowl him for nought. The match was over after two days, Essex being bowled out twice in a day and going down by the margin of an innings and 451 runs. Afterwards the Purchasers Club,

a charitable group whose invitations for membership were only extended to people who had performed some particularly funny or unusual feat, made Tom Pearce, the Essex captain, a member for being the only county captain whose side bowled out Australia in a day that year. How the counties today must long for the crowds of those times – 16,000 packed into Southchurch Park on both days.

It is unlikely that Southend will ever see such totals again – either of runs or spectators – but its relaxed, holiday atmosphere will remain the same, except when dampened by the weather. Certainly it was the atmosphere of the place which so endeared Southend to R.C. 'Crusoe' Robertson-Glasgow and one could do no better than finish with his picture of the ground, remembered from when he played for Somerset there in 1921.

I have a weakness for Southend, and in later years, when reporting cricket for the *Morning Post*, I never failed to impress on my employers the importance and brilliance of its Cricket Festival. In August, the homely smell of mankind in the streets was set off by the abundance of whelks, cockles, and stick-jaw rock. Rides were to be had on the miniature railway to the end of the pier and in mechanical boats on the lake below the Palace Hotel. Nowhere else have I

found such invigorating air; and morning brought no sense of lassitude or remorse to the nocturnal reveller.

The cricket ground was adorned at one end by a lake, on which prophetic ducks floated, and quacked as nervous batsmen made their way to the crease. Festooned around were private tents, whose occupants said and drank what they liked. One of them belonged to the Mayor, another to the Yachting Club. In both of these the hospitality was warm, and from the latter marine telescopes were sometimes directed on to the cricket.

ILFORD

The ground at Valentine's Park, Ilford is now the only metropolitan ground which Essex visit and the week in June, with two county championship matches and one Sunday game is usually guaranteed to attract good crowds. The park, extending to nearly 150 acres used to surround the stately home of a Mrs Ingleby and it was from her, in 1897, that the Ilford Cricket Club obtained a lease on eight acres to make a cricket ground. The condition was that the pavilion was built under the trees so as to be concealed from view, and a few years

Opposite above *Southchurch Park, large enough for two grounds, each with its own pavilion*

Above *The mobile scoreboard at Ilford, a legacy of Essex's wandering days.*

later Mrs Ingleby requested that the sightscreens be lowered as they were visible from her windows.

The cricket ground lies on the west side of the park, where the boundary is formed by Cavendish Road, running between Ilford main line station and the underground station of Gants Hill – which is really an east London suburb. Today the park is the property of Redbridge council who maintain it and they do a good job. It is a London park at its best, with gardens, tennis courts, four bowling greens, a boating lake and a bandstand. If the visit of the county is blessed by good weather applause around the ground will punctuate the more regular shouts and laughter of children playing and the regulars in the crowd, staying all day or even all week, are joined by the more itinerant spectator.

When the county arrive with all their trappings the surroundings of the cricket ground are transformed. On either side of the modest pavilion on one corner are marquees – some for sponsors – and temporary seating for the members' enclosure. More temporary seating is erected on the fixed terraces along the Cavendish Road side, and at the far end from the pavilion, where, with any luck, the large beds of roses will be in full flower. Beyond this end are both the bandstand and boating lake, strategically placed for the diversion of children.

The marquees in particular give the impression that Ilford is a small ground when dressed up for a county match, but this disguises the potential for large crowds. In 1986 roughly 8,000 attended on the Saturday of the week and 10,000 the next day for the Sunday league game. As it is the closest ground for Essex's London-based supporters, as well as being less than half an hour from Chelmsford (traffic permitting), this perhaps is not altogether surprising and should remain a powerful influence on whether the county club continue to make their annual excursions.

Essex's fixtures at Ilford have usually been confined to county games but, in 1972, Greg Chappell marked a rare visit by a touring team by scoring 181 – the best innings seen at Ilford in recent years. It obviously set him up, for a few days later he scored 131 for Australia in the Second Test at Lord's which combined with Massie's extraordinary performance of 16 wickets to assure his side victory.

The Ilford club can be justly proud of the contribution they have made to Essex cricket with the players they have supplied and at no time has this been more true than during Essex's recent string of successes: Graham Gooch, John Lever and Alan Lilley all graduated from Ilford, a record few clubs can rival. During Ilford week in 1978 Gooch and Lever, both already well-established Test players, gave their home crowds a feast of their talents. In the first match against Kent Gooch scored 108 in the only innings Essex needed and, in one spell of bowling, Lever took four wickets for six runs. In the second match, against Northamptonshire Gooch combined with Ken McEwan to establish a new second-wicket partnership record for the county, their score of 321 – Gooch 129, McEwan 186 – passing the old record of 294 set up by Avery and Gibb in 1952. Their effort was complemented by Lever taking 13 wickets in the match. Surprisingly enough, however, the veteran left-arm bowler has never produced anything for his home crowd like a spell by the batsman, Gooch, when he demolished Worcestershire in 1982, taking seven for 14 in 11 overs.

KENT

CANTERBURY

Canterbury in 1910, the pavilion and annexe as they are today.

Few people would dispute Kent's claim to have been the first cradle of organized cricket. The first three chapters of H.S. Altham's definitive *A History of Cricket* are entitled: 'Archaeological', 'The Early Game', and 'Kent, the First Champions'.

Therefore it is perhaps not surprising that prior to the official formation of the county club in 1870, Kent played on a total of forty-six grounds and that since then they have visited eighteen. Of these five still host county championship matches, but there have been some sad losses: Foxgrove Road, Beckenham; the Rectory Field, Blackheath; and the Private Banks, Catford Bridge in the suburbs of London, the Bat and Ball at Gravesend and the Angel at Tonbridge, and, most of all the Crabble Ground at Dover. The Crabble

had great character and individuality with its decorative pavilion perched beneath a steep chalk hillside where, for the energetic, an open plateau provided a bird's-eye view of proceedings. It was here in 1937 that four Kent batsmen – Ames, Woolley, Ashdown and Watt – made 271 runs in seventy-one minutes, the fastest piece of collective scoring on record.

Of the surviving quintet the jewel and headquarters remains, as it has always been, the St Lawrence ground at Canterbury. Geoffrey Moorhouse wrote in *The Best-Loved Game*, 'If I had to show a foreigner his first cricket match, I should ideally like it to be here, during Canterbury Week'. Coming from a Lancastrian that is praise indeed. For some people, like the oast-houses and orchards of 'the Garden of England' all around, it is

almost too much of a good thing; 'self-consciously pic-turesque', as one commentator ventured. I would prefer to agree with Moorhouse, if for the most partisan of reasons that I have lived in Kent all my life and watched cricket at Canterbury more times than on all other grounds put together.

County matches are played at Canterbury through-out the season and the tourists' match is traditionally held there. But the ground comes into its own for the first week of August – or thereabouts – for what has always been known as Canterbury Week. It is not a festival, and never has been since its foundation in 1842 – making it the oldest such occasion – and to stress this there is the 'Week' office in the back of one of the main buildings.

The outstanding feature of Canterbury Week is that it remains an occasion. This is partly because for all

sorts of people in Kent cricket is not only taken seriously but is part of their way of life and Canterbury Week is the opportunity to celebrate this. For the two county championship matches the crowds are as large as you will see anywhere; certainly when I went in 1987 there were more people than I saw at any other championship match that season. Unfortunately they were treated to some of the most dismal cricket most people could remember.

Such setbacks, however, are only minor dampeners. As well as the setting – which we shall come to – there is still a band who march around the outfield at lunch-time; there is still Ladies Day on Thursday and ladies still wear hats – proper ones, not the floppy varieties – and not only in the tents but all round the ground in the public seats.

The fact that Canterbury Week remains a social

occasion derives partly from its origins, which lie not only in cricket but also in the theatre. The tradition was established that cricket matches in the day would be followed by theatricals in the evening by a group of amateur performers called the Old Stagers. Nearly 150 years later the Old Stagers still perform during Canterbury Week. Some leading members of the group were among the first members of England's oldest wandering club, I Zingari, and thus an important connexion was established.

The ground lies on the south-east side of the city, an easy walk from the East station but quite a step from the West one. The main entrance is off the Old Dover Road, opposite the Bat and Ball pub, but ideally you should go round to the far side of the ground and come in from the Nackington Road. From here you should walk diagonally through the ranks of parked cars and end up on the left of the building in front of you. This is the best place for the first view of Canterbury.

Along to the left is open seating with a wide grass passageway behind and then an embankment – sought after by those who like to watch from their parked car or have it handy for a picnic lunch. At the end the main group of buildings curve round the far side. First is the most recent, the New Stand, opened by the club's patron the Duke of Kent – who usually attends one day of the Week – in 1986 and built at a cost of £600,000. The New Stand contains the shop and a public bar on the ground floor, with above a dining-room for members who also have the open seating in front. The top floor

Above *The ground in 1946 with the concrete stand built between the wars and later renamed the Woolley stand, beside the pavilion*

is the inevitably named Executive Suite, where a maximum of 200 privileged persons pay £200 per annum to enjoy the restaurant, armchairs and bar and one of the best views of play from the seats on the balcony outside.

Next is the ground's largest covered stand. Two-tiered, it was built in 1926–27 and first given the eponymous name of the Concrete Stand. In 1973 it was elevated and renamed the Frank Woolley stand after the county's greatest cricketer.

The pavilion commands a view down the wicket and, despite the necessary sightscreens which usually obscure most of its ground floor, remains among the most elegant on any county ground. Externally it has hardly changed since it was built in 1900. In 1970 the interior was rebuilt and it was renamed the Stuart Chiesman pavilion after the benefactor who made the renovation possible. The main Long Room with its bar at one end is now a veritable treasure-trove of Kent history, the walls lined with paintings, photographs and boards listing the various officers of the club. The painting by Chevallier-Taylor of Kent v Lancashire, 1906, confirms how little the pavilion has changed externally while, close to the bar, is Kent's greatest figure – Lord Harris – at the wicket, his bat raised and wearing the bow-tie and hat-band of the Band of Brothers. Captain of Kent from 1875–89, Lord Harris organized and dominated their development for half a century.

At the same time as the refurbishment, an extension was built, linking the pavilion to the neighbouring 'annexe', a two-storey covered stand built in 1909 in the same style as the pavilion. The new building in between contains the players' dressing-rooms and dining-room. In the dining-room the walls are lined with photographs of every player to have been capped for Kent since the 1880s, a remarkable collection, whose display like those in the pavilion and the gallery behind the annexe, is the work of Kent's joint-curators, E.W. Swanton and Chris Taylor. In those early years players had to appear in Canterbury Week to win their cap and the badges of the white horse were crocheted on by the captain's wife, Lady Harris.

Looking from the far side of the ground towards the pavilion and annexe the main tower of Canterbury Cathedral is visible above the players' building in between. Many an archbishop has visited the ground during Canterbury Week and a visit to the cathedral, if only to see the tomb of the Black Prince or the place of Thomas à Becket's murder, is compulsory.

The ground in the 1920s, with cars in what have become traditional places for parking and watching

Next to the annexe is the old scoreboard and from here open seats continue round the edge of the ground until they meet – during Canterbury Week at least – the sweep of white tents which carry on to the sightscreen at the Nackington Road end. It is the tents, with their bright flags and canvas chairs in front which complete the picture of Canterbury Week. Pride of place next to the sightscreen goes to the club's President for the year – his flag the county colours of the white horse on a maroon background. Next door is the grey and black of the Band of Brothers, the county's premier club and a driving force behind Kent cricket – especially in the early decades – who have I Zingari as visitors. In one tent the Old Stagers share quarters with the county regiment, formerly the Queen's Own Buffs, now sadly just the Queen's Regiment and, as one would expect, Canterbury's mayor has his own tent too. Most of the others are still used by clubs and cricketing bodies – rather than companies – as they have always been.

In front of the tents, a good few yards out onto the playing area, is the one feature of Canterbury most people have heard of – the tree. It is a lime and although most estimates of its age are fairly hazy it was almost certainly growing when cricket came to the St Lawrence ground and it is a peculiarity no other county ground can boast. In the 1920s Colonel A. C. Watson of Sussex hit a six clean over its uppermost branches.

The one building at the Nackington Road end, beside which the visitor is standing, is the oldest on the ground. Originally built in 1897 it was the 'Ladies Stand' or more often the 'Iron Stand' and it has never contributed aesthetically to Canterbury's appearance. In 1973 it was refurbished inside with sixteen private boxes above which stretches the main scoreboard, and renamed the Leslie Ames Stand.

Ames, with Woolley and Colin Cowdrey, forms an illustrious Kentish trio who scored 100 hundreds. Their careers also span most of this century without break, from 1906 when Frank Woolley first played at the age of nineteen and Kent won their first County Championship, until 1976 when Colin Cowdrey played his last match. They each enjoyed numerous highlights at Canterbury: Woolley, a product of the Tonbridge Nursery, of whom Robertson-Glasgow said: 'When you bowled at him there weren't enough fielders, when you wrote about him there weren't enough words', made his highest innings for the county of 270 against Middlesex here in 1923; Les Ames scored his 100th hundred on the last day of Canterbury Week in 1950; and Colin Cowdrey scored a hundred in each innings against the Australians in 1961. Few counties have been given such unbroken pleasure by three players.

Woolley's 270 was the highest score by a Kent player on the ground, but it failed to beat the record set in 1876 by W.G. Grace when he scored 344 for the MCC, then a first-class record and which set him on the way to scoring 839 runs in ten days. W.G. features rather a lot in the Canterbury records, for his 10 for 92 in an innings and 15 for 147 in the match for the MCC in 1873 have never been bettered by visitors to the ground.

They have however been beaten by a Kent man – 'Tich' Freeman, the diminutive Kent bowler who, between the wars, spun his way to 3,776 wickets – a total only bettered by Wilfred Rhodes. Freeman was the only man to take over 300 wickets in a season. When he retired from cricket he called the house which he shared with his reputedly domineering wife, 'Dunbowlin'. When there was a long delay at the start of Freeman's

funeral one friend was reported to have murmured to his neighbour 'she probably hasn't let him come'. Freeman does not have a memorial of his own on the ground but another Kent spin bowler, Colin Blythe, does. It stands near the main entrance, as does the one to Fuller Pilch, the best batsman in England in the mid-nineteeth century and one-time groundsman at the St Lawrence. Colin Blythe is among the most fondly remembered of all Kent players; his career was ended tragically early when he was killed in action in 1917.

Canterbury has a great deal of history but, like most people, I prefer some of the moments I have witnessed personally. I used to go with my family to most days of Canterbury Week: my parents used to sit on the benches between the tents and the Leslie Ames stand and my brothers and I sat on the grass in front, independent but in sight. Occasionally my parents went for lunch or tea in a tent and we either joined the throng of would-be Cowdreys on the pitch, or drifted around the back of the pavilion for the chance of players' autographs, or hung about the back of the tents to laugh at the red faces and boaters.

This was the time when, in Christmas and Easter holidays, we were coached in the indoor school over on the hospital side of the ground. Our coach was the quiet and gentle Doug Wright, the leg-break bowler who took a record seven hat-tricks and who always made you feel that you might play for England yourself, even if he knew you would be pushed to make the school colts.

Above *The New stand visible beyond the famous lime tree and the annexe on the right*

I have the most vivid memories of two games, one in 1965 when I was nine, the other two years later. It must have been one of my first visits to the ground in 1965, for Kent's game against the visiting South Africans. It got off to a wonderful start with a fielding exhibition by Colin Bland – in front of the pavilion where the players still warm up before a match today. That was only a light appetizer for the great event was to see Graeme Pollock score a double-century. As I was a left-hander I modelled myself on this innings for years afterwards. It was chanceless and brilliant and the prelude to Pollock's much more famous innings in his next match, 125 against England in the Trent Bridge Test.

The other match had batting of quite a different calibre. Playing against Yorkshire – regular visitors in Canterbury Week at one stage – Alan Brown, the Kent fast bowler with the most agricultural of batting styles, swiped 33 runs in very little time, including 4, 6, 4, 4, off the mighty Freddie Trueman. Few people, let alone a tail-ender, had ever dared this sort of behaviour and Trueman was looking like the proverbial village blacksmith. He got his revenge, however, making exactly the same score as Brown in about the same time, and at one point hit Brown into the top storey of the concrete stand. It was a schoolboy's dream come true.

Early in the following year my uncle decided that he would make me a life-member of Kent, to mark, as he said, the performance of England in the West Indies to which Kent – in the persons of Colin Cowdrey and Alan Knott – had made such a decisive contribution. The cloth-covered, maroon membership pass, with its extra badge for my 'friend' was a prized possession, if only because it gave me immediate superiority over my non-member brothers; although it once got me into a spot of bother when a well-meaning attendant hauled me off to the secretary's office for verification, not believing that someone so young could own something so important as life membership. Thinking about it now, my uncle's desire to mark the occasion in such a way seems highly indicative of the commitment people in Kent feel towards cricket, especially that of their county.

It is this commitment which remains clearly evident at Canterbury Week. The ground has changed and been modernized as most others have, but in close sympathy with the existing surroundings and atmosphere. If Canterbury remains one of the most delightful county grounds, it is also now – of the non-Test grounds – the most complete. For a great many of the spectators cricket is not only a game to be played but something to be celebrated and it is this which provides the essence of Canterbury and its Week.

TUNBRIDGE WELLS

Tunbridge Wells's cricket ground has, like the town which embraces it, a feeling of security and contentment. Much of this derives from the surroundings, for the ground is in a slight natural hollow and tightly enclosed all round by trees, through whose branches hardly a brick or chimney protrudes to spoil the view. And it is for one aspect of these surroundings that Tunbridge Wells is best known – the rhododendrons. Every year Kent play at Tunbridge Wells in early June, to coincide with the banks of mauve rhododendrons in flower. As at Canterbury it has a 'Week', with two county championship matches and with marquees and flags. In the old days all of Kent's games were played in a series of Weeks on the various grounds and today they survive at Canterbury, Tunbridge Wells and Maidstone. Folkestone and Dartford now host one game each.

The rhododendrons were a bit dilatory in 1987 and only the earliest buds had broken into full flower, but it did not really matter as the ground is by no means dependent on their charms. Tunbridge Wells is known as the Nevill ground, named after the family of the Marquess of Abergavenny, who despite their Welsh connexions have been based in Kent for many generations and have their home at Eridge Park, only a few miles south of Tunbridge Wells. Like so many Kentish families they have been long-serving supporters of the county's cricket and have provided two Presidents of the club.

In a town with so sedate a history as that of Tunbridge Wells any act of violence is surprising. Surprising, but not impossible, for not many years after the first county game in 1901, the cricket ground suffered when, in 1913, the original pavilion was burnt down by suffragettes. One loss in the fire was the records of the Bluemantle's club who have been associated with Tunbridge Wells since their foundation in 1862. The club takes its name from an officer of the College of Arms, Bluemantle Pursuivant, and is allowed to use his arms of 'A Mantle Azure doubled Ermine edged and corded Or'.

The replacement pavilion is there today, an attractive white wooden building with a tiled roof. In front are open terraced seats for members and inside photographs of Kentish performances are alongside ones of the Tunbridge Wells CC. The pavilion's two main peculiarities are above: the tortuous spiral staircase up to

the press box, positioned in the building's large central gable, above whose windows is the clock; and the scoreboard divided into two halves by the gable with, on one side, Total, Wickets and Batsmen's scores and on the other, the rest of the details. For those who prefer a more uniform presentation there is another scoreboard at the far end of the ground.

Between pavilion and scoreboard are first, the Ladies Stand, a modest covered structure, and then the row of marquees without which no Kentish ground seems complete. Some of them have the same occupants as at Canterbury – the President and Band of Brothers for instance, while others bring a more local flavour such as the Tunbridge Wells CC itself and even Tonbridge Rugby Club.

On the other side of the ground there is a scattering of marquees, one for refreshments, another housing the county club's shop, but mostly the boundary is lined with old-fashioned folding wooden chairs. Between here and the pavilion is the public stand – similar in appearance to the Ladies' stand, but slightly larger and filled with plain wooden benches. It is sometimes called

the Sussex stand and if the county border does not actually run across the ground as some people would have you believe, you could almost hit a six into Sussex.

Partly due to the clay soil below, the Nevill wicket has a reputation for being slow to dry, and at the same time the ground's low-lying, tree-enclosed situation often assists the bowlers – particularly the seamers. Only six batsmen have ever scored a double-hundred on the ground, the most recent being Bob Woolmer's 203 against Sussex in 1982, the highest was a characteristically majestic 290 by Hammond in 1934 when Gloucestershire made the Nevill's record total of 563. No doubt many Kent supporters around the ground sighed for what might have been in 1981 when, playing for Leicestershire, David Gower, who was born in Tunbridge Wells, scored 115 with his usual easy grace.

Above *The Nevill ground: the pavilion with its split scoreboard and the Ladies' stand to the right*

Overleaf *Maidstone in 1947, the River Len in the background and Mote Park away to the right*

MAIDSTONE

In a county whose history is unusually rich in noble cricketing families and the tradition of country-house cricket, it is apt that one of Kent's grounds should lie in what was the private park around such a country house. The third of Kent's Weeks is held at Mote Park, on the south-east side of Maidstone, home of the Mote CC. The club was founded in 1857 and a measure of its distinction is the fact that since then it has supplied well over one hundred players for Kent.

If less impressive in appearance and facilities than either Canterbury or Tunbridge Wells, Maidstone has great charm, relying largely on the natural appeal of its surroundings. These are considerable. On two sides groups of trees lead away into the main body of Mote Park. To the north is a view to the wooded line of the north downs, uninterrupted by the houses lying in between as they are concealed by trees and by being in a slight dip.

The eighteenth-century house lies across the park from the cricket ground. It was originally the home of the Earls of Romney, and it was they who made the ground available to the Mote club. Kent were playing here by the end of the 1870s, although the experiment in 1881 of holding all five of the county's home fixtures at Mote Park was apparently not a success, as crowds were decidedly thin.

1895 was to see the arrival of the Mote's foremost patron when Marcus Samuel bought Mote Park. Marcus Samuel was Jewish and an extremely successful financier. In 1903 he was made a baronet and, in 1921, elevated to the title of Viscount Bearsted (after the neighbouring village to the Mote). More relevant, he was interested in cricket and the Mote benefited enormously from his support.

In 1907, as a gesture towards the club's jubilee Kent agreed to hold a Week on the ground, which they had previously refused to do. At the end of the season it was made known that the Week would only continue if the ground was levelled. This was carried out, Sir Marcus covering half of the cost and as a result the wicket was laid running north–south whereas previously it had been east–west. Not long afterwards it was decided that the pavilion was insufficient for the needs of county cricket and again Sir Marcus stepped into the breech, paying for the new building erected in 1910. It survives today little altered, a two-storey building with a tiled roof and central black and white gable containing the clock.

Sir Marcus gave the Mote its most distinctive legacy in the small building to one side of the main pavilion which is one of the most delightful curiosities to be found on any county ground. It is built in the style of an ornamental cottage with herringbone pattern brickwork and a covered verandah in front and Sir Marcus used it as his private pavilion for the entertainment of

Above left *The pavilion at Maidstone*

Above *Maidstone's Tabernacle, one of county cricket's architectural curiosities*

friends during matches. As a result of Sir Marcus's racial origins it was humorously referred to as 'the Tabernacle' and the name has stuck. Today it provides a temporary office for the county club during the Maidstone week, as well as an enclosure for the ever-present Band of Brothers.

From the Tabernacle simple bench seating extends around the top side of the ground with, on the grass embankment behind and around the far side, an even more basic arrangement of sawn planks supported on rustic sawn logs. For a day's cricket-watching they are both uncomfortable and unsafe. On top of the embankment stand the two marquees housing the county club's mobile shop – red striped – and the bar and refreshments – blue striped – with also a far smaller one for the scorecards' printing-press in plain white. On the far side from the pavilion a fine stand of oaks point to the foresight of the eighteenth-century Romneys, although they could conceivably be older.

This is the least visited part of the ground but things get immediately busier as one passes the scoreboard, for from here the familiar line of marquees fill the boundary along the lower side of the ground. They are perched on top of a steep embankment, below which is a wide terrace similar to one containing the cricket ground, and housing a rugby pitch. At the end of the marquees is an open concrete stand and, next to the pavilion the recently built squash club confronts the ground with a somewhat stark brick wall broken only

by a small central balcony. The chairs in front of the squash club as well as the pavilion itself and the small enclosure on the far side are the domain of Kent members.

In 1927 the Mote was the scene of one of the great batting assaults in county cricket, by the most cavalier figure in Kent's history, Percy Chapman. Chapman's brilliant cricket at Cambridge between 1920–22, three of the strongest of all University sides, led him to be chosen for England in 1924, the year before he first played for Kent. In 1926 he captained England to the now legendary victory over Australia at The Oval, to win the Ashes for the first time for over twenty years.

Chapman's onslaught at the Mote was reputedly provoked by the extremely fast and, too-often, short-pitched bowling which Lancashire's Ted McDonald was serving up to the Kent batsmen. With the score at 70 for five the incensed Chapman strode to the wicket. Just over three hours later he returned having scored 260, hitting five sixes and 32 fours. The two hundreds both came in about the same number of minutes, the final fifty in a quarter of an hour. It was Chapman's only double-century, but after such a performance he never really needed to score another.

Lancashire have often been visitors to the Mote and at times enjoyed conspicuous success. In 1881 they bowled Kent out for 38, their lowest total on the ground and just over a century later – in 1984 – their opener, Graeme Fowler, scored 226, the last of only three double-hundreds to have been made on the ground.

Many people primarily think of Mote Park as the scene of one of the outstanding landmarks in Colin Cowdrey's career. In 1973 he came to the Maidstone Week with 98 hundreds. In the first match, against Somerset, he scored 123 not out and, three days later, in front of an expectant crowd he made 100 not out to give him his 100th hundred.

FOLKESTONE

Since the sad demotion of the Crabble, Folkestone has become Kent's only seaside ground and although the county's visits have currently been decreased to one sole fixture it is to be hoped that the ground is not completely deserted.

For most cricket grounds an atmosphere of enclosure, be it provided by trees or buildings, often provides a satisfying sense of security. At Cheriton Road, Folkestone, there are no such concessions. Far from it; the view across the ground to the prospect of the North Downs is as open and panoramic as you will find on any county ground and at times makes for bracing conditions.

As is almost inevitable, the view is no longer uninterrupted as it was when first-class cricket came to Cheriton Road in the 1920s, but it must be said that the houses which have sprung up are both sufficiently distant and inoffensive to be tolerable. Whether the ugly spectre of the channel tunnel, which will disgorge on the surface only a few miles away, will have an adverse effect remains to be seen. I doubt that crowds at Cheriton Road will be swollen by visiting Frenchmen.

During the inter-war years Folkestone enjoyed a balmy period as one of the most fashionable resorts on the south coast. Now that has gone, the Lees along the front sees few holiday-makers unless they are en route to the continent from Folkestone's busy port, the bandstand is empty and the opulent Grand and Metropole hotels are flats. In 1925, however, the town's desirability was decisive in the establishment of the Folkestone festival, which became an annual event at the end of the season until the Second World War. County cricket followed shortly afterwards, and Kent played their first

county match on the ground in 1928.

The ground itself had been first used twenty years earlier and originally belonged to the Earl of Radnor, who owned most of Folkestone and the surrounding land. In the style of a true patron Radnor advanced the £1,000 necessary for building the pavilion and employed the architect Reginald Pope to design it. There should have been no problem with the wicket for its laying-out was supervised by Alec Hearne, the Kent pro whose father had been a famous groundsman for Kent at Catford Bridge.

It is from Pope's pavilion that one has the view to the North Downs. Looking out of the pavilion, with its red-tiled roof and wooden balustrade, the fairly basic covered stand curves away to the left and on the right is a curving row of marquees. In the far corner on this side is the scoreboard.

Major features of the festival were matches between Gentlemen and Players, visits by the MCC and, occasionally, the visiting tourists. In 1933 Les Ames achieved the distinction of scoring two double-hundreds on the ground, 201 for the Players against the Gentlemen and 295 – the highest score of his career – for Kent against Gloucestershire. A few years earlier, in 1927, Patsy Hendren had provided the highlights of the MCC's match against Kent by scoring a hundred in each innings.

Whether he was able to get through the wicket's thin covering of topsoil to the sand immediately below or not, 'Tich' Freeman had a field-day at Folkestone in 1932 when his 17 for 92 against Warwickshire made him the first bowler ever to take 17 wickets in a match twice. No one has done so since.

As well as individual performances, in 1970 Folkestone witnessed two consecutive victories by Kent which effectively clinched one of the most improbable of county championship victories. After a series of very ordinary performances the county lay bottom of the championship at the beginning of July. By the time they arrived at Folkestone for their last two home games of the season they were well on the way in their climb to the top. In the first game Nottinghamshire were defeated, despite Sobers scoring 123 and enabling his side to declare at 376 for four; Kent's response was led by Luckhurst with 156 not out. In the second Kent only needed to bat once, scoring 421 for seven declared, to defeat Leicestershire by an innings. Thereafter there only remained the formality of a few points at The Oval against Surrey. For Colin Cowdrey and his side Folkestone Week of that year brought about the seemingly impossible and the Championship returned to Kent for the first time since 1913.

Above *Cheriton Road, Folkestone, a panoramic view to the North Downs*

Below *Looking across the ground to Folkestone's pavilion and stands*

DARTFORD

Hesketh Park, Dartford, is a modest, suburban cricket ground such as are the backbone of club cricket all over the country. If the annual visit by the county is a highlight which also causes some upheaval and has at times been threatened, it is well deserved and greatly enjoyed. As the only surviving ground in Kent's London area and the Medway towns – the last of the others, the Rectory Field at Blackheath saw its final visit by Kent in 1971 – Hesketh Park serves the membership in the most populous part of the county.

It is the youngest of Kent's grounds, having staged its first match in 1956, although cricket in Dartford can claim a far longer history dating back to the game on another ground between Kent and Surrey in 1709. The present pavilion was built the same year of the county's first visit while the old – and far more attractive one, with its deep tiled roof – was sensibly retained. Facing the wicket from square-leg, it houses press and scorers.

The building of the new pavilion involved a tale of the utmost complication – and ingenuity. Hesketh Park, in which the cricket ground is situated and which also contains other sports facilities and some good municipal gardening, was given to the borough council by one Everard Hesketh, a strict teetotaller. Hesketh's only condition was that no alcohol should be sold on the ground. Therefore when the new pavilion came to be built the council purchased enough land from its neigh-bour at one end to build the pavilion with its rear half off the Hesketh land and thus able to have a bar without breaking the terms. The public refreshment tent is also pitched off the forbidden territory.

In 1966, only ten years after Kent's first visit, the county were bundled out for 82 by Essex on a questionable wicket and did not return again until 1970 by which time valiant work by the Dartford club and their groundsman had brought about a dramatic improvement. Since then and partly as a result of the ground being relatively small, there have regularly been very high scoring games – with a total of over 1,000 runs in four innings on a number of occasions.

In 1973 Worcestershire scored 463, largely thanks to a double-century by J.A. Ormrod and in 1985 Kent managed to pass this to establish a record total for the ground of 476, against Essex. The most dramatic innings to have been seen on the ground was played by Lancashire's Clive Lloyd in 1970 – as if to celebrate the return of county cricket to Hesketh Park – when he hit seven sixes and 18 fours on the way to 163 in 140 minutes. Probably the most satisfying for the Dartford crowd came in 1982 when Neil Taylor, a Dartford club player, scored 143 not out against Warwickshire. It was a representative Dartford match; Asif also scored a hundred for Kent and Kallicharran one for the visitors, nearly 1,200 runs were scored in three days and the result was a draw. Hesketh Park more often provides entertainment for the crowd than results for the teams, but perhaps that is not always a bad thing.

Previous page *Hesketh Park, Dartford, shortly after its introduction to Kent's county circuit*

SUSSEX

HOVE

Hove is a paradoxical ground. To the casual visitor it is nothing to look at, with blocks of flats at both ends and an appalling heterogeneous clutter along one side which is the pavilion and attendant quarters. And yet people love it. More times than I could mention the response to 'your favourite county ground?' is Hove – or Brighton for old timers. And yet most of them do not know why; something to do with being by the sea, the atmosphere of the town, Sussex's long but eccentric history – they are all there, strangely intangible.

R.C. Robertson-Glasgow, a man not normally lost for the right phrase was one of their number.

But Brighton was the best. Was it the sea-fret that sharpened the turf there and, in a never-to-be-explained manner, helped the often derided swerver? But it had, for me at least, a mysterious pleasure, a secret none can utter . . . And the town itself exhaled an air of abandon, some inheritance from the Regency, as if it contained and encouraged a world of men taking a holiday from work, reason and their wives.

It is a genial mixture of raffish and run-down, like the numerous blazers in the pavilion bar, most sporting military buttons and yet many with frayed cuffs. Sussex cricket has never been rich and rarely successful, but it has sparkled with flashes of brilliance and lovely characters: Ranji, Fry, and Duleep; Tate, the Gilligans, and the Langridges; what more can you wish for? And the patrons have been noble to a degree; between 1897 and 1948 there were only eight commoners among the Presidents, the rest were all titled folk and headed by three Dukes of Norfolk – Sussex and England's premier family.

Hove, looking across the ground from the pavilion, revealing the ground's slope from left to right

Above *Hove's Tate gates, a suitable memorial to one of their favourite cricketers*

Above right *The Ladies' stand, adjoining the pavilion, shortly after its construction in the 1920s.*

The ground itself is fairly quirky, not least for the enormous slope from the uppermost north end to the seaward south – a drop of twenty feet from boundary to boundary. Maurice Tate used to bowl down the hill, as most fast bowlers like to do, using the breeze – usually damp in mornings and evenings – off the sea a few hundred yards away which is damp in the mornings and evenings. On the day I visited Middlesex's Wayne Daniel was in action and distinctly hostile. Before too long Sussex's captain, Paul Parker, was back in the pavilion after a nasty-sounding blow which inflicted a cracked wrist.

'Crusoe' remembered Tate 'galumphing' in to the wicket, but he galumphed to extraordinary effect. For three seasons – 1923–25 – he took 219, 205 and 228 wickets at the same time as scoring 1,000 runs in each. After discussing Tate's batting in *Barclays World of Cricket*, Ian Peebles concluded, 'But this was a small matter in comparison with the glory of Tate in his opening overs at Hove on a green wicket, freshened by a slight sea haze. Uneasy was the captain who had won the toss and decided to bat'.

Maurice Tate is immortalized in the ground's main gates, beside which is the Sussex Cricketer pub, which looks as though it has been over-smartened and was probably nicer as the County Cricket Ground Hotel. He should also be remembered as a member of one of Sussex's many cricketing families: Lillywhites (four), Tates (two), Gilligans (two), Griffithses (two), Busses (two), Parkses (three), Langridges (three), Wellses (two), Oakeses (two), Coxes (two) and Greigs (two).

Tate's captain and bowling partner, Arthur Gilligan is the other most prominently remembered Sussex player at Hove. Along the seaward boundary is the indoor school named after him. On its roof is an open stand which provides as good a view of play as anywhere on the ground, although it seems quite distant – Hove is a large ground – and the sun is on your back. The county club seems to have pulled off an unexpectedly nifty piece of bargaining here, for as the pillars of the block of flats behind stand on Sussex ground the developers paid for the indoor school. In 1984 I.V.A. Richards became the first man to hit the ball right over the Arthur Gilligan Stand, which is twenty-six feet high, and the shot had a carry of 130 yards.

Between here and the pavilion conglomerate alternating blocks of new blue-and-white seats curve around the corner of the ground, but Hove's most inviting spot is the north end with its rows of blue deck-chairs. In one corner is the George Cox memorial garden –

remembering Cox senior who took nearly 2,000 wickets and played for the county aged fifty-three. Along the back, cherry and crab-apple trees are in blossom early in the season. The ample space for car parking makes for great convenience. Although they catch the sun the deck-chairs are often breezy and tweed caps, rugs and woollen scarves are much in evidence.

On the east side of the ground is Hove's one architectural flourish and a gesture to the Brighton of George IV: the main scoreboard and clock-tower. White stucco, like many of the town's rows of houses, it is surmounted by its imposing clock cupola and weather-vane and, as if to emphasize its inspiration, it carries an advertisement for the Regency Building Society. It is called the Harmsworth scoreboard, for the newspaper family paid for its construction in 1930.

Also on this side of the ground there used to be two rather basic looking covered stands known as the 'chicken-coop' and the 'cow-shed'. They were both unattractive and uncomfortable and in 1987 the surviving 'cow-shed' was pulled down.

Hove's most incongruous sight is the collection of outsize eggs which are positioned around the boundary – as they are on all Sussex grounds. They are an advertising stunt by the Stonegate County Eggs company who used to offer £3,000 to any batsman who could hit one full-toss. The expansiveness of their gesture was sharply reduced after 1986 when Paul Parker hit one at Eastbourne and the prize is now £1,000.

The appearance of the pavilion belies the unexpected treasures to be found inside and in the adjoining buildings. From the club offices at the bottom to the Ladies' Stand at the top there are also the scorers and a smaller scorebox, the press, the library, the players' dressing-rooms and dining-room, members' bar and dining-room, and spectators' seating of one sort or another. Along the front of the pavilion it is wooden benches, all donated in memory of Sussex supporters like 'Jack Richardson, who loved his cricket'.

The scorebox was reconstructed in the 1930s in memory of Ranjitsinhji, and well might he have a memorial on the ground. Seeing Ranji in full oriental splendour Maurice Tate was moved to describe – albeit somewhat enigmatically – His Highness as 'a veritable 'indoo'. In the pavilion at Hove he smiles down from his portrait, benign and twinkling, dapper as ever in a silk shirt. He played for Sussex between 1895 and 1920 and was captain from 1899 to 1903. His batting was one of the brightest jewels of the Golden Age and his run-scoring phenomenal. In 1899 he scored 3,159 runs and the next year 3,065. He scored 14 double-hundreds for Sussex, six of them at Hove and the best 202 against Middlesex in 1900, when the rest of his side could only muster 70. Perhaps more impressive was his 100 and 125 not out in one day, v Yorkshire at Hove in 1896.

Ranji's name is forever linked with Charles Fry, and Neville Cardus wrote of them that, 'The conjunction at the crease of C.B. Fry and K.S. Ranjitsinhji was a sight and an appeal to the imagination not likely ever to be repeated.' Fry joined Sussex in 1894 and took over the captaincy in 1904. His exploits became equally legendary, not least his six hundreds in succession in 1901. Of his 13 double-hundreds for Sussex, seven were made at Hove, including 229 against Surrey in 1900 following 125 in his first innings.

When Ranji and Fry were batting at Hove there were few men who could steal the limelight, but in 1903 G.L. Jessop did so quite dramatically when he scored 286 in 175 minutes, out of a total of 355 for Gloucestershire against Sussex.

Between the wars the memory of Ranji was perpetuated at Hove by his nephew K.S. Duleepsinhji. Most people who either watched or knew Duleep almost shed a tear whenever his name is mentioned. They would all agree with Robertson-Glasgow that he was 'a very perfect gentle knight'. In his all too short career with Sussex, ended by the onset of tuberculosis, he more than lived up to the example of his uncle. In the three seasons from 1929–31 he scored 7,791 runs – more than any other batsman in England. He reserved one of his greatest performances for Hove: on the opening day of the 1930 season he scored 333 against Northamptonshire, which remains the second highest number of runs scored in a day in England and beat Ranji's record score for Sussex of 285 not out.

Duleep's 333 remains the highest score at Hove, but when Lancashire visited in 1937 Eddie Paynter played an innings which ran him pretty close. In five hours the little Lancashire left-hander scored 322 and, according to the *Manchester Guardian* correspondent, did not give a chance until he had scored 260.

You will find plenty about Ranji, Fry and Duleep in Hove's library, up a narrow staircase and next to the scorer's room. It is one of the unexpected treats of the ground and the domain of Harold 'Ossie' Osborne, the Honorary Librarian for many years and unquestioned authority on the ground, county club and its history. He will remind you that Sussex is the oldest of the first-class counties, having been founded in 1839 and that in those days it was the county of William Lillywhite, 'The Nonpareil', James Dean and John Wisden, Founder of the Almanack. They played on three grounds, last of which was Brighton's Brunswick ground whence, in 1872, the turf was moved to establish the present ground, in what was then a barley field. He will also tell you how Sussex's first outstanding captain was W.L. Murdoch, an Australian, and that country's best

batsman until Trumper. There is plenty more, including Mr Osborne's card index of every Sussex player.

The pavilion long-room with its bar at the back has an unusually rich array of photographs. Beyond, in the restaurant below the Ladies' Stand, I found a proper chef, complete with tall white hat, producing enticing hot food which included a full-blown English breakfast. I reflected that in 1911, after he had swum in the sea as the Nottinghamshire men invariably did when they came to Brighton, it being one of the only times they visited the coast, Edward Boaler Alletson probably consumed such a meal before putting Sussex to the sword in one of the most remarkable exhibitions of hitting ever seen.

'Ted' Alletson announced his intentions shortly before going in to bat, in reply to his captain's despondent conclusion that there was no chance of avoiding defeat. 'Then I'm not half going to give Ted Killick some stick.' He did, and anything else the home side cared to offer. Killick was hit for 34 in one over – the record until Sobers's effort in 1968 – and Alletson scored 189 in ninety minutes, the last 142 of which came in 40 minutes. It was the highlight of his career and the Duke of Portland, on whose estate Alletson lived, gave him a gold watch to mark the event.

No batsman, other than arguably Gilbert Jessop at Hastings, scored faster than Alletson on that day, but in 1938 Hugh Bartlett, a young left-hander who had already proved himself an outstanding University cricketer during three years at Cambridge scored 157, including 100 in fifty-seven minutes against the Australians. He is remembered in the pavilion, as are the two Langridge brothers, James and John (J.G.), who gave the county unrivalled service. Between them they played nearly 1,200 games for Sussex. James scored nearly 32,000 runs and took nearly 1,500 wickets while John's total of 34,380 is a Sussex record. 1933 saw two remarkable performances at Hove by J.G.: against Glamorgan he made 250 not out, the highest score of his career, while with E.H. Bowley he put on 490 for the first wicket against Middlesex. It remains easily a record for Sussex and only Holmes and Sutcliffe's 555 and Brown and Tunnicliffe's 554 are higher for any wicket in England.

As one would expect, Sussex's victory in the inaugural Gillette Cup in 1963 is recalled in the pavilion, as is their retention of the cup the next year and their captain on both occasions, E.R. Dexter. Dexter is more remembered for his batting for England rather than for Sussex as, in a similar way, Sussex's outstanding bowler of the post-war period, John Snow, gave his best performances for his country.

Since the war Sussex's fortunes have continued as

A plaque marking the centenary of cricket at Hove

through most of their history. The county has continually been blessed with stylish and often outstanding players: David Sheppard and the Nawab of Pataudi; Jim Parks; Dexter himself and Tony Greig. Few players have announced themselves in the style of Tony Greig when, in 1967, in his first match for Sussex, the gangling, blond-haired twenty-year-old scored 156 to save his team against Lancashire. In recent years Imran Khan has been one of a distinguished group of overseas players including Kepler Wessels and Garth Le Roux. And yet the County Championship has yet to be brought to Hove.

But one would not like to see too much change at the headquarters of Sussex cricket. A face-lift would bring unavoidable loss of character and atmosphere. All of the 4,500 members would dearly love their team to be champions; but possibly not if it meant Hove

becoming a place of executive boxes rather than deckchairs, with plastic seats in front of the pavilion instead of the old wooden benches, and if it meant a team of unfailing consistency rather than sparks of brilliance. Hove and Sussex have some of the most glamorous memories in cricket history and if the old family home is a bit tatty, there are healthy signs of progress such as the thriving shop inside the Tate Gates. The old Duke of Norfolk, one of Sussex's most loyal patrons, used to say that he never bothered to dress up when he went to London because no one would recognize him there. One feels that Hove does not need to dress up to impress anyone, and so long as people continue to enjoy going there, that, surely, is the most important thing.

EASTBOURNE

Hove instills Sussex cricket with a strong flavour of the seaside which is strengthened at Eastbourne's famously-named ground, the Saffrons. The ground is, in fact, some distance from the sea but Eastbourne is first and foremost a place for the bucket and spade and as well as hosting county cricket the Saffrons has always been a favourable haunt of club sides touring during the late-summer holiday season.

I must confess to being initially disappointed at the Saffrons. I had expected the ground to be as depicted in Yardley and Kilburn's *Homes of Sport*, a photograph taken from the football pitch side, showing an idyllic tree-lined enclosure, with marquees and a central pavilion with its flag and the line of the Downs in the background.

Things were slightly different. The marquees were there, but they were not so tall and were gaudy blue-and-white, not plain white. The pavilion has been rebuilt and although there are plenty of trees they seemed further away than I had expected, and the Downs did not provide the expected backdrop. These were all details compared to the major difference brought about – inevitably – by a recent development. The pavilion side of the ground is now dominated by

two monolithic blocks of flats. They are the sort of buildings that you imagine fill the Moscow surburbs.

When I arrived the weather was as one associates with the Saffrons: very hot and bright, and which prompted Jim Kilburn to write that the Saffrons was a ground which often induced 'a little folding of the hands between lunch and tea'. It did not last long however, and any chance of a result against a characteristically competitive Nottinghamshire was dispelled by torrential rain which brought home how much the Saffrons is a fair-weather ground. Unless you were in a marquee, cover was as scarce as for the families desperately packing up towels, picnics and wind-breaks on the beach.

Whatever my misgivings, so long as you are looking away from the pavilion, the Saffrons has both individuality and charm. The main group of marquees stretch round from the pavilion – the closest to which, the Sussex CCC Committee's, is the only white one – to the sightscreen and scoreboard next door at the north end of the ground. Through the gap in the trees is some of the ground's abundant car-parking.

On the far side from the pavilion is a temporary tiered stand beyond which is the home of Eastbourne Town Football Club. In fact the Saffrons has always been used for various sports, ever since cricket was first played here in 1884, as is stressed in the name over the

pavilion entrance: Eastbourne Saffrons Sports Club. Next to the football pitch is the bowls club, its sedateness ensured by a protective paling fence. I felt that the atmosphere would probably have been greatly more competitive in the Compton Croquet Club, set back beyond the main group of marquees in Larkins Field on the far side of the ground, which boasts five immaculate croquet lawns and a scattering of formidable-looking elderly ladies, all in whites with matching sun-hats, swinging their mallets purposefully as they strode after their balls in sensible white lace-up shoes.

In 1947 the rebuilding of the pavilion was necessitated by a fire and it was reconstructed again in 1978. Brick, with a shallow tiled roof, inside the exploits of the Eastbourne club cover the walls of the bar and generous-sized windows allow a good view of the play. In front there are a few rows of seats for members. There are two other lesser pavilions at the Meads Road – south – end of the ground, one the members' or Harry Bartlett pavilion, the other the First World War memorial pavilion.

From the main, players', pavilion, you get the Saffrons' most lasting view, across the wicket running at right-angles to the roofscape of the immediate town with, dominant, the wonderfully vigorous tower of the Victorian Town Hall (1884), and to one side the spires of the Roman Catholic church and of St Saviour's.

Certainly there is no need for a pavilion clock at the Saffrons: the Town Hall tower one is easily large and close enough and the echoing chimes each quarter remind batsmen to keep pushing along.

In the past this has often been necessary at the Saffrons, renowned as a batsman's wicket to the extent of sometimes being over-docile. Duleepsinhji secretly reckoned that Maurice Tate never really tried at Eastbourne – it was always hard work for little reward. Duleep maintained he could tell because when Tate was trying, such was the size and impact of his boots that he would start digging a front foot-hole after four or five overs, however hard the ground, and one never appeared at the Saffrons.

The one occasion when the wicket did not suit the batsmen came in 1982, when the Saffrons and its admirers had a nasty shock. Replying to a score of 261 by visiting Northamptonshire, Sussex were bowled out twice for 84 and 119, the spinners Willey and Steele taking full advantage of a crumbling top. Sussex lost by an innings and 58 runs and the wicket was reported to

Above left *The Saffrons in the 1950s, before building development spoilt the view over the Downs*

Above *The unchanged view of the Saffrons, towards Eastbourne and the town hall's clock-tower*

Lord's by the umpires, Dai Evans and Billy Ibadulla, as 'unfit for first-class cricket'. The *Guardian* correspondent remarked, 'Even now the idea of Eastbourne being reported to Lord's seems akin to the questioning of a Mother Superior's chastity'.

In the event the Saffrons put its house in order with commendable speed and the impending desertion by the county never took place. After the cricket week the following August *Wisden* was able to pronounce that the wicket was greatly improved.

This was not the first time controversy had come to the Saffrons, although on a previous occasion it was more a question of personalities. By the 1930s it had become something of an annual tradition for Lancashire to be one of the visiting counties to the Saffrons. One would have thought that a county of Lancashire's calibre would always be welcome, but it appears that the burghers of Eastbourne did not agree. At the annual meeting of the Eastbourne CC in 1931, the mayor of the town, in support of one of his associates, pronounced:

> I agree with Alderman Kay that we are in an unfortunate position in always having a certain county from the north. I will not mention the name. [Laughter]. We are rather tired of them. We have made a protest to the county, and as we were too late this year we have asked them to make a note of it and see that some other county may have the honour in 1932.

Perhaps it was the laughter that riled them, but, not surprisingly, the Lancashire pros were furious. As a result on the first day of their match at the Saffrons they refused point-blank to attend the traditional opening-day lunch given in their honour in one of the marquees, because the hosts were the Mayor and Corporation.

How surprising that Lancashire should be so shunned when one thinks that it was a Lancashire man, A.C. MacLaren, who, ten years earlier, had given the Saffrons its finest hour. MacLaren, in his fiftieth year, was captaining a side of amateurs he had assembled to play Warwick Armstrong's Australian side who came to the Saffrons unbeaten. Their captain had every intention that they should remain so and return home the first unvanquished visitors to England. It was not to be. MacLaren's team, largely made up of the brilliant Cambridge side of that year, including the three Ashton brothers – Gilbert, Hubert and Claude – and Percy Chapman, won an extraordinary game by 28 runs. At first their chances appeared hopeless when they were bowled out for 43, but they scored 326 in their second innings, the veteran South African all-rounder, Aubrey Faulkner scoring 153, having taken four for 50 in the

Australian first innings, and the tourists failed in their chase for 196.

What a way for Archie MacLaren to bow out of cricket! Indeed the scene was completed by the presence of MacLaren's greatest admirer, Neville Cardus, who had obviously let his personal preferences get the better of him rather than go with the other leading pressmen to Lord's to watch a crucial championship match. It was an opportunity Cardus was not going to pass up.

From the pains which entered the body of English cricket at Trent Bridge in May the good Lord has at long last delivered us. This afternoon, on the sunny Saffrons cricket field, the Australians' colours have been hauled down: the mighty men that authentic English elevens have found unconquerable in ten successive Test matches have been beaten, beaten by a fictitious England eleven under the leadership of

our greatest cricket captain, and, moreover, beaten by a side that was routed in a first innings for 43 paltry runs.

R.R. Relf, one of another Sussex family, for his two brothers also played for the county, enjoyed batting at the Saffrons: in 1909 he scored 272 not out on the ground against Worcestershire and, in 1920, 225 against Lancashire. I would have liked to have seen Somerset's Harold Gimblett make 310 in 1948, the highest score of his career.

If the Saffrons has changed considerably in some aspects it is still home for festival cricket and Eastbourne faithfuls have years like 1981 to savour; when the sun shone all week, and when crowds totalling 25,000 watched Sussex win twice, the second time after a desperate run chase when Imran Khan scored a hundred in 88 minutes to bring victory with five balls to spare.

HASTINGS

At the end of the 1986 season it was announced by the powers that be in Hastings that the Central cricket ground would be made into a shopping centre and the cricket moved to a new ground at Summerfield. Apparently a Hastings councillor described the plan as a 'major step forward'. I would be more hesitant until I have seen both the new shopping centre and ground. Whatever they are like the loss of the Central ground beneath the bulldozer will be greatly mourned, for it has had a long and often exciting history.

As you approach the ground from its south-east corner, from the town's present main shopping area just

The Central ground Hastings today, famous for its festival and many heroics by Gilbert Jessop

next door, a prominent notice-board informs you that you have entered the Hastings and St Leonard's Central Cricket and Recreation Ground, that it is administered by a charitable trust and that it was originally called Priory Meadow. The ground was laid out in 1864 and was land made available by the estate of the Cornwallis family, better known for their cricketing connexions in neighbouring Kent.

Situated in the middle of the town there is little about the ground's surroundings which suggest seaside, holiday cricket other than a freshness in the air and quantities of seagulls who are either calling from surrounding houses or occasionally gathering in groups in the outfield. The ground is largely enclosed by rows of tall houses – particularly those of Devonshire Road behind the small refreshment pavilion and scoreboard. On the far side are the open tiers of the Alfred Coote stand behind which runs the busy shopping street of Queens Road. Especially when looking in this direction, the ground has a bowl-like feeling, uneven rows of houses climbing the hill behind to the ruins of Hastings Castle – a reminder of the town's defensive importance as one of the Cinque Ports.

The woodwork of both the refreshment pavilion and the players' pavilion – in the north-west corner of the ground – is painted duck-egg blue, which adds to their decorative appearance. Along the north side is the fairly basic members' grandstand, the only permanent covered stand on the ground. The wicket, which is pitched north–south, has had a consistently good reputation and the short side boundaries have often encouraged exciting batting.

This has been suitable to the Festival which began on the Hastings ground a century ago in 1887. Visits by Sussex began in 1895 and have continued in most years ever since. Until the 1960s there were two county games,

though this has now become one, and there have been intermittent years with no game at all. In the old days it was an occasion: marquees, enclosures of inviting deck-chairs, bunting in the town and holiday-makers swelling the crowds.

Traditionally the Festival was always in September. After its initiation there was a lapse from 1901–23. Then, in 1926, the Folkestone Festival was started, which proved overwhelming competition. Hastings was revived after the war, in 1946, but the last September game was played in 1965 when Sussex took on A.E.R. Gilligan's XI, which had been a regular fixture for some years. Since then Sussex's games have been played at different times of the season.

In what better way could the revived Festival have got a helping hand in 1947 than for Denis Compton to score his 17th hundred, thereby breaking Jack Hobbs's record set in 1925? Before the war, in 1929, Duleepsinhji achieved the best of his three doubles of a hundred in each innings, when he scored 115 and 246 against Kent. It was at a time when Kent's 'Tich' Freeman held sway over the majority of county batsmen. Duleep scored a hundred before lunch in his first innings and H.S. Altham remembers him 'tearing Freeman to shreds'.

Other captains of Sussex have played memorably attacking innings on the Central ground. In 1968 Dexter scored 203 against Kent, his only double-hundred for Sussex. It was a remarkable innings, not only for the power of Dexter's batting, which brought him the second hundred in 103 minutes, but also because in 1965 he had broken a leg and effectively retired from first-class cricket. This was the first innings after he had been persuaded to play again for Sussex – it proved a

Above *Yorkshire's Brown and Tunnicliffe, batting in an early festival game at Hastings*

72

scintillating, if brief, swan-song which led him to be picked for the last two Tests of the season when he had not played for England since 1965.

In 1975 Tony Greig scored the only double-hundred of his career against Warwickshire at Hastings. Going in as Sussex's captain when his side were struggling at 24 for three, he hit 226 in just over four hours. His end came when, having scored four sixes in a row off P.J. Lewington, the fifth was heading the same way until it fell just short of the long-on boundary to be caught by Dennis Amiss. Thanks to Amiss and his opening partner John Jameson, who put on 188, Warwickshire were able to score 355 in 250 minutes to win an enthralling match.

The traditional adversaries at Hastings have always been Kent, whose border is only a few miles away on the edge of Romney Marsh. There have been many duels and the two counties' fortunes have ebbed and flowed – often to extremes – over the years. In 1972 the home side won decisively by 10 wickets, bowling Kent out for 54 and 199, Greig taking 11 for 46 in the match. And yet, the very next year it was Kent's turn, with victory by the huge margin of an innings and 161 runs. Having scored 282 on the only dry day of the game Kent skittled Sussex out for 67 and 54. On the third day play could only start at four o'clock when the Fire Brigade, with keen help from Kent players and supporters, had mopped up the saturated pitch. Even so it left plenty of time: 20 overs later Underwood had done the damage with eight wickets for nine runs.

Derek Underwood will have the most affectionate memories of the Central ground, for this was one of a number of startling personal performances here. In 1964, in only his second season for Kent, he took nine for 28 – which remains his best bowling analysis. Twenty years later, in the twilight of his career he took on the unfamiliar guise of batsman to score the first – and only – hundred of his career (111, out on the unlucky Nelson).

It may seem strange, to return to the early years of Hastings' first-class cricket, but historically the ground will always retain almost legendary fame thanks to the exploits of one man, Gilbert Jessop. Even by his own standards, between 1898 and 1907, Jessop played a series of innings at Hastings which almost defy belief. In 1898, playing for the Rest of England v A.E. Stoddart's XI, he scored 112 not out in 60 minutes. The next year, again for the Rest of England, against the Home Counties, it was 100 not out in 68 minutes. In 1900 he

scored 123 not out in 55 minutes for the South v the North. Two years later he was back for the Rest of England against Sussex and Surrey with 109 in 77 minutes.

In 1907 Jessop scored 119 in 55 minutes for Gloucestershire v Sussex, but his second appearance at the ground that year, for the Gents of the South v the Players of the South saw his most explosive innings. He scored 191 in 90 minutes, including 100 in 42 minutes. It was his greatest display of hitting. As well as 30 fours he hit the ball out of the ground five times – in those days it was only a six if it went out of the ground. The story has it that the walls of a modest non-conformist chapel still bear the scars of his assault. One of his sixes cleared the entrance gate and smashed a shop window, another went through the window of a house in Station Road – when the owner, fearing for his safety, refused to return the ball. It has always intrigued devotees of cricket records that, had Jessop's eleven 'over the rope' hits (only given as four, not six) been counted as sixes, as they were by the time 'Ted' Alletson made his onslaught at Hove in 1911, Jessop's innings would have beaten Alletson and been the fastest double-hundred of all time. The local paper had the last word, reporting that, 'an otherwise insignificant match was redeemed by some bright play by Jessop'.

Right *Hastings in its hey-day, 1901: Lord Hawke obliging a youthful Edwardian autograph hunter*

HORSHAM

First-class cricket in Sussex is essentially a seaside affair. At a less exalted level it is also a county blessed with some of the most picturesque village grounds in England and, as much as any other place where county cricket is played, Horsham evokes an air of the village game. One person, at least, agreed – Dudley Carew, in *To The Wicket*.

Cricket literature perhaps is inclined to babble over-much of green fields, and the sun on the ale-house, brother at times shines a little too strongly, but for all that Horsham is a ground which tugs at the heart and the memory. It is approached through a churchyard and over a bridge spanning a brook. Round one side of it runs a railway, and every now and again a train, which is doubtless prosaic and much like any other train, but somehow contrives to seem oddly primitive and unreal, puffs round and causes the bowler to pause in his run. There is a little wooden pavilion square with the wicket, a number of appropriate tents and an atmosphere which contrives to hold the spirit of a country festival and of a game not too far removed from the village green by averages and sophistication.

Horsham, where the church spire has always dominated the ground's appearance

Little has changed, although the passing trains no longer puff smoke. The church whose spire is such an important feature is still there hard by the ground. Dudley Carew's book was published in 1946 when Horsham still enjoyed its Festival Week, whose hey-day was probably in the 1930s, although first-class cricket has been played on the ground for over a hundred years. The inter-war period was the time when Horsham was the domain of Alfred Oakes, known as 'Joker', who was the groundsman and lived in the groundsman's cottage on the ground for sixty years. His two sons, Charlie and Jack were both born in the cottage and both played for Sussex.

Oakeses and Coxes, these are the Sussex families associated with Horsham for both George Cox senior and junior – father and son – were born and bred a couple of miles away in Warnham and both played for Horsham. George senior made his mark on his home ground in the most emphatic manner when, in 1926, he took 17 for 106 against Warwickshire to return the best match analysis by a Sussex bowler, including nine for 50 in one innings.

In 1934 Horsham witnessed a landmark in the departure from county cricket of England's greatest batsman, Jack Hobbs. Hobbs was never noticeably ambitious but, towards the end of his career, the goal of 200 hundreds became something he would have dearly loved to achieve. It kept him going into the 1934 season, by which time he was fifty-one. In George Duckworth's benefit match at Old Trafford he made the 197th – which was to be the last. It was in the second match of Horsham Week, when he was run out having scored 79, that he realized it was too much. Acknowledging that the goal had eluded him, he dropped out of the Surrey side.

From the 1960s there was no county cricket at Horsham for, sadly, a long time. Cambridge and Oxford Universities visited in 1971 and 1974 respectively, but it was not for over twenty years, in 1983, that there was a county championship match on the ground. As if to stress how remiss the desertion of the ground had been the games in that year and the two following were full of entertainment, with plenty of runs scored.

There was no match in 1986, however, and although Sussex did return again in 1987, one feels that Horsham's days as a ground for annual county championship cricket are over. All the same, those balmy times of the festival provide lots of memories.

HAMPSHIRE

SOUTHAMPTON

Since 1987 the appearance of Hampshire's county ground at Southampton has been dramatically altered by the addition of a new 'hospitality' building containing six luxurious executive boxes and an expansive dining-room. The tall, arched fronts – echoing those of the pavilion and stand – and tiered seating of the boxes give an excellent view of the cricket, but the brilliant white colour of the building is possibly rather sudden, especially considering that Southampton must be amongst the sunniest grounds in the country.

In 1952 Jim Kilburn and Norman Yardley wrote about Southampton, 'Nearly all the seating is uncovered and general amenities are rather limited but both the opportunity and the will for improvements are there, awaiting only favourable circumstances for translation into action'. It has to be said that, other than the new building, and the offices opened in 1956, things have not changed that much. Most of the seating is still uncovered boards mounted on tiered scaffolding, other than the fairly primitive covered stand at the far end from the pavilion, built of corrugated asbestos. The ground's seating capacity is about 6,500 and, with modern developments outside the ground limiting any expansion, it is unthinkable that 15,000 would squeeze in as they did to watch the Australians in 1934.

The less immediate surrounds, however, have changed considerably. At the far end from the pavilion the greyhound track has gone to be replaced by an estate of hutch-like council houses, although this is still called

Southampton, with the brand new hospitality suite extending the line of buildings from the pavilion

The view to the flats with their flower-laden balconies adds to Southampton's scene

the greyhound end. In 1930, when the Australians came to Southampton the eccentric George Brown who opened the Hampshire innings, hit the first ball he received from Australia's second bowler, Fairfax, straight out of the ground into the middle of the greyhound stadium. Brown scored a great many runs for Hampshire and still figures in three of the county's ten record-wicket partnerships. But he was genuinely eccentric. On tour in India in 1926–27 he amused his team-mates with his canine impersonations, going round on all fours barking loudly and biting them on the ankles. This was all very well until he tried it on the Viceroy, with unfavourable results.

If Brown started the match against the Australians in style, there were more dramatic events to follow. Don Bradman arrived at the ground needing 46 runs to complete his 1,000 runs before the end of May, but he had only the first day of the match to do so. Hampshire batting first seemed to have deprived him of the chance until Grimmett's seven for 39 brought the county's innings to an early close at 151. Bradman went in first but only reached 47 thanks to the characteristically sporting gesture of Lord Tennyson, the Hampshire captain, who kept his men in the field in heavy rain until the milestone was achieved. The next day Bradman went on to 191. He was to repeat the feat of 1000 runs in May at Southampton in 1938, a unique record for both ground and batsman. Again the rain threatened to deprive Bradman and there was no play on the first day. Nevertheless, after Hampshire had been bowled out for 151 he was as unstoppable as ever, scoring 145 not out.

Along the side of the ground opposite the executive building three two-storey blocks of flats look as uninspiring as the council houses at the greyhound end, until, on closer inspection, the horticultural skills of the residents are revealed. Almost without exception the generous balconies which give an enviable view of the cricket, are decorated with hanging baskets, pots, tubs and boxes filled to overflowing with bright summer annuals. Nor is this the only gardening surprise Southampton has to offer – Hillier's, the Winchester arboretum and garden centre are among the board advertisers, prominent behind the tiered seats on one corner of the ground.

To a man of Kent the pavilion and ladies' stand next door give a fleeting impression of a less interesting version of the pavilion and annexe at Canterbury. In some ways the two buildings sum up the appearance of Southampton: they are certainly not ugly and their open fronts on two levels suggest symmetrical elegance, but this does not overcome an essential blandness. It is a pity that the dormer louvres were done away with on the pavilion roof when both buildings were reroofed with rather too bright red tiles and one wishes that, like Canterbury, the clock was more boldly displayed, rather than almost unnoticeable on the balcony of the small addition built in 1965 to join pavilion and stand. Inside the pavilion, in the long-room bar and next-door cafeteria, there is plenty to look at, with photographs, cigarette-cards and other reminders of the county's history as befits a county ground. And outside the main door is the gleaming innings bell which came, as one might expect at England's premier home for passenger liners, from the Athlone Castle.

Next to the pavilion is Southampton's smallest building – the home team's dressing-room – which also has the most character. It is gabled Edwardian in the style of the much larger houses which used to stand behind the pavilion end of the ground, only one of which survives. It was a welcome change to most county grounds where you are often hard pushed to get a glimpse of any of the players today, let alone talk to them, to see the Hampshire players happily going up and down the steps to talk to friends or managing to cross to the offices next door without scowling at the young autograph-collectors, for whom it is not surprisingly a happy hunting-ground.

Not everything was roses though when I visited Southampton on the last day of the match against Pakistan's tourists. Imran wanted to give his bowlers practice while Hampshire's captain, Mark Nicholas, quite rightly preferred to reward the larger-than-usual crowd by declaring his team's innings so that Pakistan could score some quick runs and set Hampshire a target. Angry words were exchanged in public but like most people I had to agree with the Hampshire supporters that the situation was far more representative of the rest of Pakistan's tour than normal events at Southampton. The days when the visit from the tourists was the highlight of a county's season seemed far away.

Southampton's most lucrative addition in recent years, the squash and social club, is prominent as you enter the ground through the main gates to the car park. An outsize Hampshire County Cricket Club badge on the wall reminds you that this is all part of the club. This is made even clearer inside. Although the sporting activities are varied: four squash courts, a gym, cricket nets and a health and fitness centre suitably called the 'Bodyline Suite', the flavour is definitely cricket, with photographs of past captains up the stairs, an amusing cartoon montage of players and other Hampshire cricket figures, and in the main 'function' room – the Desmond Eagar Room.

Desmond Eagar was the type of person that every first-class county should be lucky enough to have benefited from at some time during its history. He joined Hampshire from Gloucestershire as captain and joint-secretary in 1946 and continued as captain until 1957. He remained as secretary until his death aged 59, in 1977. Eagar's captaincy did a great deal to set the county up for their first Championship win in 1961, while his tenure of the secretaryship was incalculably beneficial towards the general harmony and financial well-being of the club. At the same time he was a distinguished cricket historian.

In Harry Altham, moreover, Hampshire can claim one of the most accomplished cricket historians of all time. Altham has been, like Eagar, one of the most influential and revered figures in the club's history. He came to Hampshire as a master and cricket coach at Winchester and played for the club between 1919–23. Far more important were his spell of nearly forty years on the committee and his Presidency from 1946 until his death in 1965.

Altham was also one of three Hampshire men who give the county an almost unrivalled connexion with the administration of MCC. The county's first outstanding player and captain for six seasons was F. E. Lacey, who scored 323 at Southampton against Norfolk in 1887 – at the time the highest score in a county match. He went on to become Secretary of MCC from 1898 until 1926 and as a result receive the first 'cricket' knighthood. He was followed after an interval by Ronnie Aird, who played with success for Hampshire from 1920–38 and was Secretary of MCC from 1953–62. Finally, Harry Altham held the key post of Treasurer of MCC from 1950–63.

The ground at Southampton was officially opened in 1885 by the club's President, the Earl of Northesk (whose kinsmen are the Earls of Southesk), who gave a lunch while his Countess opened a grand bazaar. Things did not, however, get off to an auspicious start and in the first match Hampshire were skittled out by the Surrey bowler, George Lohmann, for 32.

1906 saw the arrival at Southampton of Philip Mead, who was to become the county's most prolific batsman and play a decisive part in the improvement of their flagging fortunes. Only Hobbs, Hendren and Woolley have scored more runs than Mead's 55,061, a large proportion of which were made at Southampton. In 1921 he made 280 not out on the ground against Nottinghamshire, the highest score of his career. Mead remains Hampshire's most revered player and in 1956 he opened the new office building with Harry Altham – although sadly by then he had completely lost his sight.

Although by no means a scintillating batsman, he was renowned rather for his staying power, Mead inspired one of the most delightful of cricket sketches, by R. C. Robertson-Glasgow:

> He was number four. Perhaps two wickets had fallen cheaply; and there the cheapness would end. He emerged from the pavilion with a strong, rolling gait; like a longshoreman with a purpose. He pervaded a cricket pitch. He occupied it and encamped on it. He erected a tent with a system of infallible pegging then posted inexorable sentries. He took guard with the air of a guest who, having been offered a weekend by his host, obstinately decides to reside for six months. Having settled his whereabouts with the umpire, he wiggled the toe of his left boot for some fifteen seconds inside the crease, pulled the peak of a cap that seemed all peak, wiggled again, pulled again, then gave a comprehensive stare around him, as if to satisfy himself that no fielder, aware of the task ahead, had brought out a stick of dynamite. Then he leaned forward and looked at you down the pitch, quite still. His bat looked almost laughably broad.

Most people think of C. B. Fry as a Sussex cricketer, but in 1909 he took up command of a training ship on the River Hamble and joined Hampshire whom he played for until 1921. In 1911 he made 258 not out against Gloucestershire at Southampton which was the highest score of his career.

Probably the most colourful and one of the most popular players to have ever taken the field at Southampton was Lionel Tennyson, grandson of the poet, who in 1928 became Lord Tennyson. Tennyson injected

A 1950s aerial view of Southampton, the large stand serving the greyhound track at this end of the cricket ground

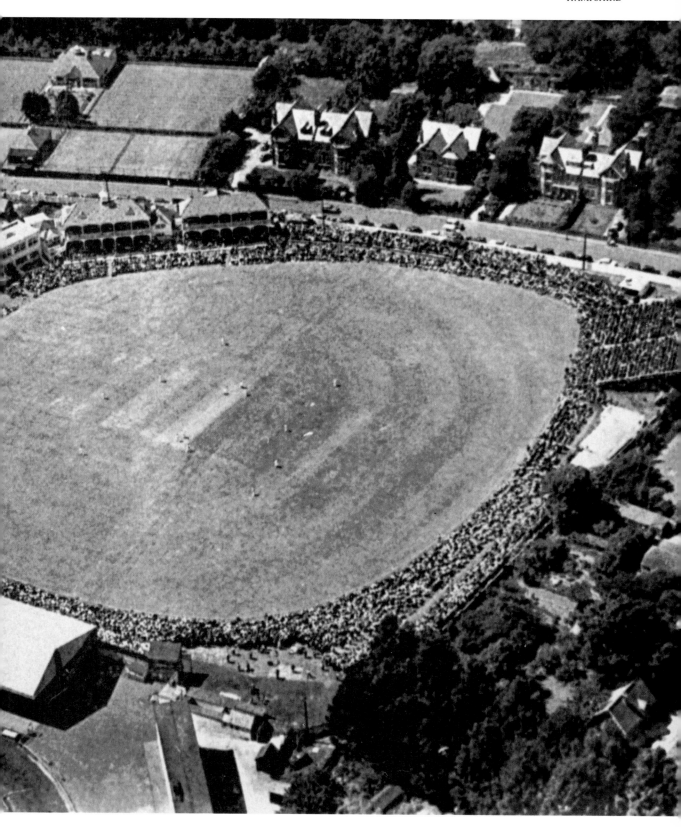

Hampshire cricket with a cavalier spirit which has resurfaced on occasions ever since. His performance on the field was as swashbuckling as his approach to the game, and never more so than when he scored the only double-hundred of his career on the county ground against the West Indies in 1928. Learie Constantine had terrorized the early Hampshire batting before his Lordship went in at 86 for five. Four hours later he had made 217.

From Tennyson the spirit of adventure reappeared in Hampshire's cricket under Colin Ingleby-Mackenzie, later Nick Pocock and most recently the current captain, Mark Nicholas. During the last two decades Southampton crowds have had plenty of entertainment, often thanks to the array of overseas stars taken on by the county. Until he became disillusioned with cricket as a result of being deprived of the opportunity to play at Test level, the South African Barry Richards, who joined Hampshire in 1968, was the best batsman in the world. When he batted with the West Indian Gordon Greenidge who arrived in 1970, theirs was the most exciting opening partnership of modern county cricket. No one who watched will forget Greenidge's innings of 259 against Sussex in 1975, when as well as scoring 24 fours he hit 13 sixes to set a record for county matches.

If Hampshire could boast a dominating partnership to open their innings, in Andy Roberts and subsequently Malcolm Marshall they have had two West Indian fast bowlers who have each enjoyed fearsome reputations. After Richards and Roberts had left the county Greenidge and Marshall were the strike forces around which the present highly talented side was built up, and reward came in 1986 with the John Player League. Success – as well as entertaining play – is a sure basis for increased support and at the beginning of 1987 Hampshire's membership had increased for the first time for many years to just over 4,500.

Many people have found Southampton an uninspiring ground but most of them would agree that it is a friendly place. Colin Cowdrey reckoned that the wicket was ideal for stroke-makers – and he should know. There is an openness which one expects in a coastal place and an essentially rural county, which is in contrast to the built-up surroundings of most midland and northern grounds. The sun usually shines and when I visited in early August 1987, a season plagued by rain more than most, Anthony Baker, the club's Chief Executive was complaining of a dry spell which accounted for the browning outfield. With a competitive and well-balanced side and a rising membership, perhaps these are the 'favourable circumstances' which Kilburn and Yardley saw the county to be waiting for thirty-five years ago.

Above *The pavilion at Dean Park, Bournemouth in the 1950s*

BOURNEMOUTH

Tell a Hampshire man that Bournemouth does not belong to his county, but to neighbouring Dorset, and he is likely to be either disbelieving or aggressive, yet so it does. Snug Dean Park is a ground with a wealth of happy records for Hampshire and has been the scene of many of the county's best achievements. Twenty years ago, Jim Kilburn wrote in the *World of Cricket* that the appeal of Bournemouth was that of, 'green foliage against blue skys, of white tenting and bright flags flying, of picnic basket and unfenced boundary'. Today it is much the same.

Hampshire's three coastal homes of cricket have different vocations: Southampton commerce, Portsmouth the navy and Bournemouth holidays. The county usually play four championship matches at Dean Park, of which the two consecutive games in August are the main occasion. This is when you will see in the town as many families with towels, beach-bags and all the other paraphernalia of the sea-side as you will people going about their daily work. Many of the visitors take their holidays to coincide with the cricket and for a long time there was a strong connexion with Yorkshire who were regular opponents at Dean Park. More often than not Hampshire were on the receiving end from the powerful northern county, but as the match at Bournemouth was among the last of the season, those Yorkshiremen who travelled south for a cricketing holiday

Lord's: An aerial view, with the white roof of the new Mound Stand prominent, the brown roof of the indoor school behind, at the Nursery end, and the Regent's Park mosque visible in the background

ABOVE Lord's: The new Mound Stand, filled to capacity for MCC's Bicentenary Test in 1987

OPPOSITE The Oval: Facing the pavilion, with the cupola of Kennington parish church visible on one side

BELOW The Oval: The famous gasholders

TOP Chelmsford: Scene of many Essex successes in recent years. The pavilion faces the wicket at right-angles with a hospitality tent to one side

BOTTOM Hove: The view from the open top of the Arthur Gilligan Stand, up the slope to the boundary, lined with deck-chairs on the far side

*ABOVE Canterbury: The New Stand, opened in 1986,
visible to the right of the well-known lime tree inside the
boundary*

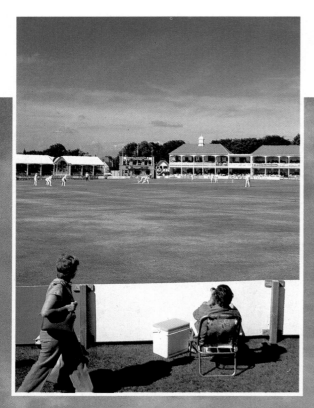

FAR LEFT *Southampton: The brown outfield is witness to the ground's habitual dryness. On the far side is the main group of buildings where club offices, players' building and pavilion are situated*

LEFT *Taunton: The view towards the elegant tower of St James's and BELOW looking towards the new pavilion with the Quantock hills forming the skyline in the background*

ABOVE Bristol: The view across the ground to the pavilion complex

BELOW Swansea: Looking from the seaward end towards the pavilion and Bryn Mill behind

Dean Park, enclosed by trees and a ring of houses

were often rewarded by their team clinching the County Championship.

Encircled by quiet streets of prosperous Victorian houses, Dean Park is among the most testing of county grounds for the newcomer to track down. When the ground was originally laid out – in 1869, making it the oldest of Hampshire's grounds – it was in open country but before long the houses began to appear, the hedges of their gardens forming the cricket ground's outer perimeter. Inevitably, modern development has brought changes, but on many sides the original houses remain, with small wooden garden gates giving direct access to the ground.

Dean Park remains, as it always has been, part of the Cooper-Dean family estate and as such is one of the few surviving privately-owned county grounds in England. The family have given continual support to both the ground and Bournemouth CC, the most recent sign of which is the scoreboard at the far end from the pavilion: 'This scorebox was constructed through the generosity of Miss A. Ellen Cooper-Dean. The Hampshire County Cricket Club will ever be grateful to her. 3rd August 1974.'

The first match was played in 1871, as is proclaimed on a board over the groundsman's shed. Hampshire's first visit came in 1897 and no doubt it was Dean Park's elevated status which resulted in the construction of the present pavilion in 1902. It was an occasion for a bit of trumpet-blowing by the local paper. 'Now, completed by this eminently practicable and presentable structure, surrounded by lovely houses, and their well-kept gardens, there is not a prettier ground in England'. Prettiness remains a strong characteristic of the circular ground, enclosed by horse-chestnut trees, pines and holme oaks, particularly when marquees complete the picture during county matches. Elsewhere the accommodation is basic: green wooden benches for members and public alike, the former enjoying the small covered stand to one side of the pavilion, the enclosure in front of the pavilion and covered seating in its upper storey, and the temporary stand of open seats on the other side. Next to the covered stand is the sort of building boasted by many grounds, Heath Robinson but effective, it is a Nissen hut with extensions on the front housing press and scorers in conditions far from lavish. Most basic of all, however, are the lavatories behind the pavilion which must rank as among the most archaic and unwelcoming in the country.

Whether today's county players would agree that the pavilion is practicable by today's standards, it is certainly presentable. The shape of the steeply-pitched tiled roof gives it a slightly unusual appearance, but beneath is an elegant white-painted balcony, supporting slender posts. It was from this balcony that Colin Ingleby-Mackenzie's team acknowledged the delighted cheers of their supporters, having given the county its first honour with the County Championship in 1961. It was one of the most popular of all successes achieved by a side whose spirit was described by their captain not long before as originating from 'wine, women and song'.

Ingleby-Mackenzie's light-hearted reference typified his cricket and captaincy which mixed flair and enjoyment. His team contained a rare mixture of talents, from the electrifying batting of Roy Marshall to the unfailingly consistent bowling of Derek Shackleton. Marshall, a white Barbadian was one of the most popular sights on any ground in England and among many exciting innings at Dean Park came the highest score of his career – 228 not out against Pakistan in 1962. Shackleton's bowling brought him a county record of 2,857 wickets in his career and provided the backbone to Hampshire's performances to such an extent that when he retired *Wisden* commented that, 'Hampshire without Shackleton will be like Blackpool without its tower'.

After Philip Mead had scored his 150th hundred at Southampton he was presented at Dean Park with a large parcel containing an inscribed scroll and a cake. When Lionel Tennyson visited the ground in 1936, having retired the previous year he got a silver cigar box – suitable and more generous.

The outstanding individual achievement at Dean

Park came, however, in 1937 when Hampshire's captain, R. H. Moore, made the county's highest individual score of 316 not out, an innings put on a good footing by a hundred before lunch. At the other end of the batting scale, the opener A. Bowell and W. H. Livsey established a last-wicket partnership record for the county against Worcestershire in 1921, their score of 192 being one of the highest for the tenth wicket in all county cricket. Bowell was a strong batsman who had scored a double-century at Dean Park in 1914. Walter Livsey, who doubled up as Lord Tennyson's valet and Hampshire's wicket-keeper, made something of a reputation with his batting, and never more so than a year later when, going in at number ten, his 110 not out was largely responsible for Hampshire's historic win over Warwickshire at Edgbaston.

Today little has encroached on the atmosphere of relaxation at Dean Park and on a sunny day, with a gentle sea breeze keeping the air fresh, it is among the most attractive places for watching county cricket. About the only eye-sore is the towering modern building of Macarthey and Stone which looms above the sight-screen from the centre of Bournemouth. By general consent it is the ugliest building in the town and according to Dean Park's groundsman, Fred Kingston, 'should have a bomb put under it'. Nothing so dramatic has ever happened in Bournemouth, certainly not at Dean Park unless you are talking about some of the cricket and it will take more than one tower-block to spoil the scene.

PORTSMOUTH

The United Services ground, home to the Royal Navy and the only 'military' ground now used for county cricket has two notable features: one architectural, the other mechanical. No other ground boasts a gateway of the quality of Portsmouth's. One feels it should really grace the entrance to the park of some classical stately home, flanked by matching lodges. In fact this was not its original location: it was once across Broad Street, at the end of the High Street, from there it was moved to the Royal Naval barracks and not until 1951 did it find its present resting place. All the same, it gives the most dramatic of welcomes, its intricate wrought-iron gates hung in the central archway of the edifice which boasts massive, double, Corinthian pilasters on either side and heavily rusticated stonework. Where the lodges would

Portsmouth's triumphal gateway, the grandest in county cricket

Portsmouth: Hampshire v Sussex, 1899. A view across the ground towards the pavilion, with a train in the background

be are perfectly symmetrical arched doorways, half the height of the main gateway, inside whose wooden doors are the ground's turnstiles. In characteristic style the frieze of the main gateway proclaims, 'JACOBUS SECUNDUS REX A REG III AN DOMI 1687'. It must be one of the few things of beauty to survive from the three-year reign of that unpopular, autocratic Catholic monarch.

Quite different, but on a similar scale, is the ground's heavy roller. Weighing in at five and a half tons it is the giant of a universally heavyweight family and one pities the poor horse – or more probably, horses – who dragged it back and forth across the ground before the war. Today it is painted a jaunty shade of yellow and, fortunately, it is motorized. In the 1950s Arthur Gawler was the groundsman and his partnership with the roller led Desmond Eagar to comment at the time that Portsmouth was, 'the best cricket wicket in the county'.

Cricket has a long history at Portsmouth and the ground was originally laid out, after it had been levelled and drained by convicts, in the 1870s. 1987 celebrated the centenary of county cricket on the ground. Suitably

enough, Hampshire played Sussex – the original opponents a hundred years before – although that match was not first-class as Hampshire had not yet qualified.

The ground is host to rugby as well as cricket and home for the United Services Portsmouth RFC. It seems illogical that it is the rugby clubhouse which is virtually behind the bowler's arm at one end, while the cricket pavilion faces the wicket at an angle from long-on. The latter is an attractive building with an upper balcony, whose balustrade supports the clock, stretching between two side blocks and a gently-pitched tiled roof. In front bright red seats add a splash of colour although their effect is minimized, as this is a large ground accommodating the rugby pitch at right-angles to the wicket at one end.

The only covered stand, positioned on the other side of the sightscreen from the rugby clubhouse is really

designed for watching rugby rather than cricket and other than a small, tiered open stand on the city side of the ground accommodation consists essentially of individual wooden seats. As if to compensate, and to provide relief for aching posteriors, it is a ground with ample space around the boundary which encourages the perambulating, rather than the sedentary spectator.

Today the ground's outlook is overshadowed and, one must say marred, by the pair of buildings belonging to Portsmouth Polytechnic beyond the north-east corner. The Polytechnic has also taken over the red-brick building on the south-east corner which used to be the Nuffield Club for the use of servicemen. Despite the size of the ground, one feels that one distraction for batsmen must be the unusually noisy and frequent diesel trains which rattle through to the Harbour station, just across Park Road which runs along behind the pavilion end.

Over the years the Portsmouth wicket has provided an unusual proportion of results as against drawn games and yet, at the same time, has lived up to the reputation of providing plenty of runs. No player benefited from this more than Philip Mead. On two occasions he shared in record-breaking partnerships at Portsmouth: in 1921 he put on 259 for the fourth wicket with his captain, Lionel Tennyson against Leicestershire and in 1927 he put on 244 for the third wicket with G. Brown against Yorkshire – the latter remains a record for the county. Pride of place, though, must go to Yorkshire's Percy Holmes who, in 1920, scored 302 not out.

You will still see some uniforms among the crowds at Portsmouth, even if the scoreboard is no longer operated by two serving seamen. Times have changed since the ground was exclusively for the use of officers and when a military man could comment that, 'a good cricket side has always been an invaluable asset to a ship on a foreign station'. And gone are the days when the Combined Services could claim a game against the visiting tourists, the first of which was against Armstrong's fearsome Australian side of 1921, when they only beat the Combined Services at Portsmouth in the

Above *Portsmouth's pride, the heaviest of heavy rollers*

dying moments of the game. That evening there were dark mutterings in the mess that defeat only came because a broken wicket made J. M. Gregory virtually unplayable. Perhaps the roller had done its job too well.

BASINGSTOKE

Since 1966 Hampshire have made an annual excursion from their coastal strongholds to the delightfully named ground of May's Bounty at Basingstoke. Prior to then the county had played eight first-class games there between 1906 and 1951, the last against Oxford University. It was a desire to attract support in the northern part of the county, combined with Basingstoke's rapid expansion which were primarily responsible for the return, since when the county's visits have been unbroken.

The ground is home to the Basingstoke and North Hants CC, a successful club who have been established since the mid-nineteenth century. At that time the ground was called the Folly and this name has continued to be used occasionally: May's Bounty tells the story of the club's major benefactor.

In 1880 the club were given orders to leave the ground as it was to be sold for building. Enter Lieut-Col John May, local brewer and mayor of Basingstoke for no less than six periods of office and the town's most generous benefactor. A keen sportsman, May determined to save the ground for the cricket club and purchased it, leasing it back to the club at a nominal rent of £10 per annum. Seventy years later, in 1950, the club were able to buy the freehold – for £450.

Although it is only a ten-minute walk from the centre of Basingstoke May's Bounty has retained a tree-lined appearance which is the ground's most attractive feature. The brick pavilion, originally built at the beginning of the century, has been regularly and considerably altered since – especially in recent years, in response to the county's annual visits and as a result of the club's increased prosperity. It retains its open balcony for players, as well as the handsome clock, set in a central gable in the roof, and the flag-pole surmounting the gable.

May's Bounty in 1901, shortly before Hampshire paid their first visit to the ground

The pavilion stands in the south-west corner of the ground and at the far – north – end is Bounty Road and the Bounty Inn. The boundary is particularly short on this side and big-hitters have often dispatched the ball over the road to land among the houses beyond.

In the early years of Hampshire's regular visits to May's Bounty the wicket was often reported to be of suspect bounce. This appears to have been the case for the match against Kent in 1974, when the unfortunate Colin Cowdrey, admittedly no longer at his most mobile, was felled by the ball after he mis-timed a hook off Andy Roberts. Cowdrey was out, having fallen onto his stumps and retired from the match. The wicket's unevenness would now have appeared to have been dealt with, however, and in recent seasons the present groundsman, Bill Hiscock, has been commended for his

Modern May's Bounty, Hampshire's only ground away from the coast

pitches each time Hampshire have visited.

If May's Bounty has yet to witness any record-breaking feats or become part of Hampshire's cricket history it appears to have carved a secure niche for itself as the county's northern outpost. What an enjoyable coincidence it would have been if Peter May himself had appeared on the ground – the odds are he would have made an occasion of it – but sadly, he was only eight when his university, Cambridge, made their one and only visit and by the time Surrey appeared as the opposition on Hampshire's return in 1966 he had been retired for three years.

SOMERSET

TAUNTON

Taunton and Somerset immediately bring to mind what one Somerset player, R. C. Robertson-Glasgow, wrote about another, J. C. White, 'Whether it was cows or batsmen, he had the treatment for the trouble'. One's fantasy of Taunton, the most south-westerly county ground, is essentially rural, where a good proportion of the crowd and members might be farmers or other countrymen who have strolled over from the market, just across Priory Bridge Road and the River Tone.

Of course the reality is different. All the same, if there are two notable features of Somerset it is dairy farming – despite the milk quotas – and the wonderful stone churches, and the county ground lies between the cattle market and a positive array of church towers. The closest of these is St James's, literally just outside the ground. When I visited Taunton the bell-ringers were practising, a bonus I had not expected but which could have not been more suitable anywhere. Somerset, who were in the field, were obviously used to it, as no one payed any attention.

The church is across the street from the main gates – which, I was delighted to see, are named after Jack White, appropriately as he took more wickets in his career than any other Somerset bowler. Many of his victims' departures were followed by a sotto voce aside from the slow left-armer to the nearest fielder such as, 'I didn't think *that* cock would last long, Glasgy; he had one of those fancy caps on'.

Taunton has recently been through something of an upheaval, of the sort the west countrymen are not used to. Through the late-1970s and early-1980s Somerset was – at least to the great majority of non-Somerset people – the county of Botham, Richards and Garner. They were also the years of the county's first successes and in five seasons they won all the limited-over competitions, including two victories in both the Benson and Hedges Cup and Gillette Cup/NatWest Trophy. Then, in 1986 came the highly publicized storm and all three superstars left.

Now, most Somerset supporters would say that things are getting back to normal. Botham, Richards and Garner undeniably attracted a great deal of publicity and support – both human and financial – to Taunton. But they were not always of the most desirable sort and, as Somerset's secretary, Tony Brown commented in a measured way, there were many who came only to watch Botham and Richards, not Somerset, whose fortunes did not concern them. As if to emphasize this, the club's membership of just over 5,000 increased between the 1986 and 1987 seasons.

The county's successes in competitions was partly responsible for the dramatic addition of the new pavilion, built in 1981. The design of the building is not to everyone's taste, its long tiled roof punctuated by an outsize central gable containing the clock, and the overall impression of red-brown modern brickwork, devoid of decoration, dark-stained woodwork and tinted glass is not exactly cosy. It is, however, impressive, a building of confidence and prosperity which won a local design award.

Inside the pavilion is luxurious to a degree few other counties can rival. On the ground floor are a dining-room and the members' bar; above are the dressing-rooms, club offices and committee room – all with their own large balconies. Perched on top, its windows filling the centre of the gable, is the executive room. If it was all expensive to create, the pavilion is already producing significant revenue, for the dining-room, committee room and executive room are all available for hire throughout the year, and the club does not stint on advertising its suitability for conferences and receptions.

The front of the pavilion is lined with rows of the plastic bucket chairs which appear to be the hallmark of a general smartening up by any ground. The whole arrangement is most satisfactory; you can wander in and out of the bar from your seat, or into the dining-room for a three-course lunch, which, in 1987, would have set you back just over five pounds. At the back of the dining-room are display cases filled with Somerset cricketana including one of the most amusing of all the 'Spy' cartoons, of L. C. H. Palairet. The picture was presented by Jeffrey Archer in 1981, Archer being an

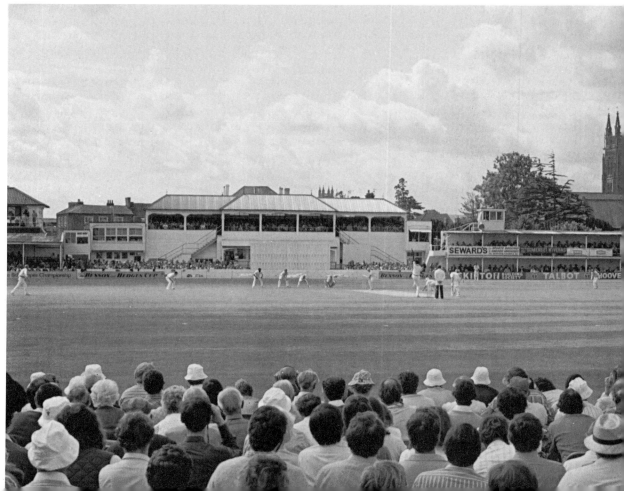

ardent Somerset supporter and president of the Somerset Wyverns – a collection of non-resident Somerset diehards.

The new pavilion has virtually put an end to one of Palairet's favourite pastimes, hitting the ball out of the ground into the River Tone. Far from being a slogger, however, Palairet was often described as the supreme stylist and he remains in the Somerset and Taunton record books for his first-wicket partnership on the ground with H. T. Hewett in 1892, when they put on 346 against Yorkshire.

If the elegant batting of Lionel Palairet represented one quality of Somerset cricket in its early days, S. M. J. Woods represented the other. Although born in Australia, Sammy Woods is *the* figure in the history of Somerset cricket. Robertson-Glasgow called him 'Somerset's godfather'. In the years either side of the turn of the century his fast bowling, big-hitting and captaincy gave

Opposite *Taunton's new pavilion, a monument to prosperity, with Peter Roebuck leading out his side*

Below *The more traditional view, from the new pavilion to the old*

Somerset cricket a certain character it has never lost and saw them establish themselves as a worthy first-class county. In 1891 they beat the champions, Surrey, at Taunton when Woods's bowling was decisive. In the last over he bowled John Sharpe, Surrey's one-eyed number eleven, to win the match and scepticism over Somerset's suitability for first-class status was effectively silenced.

C.B. Fry considered Woods the most impressively built athlete he ever saw and his appetite for life was reflected in his down-to-earth, humorous attitude to cricket. His conclusion on batting was totally characteristic, 'You're not Ranji, so aim at mid-on's nut and you'll find the ball will go over the square-leg boundary'.

If Sammy Woods was the first, Taunton has been home to a succession of the game's biggest hitters. Between the wars few people hit the ball harder than Guy Earle. A massively strong man, who first rose to cricket fame as the unfortunate captain of Harrow in 'Fowler's Match' against Eton in 1910, Earle often gave the impression that the only purpose of batting was to dispatch the ball out of the ground as often as possible. He once scored 59 runs at Taunton in fifteen minutes.

Earle was followed by Arthur Wellard, whose hitting and fast bowling made him a worthy successor to Woods. Wellard hit one quarter of his career's total of runs in sixes – some 500. His two most explosive efforts both took place at Wells, where Somerset no longer play. Against Derbyshire in 1936 and Kent in 1938, he hit five consecutive sixes in an over. On the second occasion the bowler was Frank Woolley and off the sixth ball Wellard was dropped in front of the pavilion. To complete the succession, in 1985 Ian Botham hit 80 sixes in the season, thereby beating Wellard's existing record of 66. If Botham's batting exploits for England are more renowned, it was for Somerset and in front of Taunton crowds that he most regularly displayed his hitting and fast-scoring abilities.

The new pavilion has reversed the balance of the ground at Taunton for it stands at the opposite end of the wicket from the old one which survives – in good health after a revamp following the Bradford disaster. In fact the new pavilion is at a slight disadvantage, for it faces the wicket from fine-leg/long-off, while its predecessor has a view from directly behind the bowler's arm. Purely on appearance, the old pavilion, with its white-painted woodwork and simple roof-line surmounted by delicate finials, wins hands down – though inside it did not compare. Now it accommodates sponsors and vice-presidents, and there is also a bar downstairs, but it has the disadvantage of often being largely obscured by the sightscreens.

A game between Somerset and Worcestershire at Taunton in 1910

In the old days this and the low two-storey covered stand next door made up the members' enclosure but now, of course, their domain is in the new pavilion. On the opposite side of the stand from the old pavilion is a building with the same grey roofline, giving this end of the ground some symmetry. Inside is the indoor school with six executive boxes on top and a covered stand in front.

Taunton may have moved into the modern age with its new pavilion and executive boxes, but not at the expense of all tradition. In one corner of the ground, in front of the tower of St James's, is the stand and enclosure of the Somerset Stragglers – where it has been since most people can remember. An historic club, the Stragglers have the Devon Dumplings as their neighbouring opponents.

On round from the Stragglers' enclosure, the west side of the ground remains nice and simple with backless, tiered bench seating. A row of pollarded limes behind – matched by another along the east side

opposite – contribute to the shade here, and certainly for the last session of play the sun is behind you. It is a friendly spot, however, where you feel you can move about without causing offence, and where the spectators are often akin to the family I sat next to: mother on a canvas chair with her knitting and small daughter, watching father and son practising against the advertising boundary boards during the tea-interval.

The Stragglers' stand is in front of the secondary scoreboard and the main one lies almost directly opposite, round from the new pavilion behind an open stand of spanking new tiered seats which continue on round this east side of the ground. These seats probably give the most enjoyable view of the ground, looking across to the older buildings and enclosures and the church towers beyond and are made all the more agreeable by constant sun on a fine day. The new scoreboard is a relic of Somerset's immediate past, having been paid for by Ian Botham's erstwhile backers, Saab Motors. I instinctively took against it, not for this reason, but because it replaces the old one which features in one of the most famous of all series of cricket photographs: Jack Hobbs equalling W. G. Grace's record 125 centuries in 1925.

The old man had scored his hundredth – ending up with 288 – against Somerset, but that was at Bristol. Afterwards, according to Sammy Woods Grace was given a dinner but no quantity of alcohol seemed to have any effect. 'You couldn't make the Old Man drunk, his nut was too large. About midnight, some of us thought we might start for home; but the Old Man said to me: "Shock'ead, you get two others, and we'll play rubbers of whist till two in the morning"'.

To return to Hobbs, 1925 was a great season for him; he scored 3,000 runs and headed the batting averages and, on 16 August, after many anxious weeks when it seemed that the whole country was watching him, he equalled W. G. Grace's record. In all the photographs – of Hobbs setting off for the final run, with Jardine at the other end in his Harlequin cap, and of the congratulations that followed, the old scoreboard is there in the background, with its rounded top to hold the clock which said 11.40. The next day, with the pressure off, Hobbs scored another 101 not out.

Nobody enjoys talking about Hobbs's achievement more than old Taunton regulars and the other mighty incident they delight in – although at their own county's expense – was when Archie Maclaren scored 424 which remains the highest score in England. Lancashire scored 801, at the time the highest total in county cricket, although a year later Yorkshire ran up 887 against Warwickshire.

They are equally proud of their own county's achievements and none more so than the batting of Harold Gimblett. From 1935–54 Gimblett's batting for Somerset was among the most exciting anywhere in county cricket and many people – Charlie Macartney among them, when he was watching England bat in Australia in 1946–47 – were amazed that he never played for England in more than three Tests. In 1946, Gimblett scored 231 at Taunton against Middlesex and he remains the county's highest run-scorer. But he had already passed into legend in 1935 for his first appearance for the county, at Frome, where Somerset no longer play.

Aged twenty he had had a trial for the county at Taunton but been sent home to his father's farm near Watchet with his prospects dashed. At the last minute,

however, he was summoned to play against Essex at Frome. Accounts of his long journey across the county are numerous, but however much of the way young Harold did or did not walk, it was certainly made touch and go by his missing the bus. He went in to bat when Somerset were 107 for six and nobody seriously believed that a young first-timer would stop the slide. Gimblett scored 50 in twenty-eight minutes, 100 in 63 and ended up with 123 in eighty minutes. It was the most sensational entry into county cricket of all time and set the style of his batting for the rest of his career.

In recent years Taunton has been treated to batting by Ian Botham and Vivian Richards which has rivalled any of their predecessors' for excitement. And yet what many people found hard to understand was the often dismal performance by the county in the championship which accompanied it, never more so than in 1985. In the first three matches of the season at Taunton Botham scored 90 off 77 balls, 112 (including 100 off 76 balls) and 149 off 106 balls, and yet all three games were lost. In the third of these matches Richards had made 186 and the next time Somerset played at Taunton he dwarfed all his previous efforts by making 322 off 258 balls, the highest score by a Somerset player. And yet Somerset could only draw the match and at the end of the season they were bottom of the championship.

Tony Brown is confident that things have settled down and as he watched his side heading towards an innings victory over his old county, Gloucestershire, the omens seemed good. I was pleased to see Vic Marks getting some wickets for his credentials are full of ideal Somerset characteristics: quiet and self-effacing, good middle-order bat and patient off-spin bowler, born at Middle Chinnock and educated at Blundells. Tony Brown remembers when, in his playing days for Gloucestershire, the Somerset match was a local derby, but like most of these traditional games the edge seems to have gone today and they are just another county match. Nevertheless, there was an unusually good crowd for a championship contest, even considering that it was the May Bank Holiday Monday. They were enthusiastic, applauding and commenting liberally and interested, as I joined a crowd of between fifty and 100 to look at the wicket during the lunch interval.

Leaving Taunton I could see why people always speak of it with affection. Although it has very definitely become a county headquarters in recent years, it has got over the period of rowdy Sunday league full-houses and managed to retain an essential friendliness and feeling of being a slight backwater. I am sure that I saw at least one farmer in the members' bar and the church bells rang, so all in all it lived up to my expectations.

BATH

With the notable exception of the sports and leisure centre which has loomed over one side of the ground since 1972, Bath enjoys an incomparable architectural setting. The recreation ground, which houses the cricket pitch, tennis courts, croquet and bowls clubs, as well as the home of Bath Rugby Club, lies in a natural amphitheatre next to the River Avon and on two sides houses built in the city's famous honey-coloured stone lead the eye to wooded hills beyond. Across the river to the west is the abbey, its east end and tower dominating the view in this direction beyond the rugby pitch which is adjacent to the cricket ground and used as a car park during county matches.

It is a fine setting for a festival, which the county normally hold in June, with two county championship matches. Temporary seating is erected along the rugby pitch side and along the opposite side, with the houses of Pulteney Street behind are the marquees of local clubs and sponsors. At one end of Pulteney Street is the tower of St Mary the Virgin, Bathwick while beyond the southwest corner of the ground is the tall spire of St John's Catholic Church.

The best way to approach the Bath ground is from Great Pulteney Street, one of the city's most impressive thoroughfares, down the slight hill of William Street to the pair of suitably architectural turnstiles. From here the keen eye will pick out the porticoed facade of Prior Park among the distant trees of Beechen Cliff, a house built for Ralph Allen, a Bath postmaster, whose park dropping down towards the city was designed by 'Capability' Brown and boasts one of England's three Palladian bridges.

The pavilion, the centre-piece of the members' enclosure stands on the north side of the ground, set up on a grass bank broken by wide steps in front and screened behind by tall lime trees with a copper beech at one end. In front, variety is given to one side of the pavilion by a pair of silver birches, planted in 1977 when the Australians played their match against the county here. The trees were planted by the two captains, Greg Chappell and Brian Close and the match well deserves to be remembered. Against the county he had played for in 1968–69 the Australian captain, going in to bat after Joel Garner had taken a wicket with his fifth ball for Somerset, set the standard of play by scoring 99 before lunch and going on to 113. The game ebbed and flowed throughout the three days until Somerset won by seven wickets with an hour to spare.

Jim Kilburn wrote about Bath in *The World of*

Cricket that, 'in very warm weather it is stifling and in very wet weather it is muddy'. Since the first county match against Sussex in 1880 the low-lying position and often damp wicket has assisted bowlers and frequently made batting highly testing. Only six double-hundreds have been scored on the ground, although they include 303 not out scored by the mighty Warwick Armstrong on the Australian tour of 1905, the highest score of his career.

The next year the Yorkshireman George Hirst established a unique all-round record, never approached since, when he scored a hundred and took five wickets in each innings (111 and 117 not out, and six for 70 and five for 45). Not all the successes have been at Somerset's expense, however, for in 1919 Jack White took 16 Worcestershire wickets for 83 runs.

Spare a thought, though, for poor Bertie Buse, the Somerset all-rounder and respected citizen of Bath who chose his home city for his benefit match in 1953. On a wicket which came in for severe criticism from the *Manchester Guardian*'s correspondent, Buse's hopes of a productive match were quickly dispelled since an hour before the end of the first day Lancashire had defeated Somerset by an innings and 24 runs. By taking six for 41 in Lancashire's only innings Buse unwittingly

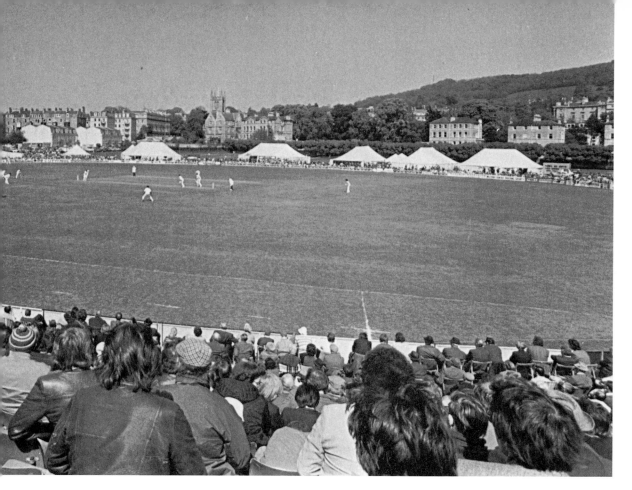

hastened the unhappy demise of his big occasion. It was
the fourth time that Lancashire had defeated Somerset
in a day.

In recent years some batsmen have undoubtedly left
Bath with happy memories. In 1981 Zaheer Abbas con-
solidated his own remarkable record when scores of
215 not out and 150 not out were his fourth instance of
a double-hundred and hundred in the same match. In
1983 Nigel Popplewell scored 100 in forty-one minutes
and 143 in sixty-two minutes, admittedly when
Gloucestershire were encouraging a declaration. A year
later Mike Gatting played an innings of 258 for Middlesex, where no assistance was given by the opposition.

If the wicket does not always match the surroundings,
Bath presents a very different Somerset face from the
county ground at Taunton and, indeed, from Weston-
super-Mare. The festival always attracts good crowds
and if the wicket produces a few surprises, then for
many people that adds to the fun.

Above *Bath, the view from the Pulteney Street side,
with the Abbey central among the Georgian buildings
on the far side*

Right *One of Bath's elegant turnstiles*

WESTON-SUPER-MARE

When R. C. Robertson-Glasgow first played for Somerset at Weston-super-Mare the ground in Clarence Park struck him as the smallest and most intimate of all county grounds. It was, 'a thing of marquees where the right stuff could be found, and deck chairs and wooden chairs under which the spade and bucket could be parked for an hour or two'.

It is much the same today, the crowds for the week's festival in August always swelled by holiday-makers, the simple square of the park enclosing a grid of residential streets and bounded by pines and holm oaks as one would expect near the sea, the pavilion – modest even by the standards of many clubs – on the seaward side the only permanent building.

All this is transformed for a week by an influx of canvas, temporary stands, a variety of seats, small caravans for press, scorers and printer and advertising boundary boards which, in this instance, bring welcome colour. Limited space around the boundaries means that the ground quickly gains the impression of being full and on a hot August day it offers traditional seaside county cricket.

The cricket ground fills only half of Clarence Park, which is divided by Walliscote Road running along behind the pavilion. A large square wall-plaque tells the visitor entering the cricket ground that the whole area was presented to the town by a Rebecca Davies, in 1882, in memory of her husband Henry. No visitor with even the smallest interest in gardening should go to Weston-super-Mare without crossing Walliscote Road into the second half of Clarence Park where they will find the most marvellous display of summer bedding. In one long, curving border groups of annuals are neatly arranged in blocks of colour: pink, white, red and blue, while in other circular beds the flowers are built up into mounds. The centrepiece is a grand fountain which was presented by the mayor in memory of Rebecca Davies herself: a fitting tribute to Somerset CC's benefactor.

Somerset's cricket at Weston was immediately inter-

rupted by the First World War, for they made their first visit in 1914 and only two of the scheduled three matches were played. The year of their return, in 1919, the Somerset tail-enders, J. Bridges and H. Gibbs celebrated the occasion by establishing a last-wicket record of 143 for the county. Jim Bridges, who made 99 of the runs, was a Weston character who, according to Robertson-Glasgow, fancied himself as a bit of a batsman and once remarked, 'If only they *knew*, that you and I, Glasgy, are as good batsmen as any in the Somerset side ... except possibly Dar Lyon and Jack MacBryan'. It appears that they never did know, for he always batted at number ten. Tail-enders have often done well at Weston, however, for in 1963 C. M. Greetham and H. W. Stephenson established the ninth-wicket record of 183 for Somerset against Leicestershire.

Probably the best innings on the ground was played by M. M. Walford against Hampshire in 1947. Walford, a highly talented athlete who won a triple blue at Oxford and played hockey for Great Britain in the 1948 Olympics, was a school-master at Sherborne and as a result his appearances for Somerset were usually limited to August. He made the most of his time on this occasion, scoring 264.

The often dry Weston wicket, where the sand is not far beneath the surface has been on occasions what *Wisden* would describe as 'spiteful', and in 1982 Somerset's second innings against Middlesex was all over in 14 overs, during which time they struggled to 57 runs. In recent years it has produced a surfeit of draws – nine out of twelve in the last six years, but that is not to say that there has not been some stirring stuff to keep the holiday-makers happy, for with a quiet wicket runs are often easy to score on the relatively small ground and in 1985 Botham hit 10 sixes on his way to 134. Vic Marks will always have fond memories of Clarence Park as well: at last, in 1984, his tenth season with Somerset, he scored his maiden hundred for the county.

Above left *Clarence Park, Weston-super-Mare. A sunny day such as is needed for seaside cricket*

Above *Clarence Park's heavy roller in action, keeping the sand beneath the surface*

GLOUCESTERSHIRE

BRISTOL

For nearly a hundred years the county ground at Bristol took the name of Ashley Down, the area of open farmland to the north of Bristol where, in 1888, the county club purchased the site for their headquarters. In 1976, however, the old-established territorial connexion was superseded by a commercial one in a manner illustrative of the fortunes of the modern county game. Faced with unrelenting financial problems, Gloucestershire CCC had accepted the inevitable necessity of selling the freehold of their ground. At the same time, the Phoenix Assurance Company, who were in the process of establishing a major presence in Bristol, were looking for a suitable site for a sports centre for employees. The deal which followed meant that – in simple terms – Phoenix paid £125,000 for the ground, the Gloucester and Phoenix Assurance Amenity Company were granted a lease under which the county club retained use of the playing area for their fixtures, and the ground took on the new name of the Phoenix County Ground.

It is hard to imagine that, in its early days, the ground was virtually surrounded by open country. Not quite though, for immediately adjacent on two sides were the forbidding grey buildings of Muller's Orphanage which extended steadily between the 1840s and 1870s until eventually it housed over 7,000 children. The orphanage buildings are still there today, indeed, being Victorian institutional architecture at its most solid, it is hard to imagine that they will ever not be, although they are now part of Bristol Polytechnic and Brunel Technical College.

Because of the position of Ashley Down close to the outskirts of Bristol and the main route out of the city to Gloucester, development around the ground was not long in coming. The fact that the cricket ground was there first did mean that the surrounding streets of houses were named after the counties and two universities who were Gloucestershire's opponents. By the turn of the century the ground was pretty well sur-

Opposite One of the piers of Bristol's Grace Gates, a monument to the great man

rounded by a maze of residential streets and today this, as well as the distance of the ground from the centre of Bristol and – at least on the day I visited – a distinct shortage of the welcome AA 'County Cricket' signs, makes discovery of the Phoenix ground fairly testing.

One of the few exceptions among the cricketing addresses in the immediate vicinity is Nevil Road, leading off the busy A38 Gloucester road up to the main gates. Not any old gates either, but the Grace Gates, set between impressive stone piers, one of which bears a tablet with the great man in the famous stance of his portrait by Stuart Wortley and the inscription, 'To commemorate Dr. W. G. Grace, the great cricketer. Born 1848. Died 1915.' This tablet was erected outside his county ground at the centenary of his birth, 18th July, 1948. The gates were severely damaged by a reckless lorry during 1987, but no doubt the repairs will be swift and to the highest standard.

In many ways it was the 'Champion's' county ground. W.G.'s family had collectively played the leading role in the foundation of Gloucestershire CCC in 1870 and he himself was directly involved in the club establishing themselves at Ashley Down and in the setting out of the ground. When the matriarch of the family, Martha Grace, who produced five sons and four daughters, died in 1884 during a match between Gloucestershire and Lancashire at Old Trafford, the game was immediately abandoned and the scorebook recorded the result: 'Drawn, owing to the death of Mrs Grace'.

With his two brothers E. M. and G. F., W. G. had been largely responsible for Gloucestershire's spectacular success during the 1870s, when they won the County Championship outright three times and shared it in another year. The county suffered a severe blow when G. F. suddenly died of pneumonia in 1880, aged 30. E. M. continued to play for the county until 1896 and stories of his foibles are legion. On one occasion he became so incensed by a barracker at the county ground that, dropping his bat, he seized a stump and not only ran across the ground in the direction of his tormentor, brandishing the weapon, but continued to pursue the unfortunate man right out of the Ashley Down gate.

W. G. may not have scored the majority of his runs for Gloucestershire, or played the majority of his games for them, but such was the strength of his personality that, as John Arlott has written, 'in the public mind W. G. *was* Gloucestershire'. One of the landmarks of his career which he did achieve at Ashley Down was his 100th hundred, scored against Somerset in 1895. The doctor was not someone to be put off by some snow in the morning and bitter cold all day. When he reached his hundred, E. M. appeared from the pavilion with champagne and glasses. Suitably fortified, W. G. went on to score 288.

As well as his entrance gates W. G. is also remembered by the Grace Room in the pavilion – a 'function' room in the style boasted by the majority of county grounds today. The pavilion itself was in its present position at the west (Lancashire Road) end of the ground when W. G. was striding out to bat in the 1890s, although only the gable containing the clock is recognizable from the original. Today the pavilion, built of grey stone which echoes that of the old orphanage buildings, has been altered and added to at regular

intervals and as a result has a somewhat haphazard appearance. Its impact is also reduced by the fact that it is set back some distance from the boundary. Forming one side is the building housing the Grace Room and on the other is the Hammond Room – a members' bar – with the open, tiered seating of the members' stand on its roof. The clock gable is no longer in the centre of the pavilion roof, but one bonus is the view for players and committee members from the open flat roof beneath the clock, which does retain the elegant old white balustrade along its front.

Despite the fact that it is now largely enclosed, the Phoenix ground retains an appealing air of spaciousness which makes it easy to imagine its days as open downland. This is partly because of the ground's large size and because, other than the old orphanage buildings, which are set well back from the ground, the houses all around have a low roof-line. Almost wholesale modernization has transformed the city centre of Bristol, but the Phoenix ground is far enough out to be unaffected by tower blocks or other recent building programmes and one imagines that the surroundings remain much as they have been throughout this century.

Changes have, however, taken place immediately around the ground, mainly to improve the facilities and seating capacity which is now 5,500 – although the total capacity is more than this. As well as the alterations to the pavilion the old covered Ladies' Stand was demolished in the 1970s and the car park inside the Grace Gates extended to this area on the north-west corner of the ground. In front, sponsors' marquees are now put up around the boundary.

At the far end is the Jessop Tavern with its public bar and to one side, on the corner of the ground with the Ashley Road entrance and public car park behind, is the new scoreboard. The largest stand is the long covered one on the south side of the ground, always known as the 'Driving Range' for in the winter it is filled with golfers striking their balls off the tee onto the outfield of the cricket ground.

The county club have high hopes of instigating a 'ten-year plan' of further improvements, although this is dependent upon the approval and mutual involvement of the Sun Alliance company who, in 1985, took over Phoenix Assurance thereby becoming the new owners of the ground. One major feature of the improvements would be a new Indoor School, towards which Paul Getty junior, who has already shown himself to be a generous benefactor of English cricket, has given

Bristol's clock cupola, no longer central on the pavilion roof, but still an elegant feature

Above *Looking from the Ashley Down end with the windows of the Grace Room on the pavilion's left*

£10,000. The improvements would also include the replacement of the wooden bench seating which predominates around the ground.

I visited the Phoenix ground when Gloucestershire were playing Kent in the quarter-final of the Benson and Hedges Cup. This accounted for the larger-than-usual crowd, the surfeit of schoolboys, the greater volume of noise and air of expectancy around the ground. I watched two teenagers solemnly recording the minute details of the day's proceedings in their score-books, content to sit in almost total silence throughout the eight-odd hours of the playing day,

and pondered on how different they were from their contemporaries who pack the terraces of football grounds.

In front of the pavilion two old boys were swapping jokes and stories of Kent's visits to the ground. One had seen Doug Wright take nine for 47 in 1939, the other remembered his first visit for the batting of Leslie Ames. I was surprised that, being a Gloucestershire supporter, the Wright admirer had not compared his effort to that of Tom Goddard, who took 17 of the Kent wickets for 106 in one day of the same match. In all, Goddard took nine wickets in an innings six times at Bristol. Charlie Parker – the most prolific wicket-taker in the county's history, and third to Rhodes and Freeman, with 3,278 in his career – took nine wickets in an innings twice at the county ground and once, in 1921, took all 10 Somerset wickets. Few counties can boast a pair of spinners of their calibre, who between them appeared over a thousand times for the county. When the two dyed-in-the-wool Gloucestershire men bowled well, in tandem on the right wicket, it was an ambitious batsman who fancied his chances.

In contrast, as we watched, the Kent spinner with a comparable reputation – Derek Underwood – was not having the best of things. His plight was made worse by the fact that the ghost of E. M. Grace's adversary seemed to have arisen. Underwood's unhappy five overs cost 45 runs for no wickets and were punctuated by a rich array of comments from the crowd. The final shot was a plea that Underwood bowl the last over of Gloucestershire's innings. As so often in cricket though, Underwood had the last laugh, scoring a flailed four with his first strike on the penultimate ball of the match and scampering through for the bye which gave Kent victory on the last.

From the present one turns – instinctively – to the past, for although the Phoenix ground does not evoke the great men and deeds it has seen in the way others do, there has been no shortage of them. After Grace came Jessop, one of the fastest run-scorers and greatest crowd-pullers the game has ever seen. It is hard to imagine 'The Croucher', his five feet seven inches diminished by his bent stance at the wicket, waiting bulldog-like to savage the offerings of the bowlers. But savage them he did, and if Bristol was not the scene of his most audacious exploits, the home crowds would certainly agree with C. B. Fry that, 'no man has ever driven a ball so hard, so high and so often in so many different directions'.

Then, between the wars, came Walter Hammond, whose batting was probably the greatest privilege Bristol spectators have been afforded. Of his 36 double-hundreds – far and away the most by an Englishman and only one less than Don Bradman's record total – Hammond made eight of them on the county ground. Hammond was playing for Gloucestershire in 1930 against the Australians, in one of the most memorable matches the ground has seen. His 89 in the county's second innings was their decisive score before, left 118 to win in the last innings, the visitors were bowled out by Parker and Goddard for 117 and the match was tied.

In more recent years the county's two outstanding and favourite cricketers have both come from overseas, Mike Procter from South Africa and Zaheer Abbas from Pakistan. Through the 1970s the whirlwind bowling and Jessop-like batting and fielding of Procter and the supremely elegant batting of Zaheer constantly delighted the crowds of loyal supporters – who also saw their county's first successes since 1877, victory in the Gillette Cup in 1973 and the Benson and Hedges Cup in 1977.

As other people have remarked, it is surprising and a pity that the Phoenix ground does not have a museum, or at least that one of the rooms in the pavilion is not given over to a high-class display of the ground's history and its highlights. One feels that it would help to give the ground – more blessed than most in the events it has witnessed – an increased stature and to enable it to identify itself more closely than it does with its rich heritage.

An early view from the pavilion, with the forbidding Muller's Orphanage behind the old stands

GLOUCESTER

The unusual name of the Wagon Works ground at Gloucester gives it a certain individuality – which is fortunate as the somewhat bleak site on the south side of the city possesses few features to attract the visitor. Jim Kilburn commented politely on the exposed position of the large, open area of the cricket ground, 'it has its drawbacks in broken weather and it is open to all the winds that blow'. In fact it is now officially the Winget ground but old habits die hard and certainly for the majority of players and regular visitors to the ground it will remain the Wagon Works, recalling the days when it was the works ground of the company which built railway carriages. Indeed close to the pavilion, built in 1979, is a building of considerable curiosity, which is actually used by the neighbouring bowling club. It was originally a railway carriage, built by the Wagon Works company to go to Argentina, but it only got part of the way, as the ship it was travelling on sank and the carriage was salvaged and returned to Gloucester.

Unlike its close neighbour, Worcester, Gloucester's cricket ground is too far from the city centre to benefit from a view of the cathedral. What a pity this is, for the marvellous fifteenth-century tower at Gloucester, rising to 225 feet, is in my opinion more beautiful than that at Worcester. One just catches a glimpse of it from the far end of the ground, away from the main entrance off busy Tuffnel Road, as it appears above the roofs of intervening houses.

The ground's appearance is not helped by the fact that the pavilion and other buildings next to it are screened by a line of plane trees along this boundary, giving the impression that the ground boasts no fixed facilities for players or spectators. As far as the latter are concerned this is true, although when the county are playing marquees at the far end, with the Mayor of Gloucester's the most prominent, temporary seating and the welcome colour of boundary advertising boards give some atmosphere and alleviate the openness which extends away at the far end to an unusually dull – even by council building standards – housing estate.

Probably the ground's most enjoyable feature is the view past one end of the line of plane trees in front of the pavilion, to the rounded dome of Robin's Wood Hill to the east. On the subject of trees, the Wagon Works ground does boast one young specimen of considerable note. It is a *Fagus sylvatica* 'Dawyck', a rather special type of beech in front of which is a large plaque proclaiming, 'Planted to Commemorate the 60th birthday of Her Majesty Queen Elizabeth II by David Lawrence GCCC, Young Cricketer of the Year 1985'. Perhaps the tree-planting inspired young 'Sid' Lawrence, who was born in Gloucester, for in the game against Yorkshire on the ground that year he took 5 for 50 in the second innings (the best bowling figures of his career at the time), to give Gloucester victory by eight wickets.

Over the years the Wagon Works club has produced a number of players for Gloucestershire, most notably Tom Goddard who was born and died in the city. Goddard played for the Wagon Works CC when their coach and groundsman was Arthur Paish, who himself had played for the county in the years of Grace and Jessop. When Goddard was awarded the first of two benefits, in 1936, he chose to play the benefit match on his home ground and it turned out to be a memorable occasion – but with a tragic outcome.

Above *Gloucester's Winget ground, with the pavilion concealed by trees*

The game was the last of the season, against Nottinghamshire, and on the first day, Saturday, everything went Gloucestershire's way with the visitors being bowled out before tea and Goddard taking 4 for 49. It was obvious, however, that the life of the wicket was limited and, after Gloucestershire had lost two wickets before the close of play Goddard was understandably concerned as Hammond strode out to bat. For in those days the financial rewards of a benefit came only from gate receipts and he knew that if Hammond was out before the close there was little chance of a large crowd on Monday. As Hammond walked out to bat he made it clear that he had no intention of letting down his old friend saying, 'Don't worry Tom, I'll bat all day Monday'. Even he could not have guessed to what extent he was to keep his word. Play resumed on Monday before a crowd of 7,000, the most to have ever attended a game on the ground, and by the end of the day Hammond had scored 317, his highest score in England. In doing so he passed W. G.'s record aggregate of runs in August of 1,278.

Goddard received £2,100, the second-highest benefit awarded to a Gloucestershire man at the time. And yet the euphoric happiness of ending the season on such a successful note was stifled within hours, for D. A. C. Page, the twenty-five year old captain of the county died in hospital a few hours after he was involved in a motor accident on his way home from the game.

Page had taken on the captaincy only one year previously, from Bev Lyon, a shrewd and enterprising leader for whom the game was played to be won and who became well known for his adventurous declarations, not least one in a game against Middlesex at Gloucester in 1929. The first two days had been virtually lost through rain, but on the last Lyon forced a result against all odds. He declared Gloucestershire's innings shortly before lunch when they were one run ahead of Middlesex's total of 184. After Charlie Parker had demolished the visitors for 121 in their second innings, Gloucestershire had a comfortable two and a half hours to score the winning runs. Lyon's laconic comment was, 'You've got to let the dog see the rabbit'.

Although Gloucester cannot really compare with either the Phoenix County Ground at Bristol or the far more picturesque Cheltenham, it plays an integral part in Gloucestershire's cricket and has witnessed a number of record achievements – albeit mainly by men from the county. Only a few years ago, in 1982, one Gloucestershire player equalled another's long standing record: against Lancashire in that year Zaheer Abbas scored 162 and 107 to equal Hammond's record of scoring a century in each innings of a match seven times.

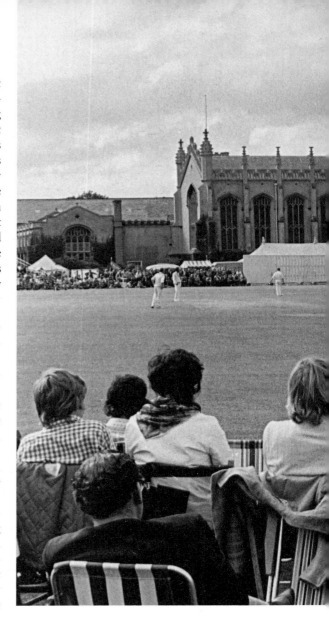

CHELTENHAM

Neither Bristol nor Gloucester would put up much competition in a league of the most memorable-looking cricket grounds. At Cheltenham, however, Gloucestershire has one of the leading contenders and the visitor's first view across the cricket ground as he approaches from the main car park, to the late-Victorian architecture of the College's hall and chapel, is one of the most impressive he will find in England.

In some ways Cheltenham is a glorious anachronism and one could be forgiven for wondering how it has survived into the world of late-twentieth century county cricket. For a start it is a school ground and as a result county cricket has to wait until the end of the summer term. It is also a festival and, at eleven days, the longest

in county cricket anywhere. Most festivals have given up the effort of producing anything festive, be it bunting in the town or entertaining cricket, and others, like Scarborough, struggle on but more often recall the glory of their former years.

Cheltenham, by contrast, is vigorously alive and retains a good many of the ingredients which once were common to all cricket festivals: for the first week and a half of August – give or take a few days – it is the main event in Cheltenham, whose streets are suitably bedecked; for many Gloucestershire folk it is an annual social occasion; for the hosts Cheltenham College, it is a source of considerable pride; there are marquees and flags and in one place stands a brightly painted double-decker bus, chartered by supporters and reminiscent of Epsom Downs on Derby Day. On a sunny day it is a celebration of cricket for the most humble and the most

exalted spectator alike, on a wet day they all suffer.

Today many of the marquees which line the boundary, from the top corner of the ground in front of the members' bar and dining-room round in front of the elegant Ionic portico of the General Hospital across the road, are taken by companies for entertainment and a day here must be an enjoyable experience for even the most disinterested cricket spectator. Elsewhere the accommodation is less indulgent: temporary tiered stands of open seats in front of the gymnasium and on the opposite side of the ground, continuing from the end of the marquees; plain wooden benches or single seats; or all manner of deck- and fold-up chairs for the self-sufficient.

Above *The College ground at Cheltenham, one of county cricket's most majestic settings*

In the earliest days of county cricket at Cheltenham the ground had a quite different appearance, for neither chapel nor hall had been built. Their tall, arched windows, stone buttresses and finials so typical of the Victorian architecture to be found at many public schools did not appear until the last years of the century and the chapel was consecrated in 1893. The enormous gymnasium was there, with its rows of arched Gothic windows, ornamental brickwork and twin towers, stretching almost the length of one side of the ground and facing the wicket from square-leg, at right-angles to the other college buildings behind the bowler's arm. Dwarfed by the gymnasium is the small pavilion, standing to one side and perhaps more than anything else, giving away Cheltenham's identity as a school ground.

The first county match was played against Surrey in 1872. Six years later the Gloucestershire committee were persuaded to extend the fixtures to two games, which they did, largely thanks to the persuasion of James Lillywhite, a member of the famous Sussex cricketing family and the College coach. On agreement of the fixtures being extended Lillywhite was paid £120, 'to run it and cover all the local expenses'. So the Cheltenham Week began and, in 1906, with the addition of a third game, it became the Festival. In 1969 one Sunday league game was added and finally, in 1975, a second to make the present eleven days of play.

During the 1870s Gloucestershire played on another school ground as well as Cheltenham, the Close at Clifton, scene of Henry Newbolt's 'breathless hush'. In 1876, W. G. Grace returned from having scored 344 for MCC against Kent at Canterbury – an innings which set up a new record for first-class cricket – to amass an unsurpassed number of runs, even by his own standards. At Clifton he made 177 for Gloucestershire against Nottinghamshire and in the third successive innings, 318 not out for the county against Yorkshire at Cheltenham, which remains the highest score by a Gloucestershire man. It gave him an aggregate of 839 runs in three innings in ten days.

The next year the county's game was against Nottinghamshire and the poster advertising the game, as well as announcing that admission would be one shilling per day, two shillings for the three days and sixpence for colleges and schools, revealed James Lillywhite to be a man of prudence and imagination. 'Should the match terminate early, a Second Match, namely Gloucestershire (*with broomsticks*) versus Cheltenham (*with bats*) will be played.' In the event W. G. showed the other half of his skill, taking 17 for 89.

G. L. Jessop was born in Cheltenham and although he was educated at the Grammar School the College ground later saw many of his most dynamic exploits. Against Yorkshire in 1895 he scored 51 in 18 minutes as well as demonstrating his often-forgotten fast bowling – at one point he had four wickets for nine runs. In 1907 he made one of his two fifteen-minute fifties at Cheltenham against Hampshire.

It is almost inevitable that any mention of Gloucestershire or of the county's grounds will include Grace, Jessop and Hammond and certainly the last gave Cheltenham crowds much to remember. If it was not the most fertile ground for his run-scoring, the festival of 1928 was the scene of his best all-round performance. In the first match against Surrey he made 139 and 143 and took ten catches. In the second game against Worcestershire he took nine for 23 in the first innings and caught the tenth wicket off Charlie Parker. In the second innings he took six for 105 and his batting in Gloucestershire's only innings, 80 out of 370 seemed almost incidental, although it was made on the most difficult of wickets.

Cheltenham has often been a wicket to favour bowlers, as the county discovered to their cost in 1896 when they were bowled out by the Australians for 17, their lowest total ever. No two men were more aware of its possibilities for spin after rain than Charlie Parker and Tom Goddard who both recorded a collection of outstanding analyses on the ground. Most individual, however, was the more recent achievement of Mike Procter who, against Yorkshire in 1979, repeated his own unique record of an all-lbw hat-trick, having previously done so against Essex in 1972.

Gloucestershire's other most spectacular import of modern times, Zaheer Abbas, also made his mark at Cheltenham and achieved a world record in the process. In 1977 he became the only batsman to score a double-hundred and a hundred in a match three times when he scored 205 not out and 108 not out against Sussex, an extraordinary statistical feat.

Today Cheltenham is one of the few grounds not to be a county headquarters which continues to play, as it always has done, an integral part in the county's cricket and it is one of the very few to have hosted county cricket for over a hundred years without a break. From photographs it is clear that the ground has hardly changed in appearance since the beginning of this century, and it is unlikely to do so in the near future. Only additions beyond the immediate surroundings, such as the office block of the Eagle Star company's administrative headquarters, which now towers behind the college chapel, have changed the outlook and the building is far enough away for its impact to be diminished.

GLAMORGAN

CARDIFF

Cricket in Glamorgan has always been overshadowed by the national game and obsession – rugby union. As Tony Lewis, captain of Cambridge, Glamorgan and England and yet, for most of his compatriots a full-back who played for Neath, has written, 'There was plenty of cricket in summer, but it was only a breather between scrummages'. It has been overshadowed in the minds of Welshmen and more literally in the sense that few Glamorgan cricket grounds seem able to escape from rugby pitches and are often found cowering alongside the hallowed turf, modest pavilions no match for huge

covered stands 100 yards long and bursting at the seams every winter Saturday afternoon.

It is not surprising, therefore, to know that cricket only came to Sophia Gardens in Cardiff because it was summarily evicted by rugby from its old home at Cardiff Arms Park. Originally cricket and rugby had existed side by side on the Arms Park site in the city centre.

Cardiff Arms Park, an aerial view showing the old rugby and cricket grounds and, in the background, the castle and impressive civic buildings

Previous page *Sophia Gardens, the 'new' home of Glamorgan cricket*

Above *Cardiff Arms Park, with the new pavilion in the corner and the North stand of the national rugby stadium overshadowing one side*

In 1921, Glamorgan played their inaugural first-class match here against Sussex. By the 1960s, however, the Welsh Rugby Union, who had long fostered ambitions of a national rugby stadium, began to look outside Cardiff for a site. The prospect of Welsh rugby deserting the capital was so appalling to Cardiff City Council, owners of the site, and Cardiff Athletic Club, the tenants, that they immediately offered the Arms Park to the WRU to develop as they deemed necessary. The cricket ground alongside the stadium would become a rugby pitch for club games and Cardiff and Glamorgan cricket clubs would be moved to the new site across the River Taff, in Sophia Gardens.

Before going any further it is worth noting that all this was possible due to the bequest of the fifth Marquess of Bute who, in 1947, handed over his family's hugely valuable Cardiff estate to Cardiff City Corporation. This included the Castle, the three sites of the Castle Gardens, Sophia Gardens and the Arms Park which between them totalled three square miles and the port, all of which was reputed to have helped make his grandfather, the third Marquess, the richest man in the world at the end of the nineteenth century.

Sophia Gardens itself is named after Sophia, wife of the second Marquess. Following the death of her husband, in 1849, only four years after their marriage, Sophia spent much of her time at Cardiff Castle. She initiated the laying out of the castle gardens and later the pleasure gardens across the river which she planned for the enjoyment of the people of Cardiff and which were opened to the public (free of charge) in 1858.

For many years the Corporation were uncertain what to do with the Sophia Gardens site and one of the many schemes which they turned down was the suggested move of Glamorgan CCC in the 1950s, due to problems at the Arms Park. When the crisis over the national rugby stadium blew up though, it meant that they had what became the obvious alternative site for cricket. Sophia Gardens has been Glamorgan's official cricket capital ever since.

Naturally many were sad to leave the Arms Park. For a start it is a great shrine and in many ways cricket benefited from the association. It was also, with St Helens, Swansea, one of the two historic homes of Glamorgan cricket, where many of the highlights and dramas of their past had been enacted: the day in 1935 when Cyril Smart hit the then record number of runs – 32 – off a six-ball over, the hapless bowler being G. Hill of Hampshire; when Maurice Turnbull hit 205 in 1932 off Larwood and Voce when the Nottinghamshire pair were perfecting their leg-theory attack; the defeat of the West Indies in 1939; and the penultimate game in the Championship winning year of 1948, when Surrey were bowled out for 47.

It was also one of the most conveniently placed county grounds for spectators, right next to the city centre and two minutes' walk from the railway station. As Philip Carling, the current Secretary remembers, 'people used to wander in and out to watch a bit of cricket during their lunch break or after doing the shopping'. If claustrophobic as a result of being enclosed on two sides by the back of the rugby ground's main stand

and by an equally monolithic modern office block, the problem of the post-war years – when on many occasions the capacity was not sufficient for the crowds – had disappeared by the 1960s with a decade of diminished attendances.

So when the move was made it was a wrench, but in retrospect it was for the good of Glamorgan cricket. Sophia Gardens is quite different from the old home, not least because it is a park ground, its openness contrastingly and immediately attractive. The east side of the ground, along which flows the River Taff, is protected by stately mature lime trees while at the far end from the pavilion, beyond the inevitable rugby pitch, is a similar line of copper and green beech.

The pavilion itself, built at a cost of £25,000 and completed in time for the first county game in 1967, is a long, low building of light-coloured brick, given character by the curiously undulating facade of its flat, white roof. Despite moving house, Glamorgan CCC have not achieved full independence, for the name on the white facade, to one side of the pavilion clock, is not their own but Cardiff Athletic Club, who are the tenants of the Corporation and from whom the cricket club have a sub-lease. Since the early-1970s, when the Corporation offered the piece of land immediately to the south of the cricket pitch to the Sports Council, the pavilion at Sophia Gardens has been sadly overshadowed by the massive, featureless, back of the National Sports Centre.

The early days at Sophia Gardens were not without problems, first on a practical level with the square itself. When a new drainage system was installed it was found that one of the channels caused a ridge half-way down the wicket, which fast bowlers managed to hit with unerring accuracy, making batting a hazardous occupation. It was muttered darkly in some quarters that the wicket had been laid out the wrong way and that it should be in line with the pavilion rather than side-on. It was not until the early-1980s that this was finally rectified by the whole square being relaid with a second new drainage system, although the wicket remains at right-angles to the pavilion.

Another problem was one of administration, for the county club offices remained in the city centre, at 6 High Street. This has now been rectified and the offices and committee room are in a temporary building, on the boundary closest to the main gate and car park and it is hoped to make the building permanent as a result of an appeal during the club's centenary in 1988.

There may have been teething problems on the new ground but, in 1969, Glamorgan triumphed for a second

The visiting New Zealand tourists leaving the pavilion at Cardiff Arms Park in 1937

time in the county championship and remained undefeated in doing so, a feat no other county had achieved since Lancashire's win in 1930. It was during the last match of the season, against Worcestershire in early September, that Sophia Gardens became part of the county's history. In front of a crowd of 16,000 Glamorgan won by 147 runs; Majid Khan scored a hundred before lunch on a broken wicket and went on to 156, Don Shepherd took his 2,000th first-class wicket and, as *Wisden* recorded,

> A week's stirring cricket had a great climax at Cardiff where Glamorgan entered their last home game happy in the knowledge that if they won they were virtual champions with an unassailable lead. And win they did. Sophia Gardens broke out in pandemonium and the celebrations ran well into the evening.

Sophia Gardens has retained one visible contact with the Arms Park, the covered stand at the river end which was dismantled and transported to the new ground. It is neither the most elegant nor extensive of stands but it is a link with the past. At one end is a commentary box for BBC Wales and in the small adjoining building sit the scorers and members of the press. (If their quarters are spartan, the latter group are better off than in the old days at the Arms Park when their quarters had been the groundsman's store.) Between here and the pavilion are open, tiered seats for members, who also have a similar block of open seats on the far side of the pavilion. At the far end of the covered stand is tiered wooden seating for non-members.

Probably the most impressive feature at Sophia Gardens is the electronic scoreboard which stands on the north-west corner of the ground, at the end of the open public seating along the west side. Its cost of £3,500 was covered by a donation from the late Sir Edward Lewis (no relation of A.R.), for many years chairman of Decca and lifelong supporter of cricket. The opposite side of the ground from the pavilion, open during most matches and occupied only by a few benches and the humble but gaily painted trailer which houses the Glamorgan County Cricket Shop, is enlivened with marquees for sponsors and their guests during the 'week' in August.

The Championship victory of 1969 was a highlight which has yet to be matched at Sophia Gardens. Of a very different type was the terrifying incident in 1971, when Roger Davis was hit full on the head by the ball while fielding at short leg and had to be revived with the kiss of life from a doctor who was watching, before being rushed to hospital in an ambulance.

SWANSEA

Sophia Gardens, with its tree-lined, parkland setting, like the grand parts of Cardiff, is untypical of South Wales and an unexpected setting for Glamorgan cricket. It is almost too English. On the other hand St Helen's, Swansea, named after a medieval Augustinian convent, is absolutely typical, as Welsh as the Eistedffod. Dylan Thomas was born and spent his childhood just up the hill behind the ground, in the Uplands district of the city. He does not appear to have been a cricket lover but John Arlott, a life-long admirer of Dylan Thomas's work once wrote a poem called 'Cricket at Swansea' which begins:

> From the top of the hill-top pavilion,
> The sea is a cheat to the eye,
> Where it secretly seeps into coastline
> Or fades in the yellow-grey sky;

St Helen's suffers from a number of fundamental perversities as far as the playing and watching of cricket are concerned. Most people, however, are happy to forgive these as endearing signs of individuality. Moreover, all Welshmen, many players and the majority of visitors look upon St Helen's with affection. Sophia Gardens may be the county headquarters, but you go to St Helen's for a taste of Glamorgan cricket and its history.

The ground lies on the west side of the city, immediately behind the Mumbles Road which goes on to curve round Swansea Bay to the promontory of Mumbles Head. Its position is the first of many peculiarities: beyond the Mumbles Road only a narrow strip of grass and the beach separate St Helen's from the sea – to which it is the closest county ground in the country – beating Scarborough by a matter of yards. There used to be a railway line as well, running alongside the road, which rejoiced in the name of the Mumbles to Oystermouth. The trains were drawn first by horses, then steam engines and finally electric ones and ran on a single track line with pull-ins for passing, like a minor road in the Welsh hills. History does not relate what happened if trains ever met in between but Welshmen are not known for giving ground easily. The closure of the line in 1960 put an end to stories about cricket balls being hit into passing carriages and travelling to either of the line's termini before being returned to St Helen's, thereby qualifying as a record hit. Anyway, after Sobers's effort in 1968, Swansea is not exactly in need of record hits.

St Helen's, Swansea, looking towards the toy fort-like pavilion perched above the terraces. A formidable climb of over seventy steps awaits the unfortunate incoming batsman

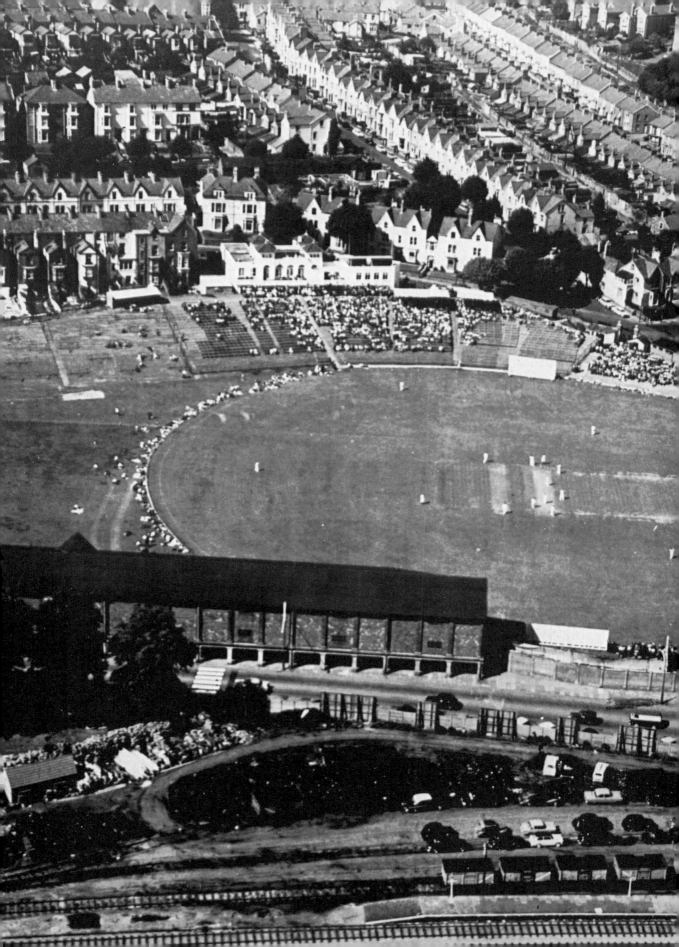

On the landward side the rows of terraced houses in Bryn Mill rise steeply up behind the embankment stretching almost the length of this – north – side and which in one place supports the pavilion. As a result, looking across the ground from the seaward side one gets the impression that the houses might one day come sliding down the hill onto the pavilion and terraces below.

Inevitably St Helen's is used for rugby as well as cricket. It is home to the Swansea Cricket and Football Club. The joint use accounts for the size, an area of four acres and distance of a third of a mile around the perimeter, as well as its extraordinary pear-like shape. At the narrow, west, end is most of the rugby pitch and the cricket ground fills the 'bulge' on the east side. The two meet in the middle where an area from roughly one twenty-five yard line to the dead-ball line of the rugby pitch encroaches over the cricket boundary – or the other way round, depending on where your loyalties lie. Successive St Helen's groundsmen have cursed the studs of rugby boots, the divots of place-kickers, or just the weekly streams of supporters who migrate unerringly across the square en route from the grandstand to the club-house.

As far as the facilities for spectators go, the rugby enthusiasts definitely have the better deal. Stretching from the south-west corner of the ground, with its back to the Mumbles Road, is the impressive grandstand, built in the 1920s. Both this, and the majority of the embankment along the far side are too far from the cricket ground for spectators and they face at the wrong angle. (Admittedly, much of the embankment is for standing spectators, which few people would tolerate for a whole day's cricket, but there is seating along the section immediately facing the cricket pitch.) For county games temporary seating is put up along the boundary where it curves across the open ground, but unless you retreat to the rugby grandstand there is no covered seating at St Helen's, making it a place for fair weather spectating. Above all, the ground is dominated by the four 140-foot floodlight pylons, one at each corner, which act as a useful guide for first-time visitors as they approach the ground.

The pavilion at St Helen's dates from 1927 but since then it has been altered almost beyond recognition. It used to be a two-storey building with dressing rooms and an umpires room below, and a colonnade and verandah above. When the embankment was extended to increase the capacity of rugby crowds the lower floor

St Helen's, an aerial view showing the old Mumbles railway in the foreground

disappeared, obscured behind the concrete while, as if to compensate, four turrets were added to the top, one on each corner. The front two were for the scorers and press but both parties have moved to new quarters and now one only is occupied by commentators for BBC Wales. It is not an ideal vantage-point for commentary, however, as the pavilion faces the pitch at a curious angle, from somewhere between the mid-wicket and long-on boundaries when the batsman is at the sea end. Inside, when there is no cricket, you would hardly know it to be a pavilion, so complete is the dominance of the photographs by rugby in general and Swansea RFC in particular.

In the circumstances, it is a refreshing surprise that the pub outside the members' entrance to the ground, on the corner of Gorse Lane and King Edward Road, is the Cricketers' Hotel. This is a place where spectators should feel at home, not least because of the ball, bat and stumps which adorn the railings outside the upstairs windows, and the mats inside which are the scorecards of a selection of Glamorgan's most memorable games. At the far end of Gorse Lane, where it meets Mumbles Road, is one of Swansea's few gestures towards being a seaside town, the Madame Patti Pavilion which stands on the corner of Victoria Park. The theatre used to be the redoubtable singer's winter garden in Dan-yr-Ogoff, until in 1920 it was dismantled, moved and rebuilt in its present position.

Ask people what they remember about St Helen's and you will get a variety of answers. For batsmen – particularly unsuccessful ones – it will be the distance from the wicket to the pavilion, including the final climb up the steps on the return journey. There used to be over sixty steps, but they have been reduced to nearer forty since the dressing rooms were moved. Spin bowlers remember the dry, dusty wicket prone to losing its top and giving the ball prodigious turn, seamers the damp sea air which encourages movement.

For spectators it depends on the weather. If it has rained they probably prefer to forget they ever went. On a fine day, however, the view is memorable. From the upper levels of the embankment on the north side, or, more especially, from the top of the pavilion, you look out across the grandstand to Swansea Bay and the regular distraction of large ships coming and going from either Swansea itself or the steel giant, Port Talbot, just round the bay to the east. To one side the lighthouse on Mumbles Head is certainly in view, but it needs to be unusually clear for one to catch a glimpse of North Devon, some twenty-five miles away across the Bristol Channel. All the same it is a prospect few cricket grounds rival.

Glamorgan may be the youngest of the first-class counties, only having been admitted to the fold in 1921, but cricket in Swansea has a long history and there are records of a game in 1780. By 1850 things had obviously lapsed, as the local paper was complaining that it was 'a disgrace to the town that in such an enlightened age there should be no properly organized club in this large and populous place'. In 1868, by which time the short-coming had been made good, the Swansea club were hosts to a team of Australian Aborigines, who won and followed their victory with a display of boomerang and spear throwing. Apparently they were well – if incredulously – received.

It was in the 1870s that the real breakthrough came with the purchase of the present site. This leads to another of St Helen's peculiarities; the ground has been made on reclaimed sandbanks, which were levelled and turfed at the then substantial cost of £2,000. Even today in some places the sand is only a few inches beneath the surface, but, contrary to local lore, the turf does not change colour when the tide is in – except for those spectators who have spent too long in the Cricketers.

From 1888 until 1921 Glamorgan were a strong force in Minor Counties cricket. During this time they owed much to one of the leading personalities of St Helen's – Billy Bancroft. Bancroft became the groundsman at St Helen's and lived in a cottage on the corner of the ground. He was also Glamorgan's first professional and one of their leading batsmen during the Minor Counties years. It probably meant more to his countrymen that he also captained Swansea at rugby and played thirty-three internationals for Wales. For many years after his retirement he could be found in the nets at St Helen's coaching young protégés.

As a result of Glamorgan being the seventeenth county to attain first-class status, they were the 'odd ones out' in the sense that for both the Whitsun and August Bank Holidays the other counties played regularly against traditional opponents. Accordingly Glamorgan were given the privilege of two matches against visiting tourists, the second one of which over the August holiday was always staged at St Helen's. These games have witnessed great scenes of Glamorgan cricket, as well as enormous crowds. In 1950 67,000 watched over the three days of the match against the West Indies. A year later, 25,000 watched the last day of an enthralling match against South Africa – and saw their boys achieve the first county win of the season over the visitors. Len Muncer was the Glamorgan hero with figures of 11 for 61 in the match and J. B. G. Thomas of the *Western Mail* recorded 'but the last forty-five minutes of this game were to prove the most historic in Glamorgan's many epic struggles against touring sides. Only then did the tide of battle turn – one side was engulfed – the other climbed to the heights of magnificent achievement'. Welsh hyperbole at its best!

In 1964 and 1968 the Australians were beaten at Swansea and on both occasions the crowd sang 'Waltzing Matilda' and 'Land of My Fathers' in appreciation. And one should not forget an achievement by Don Shepherd during the match against the 1961 Australians. Shepherd, the backbone of the county side through a record 647 appearances, is principally remembered as a bowler, and why not, as his total of 2,174 wickets is a record for the county and the most taken by any bowler who never played in a Test. But on this occasion he struck with the bat, making 50 with eleven scoring strokes.

There have also been moments to savour in many county matches. In 1937 Maurice Turnbull scored 233 against Worcestershire, including 200 in 188 minutes. From when he joined the county as captain in 1930 and a year later took on the secretaryship as well, Turnbull was the driving force and inspiration behind the financially unstable club and a team who were becoming used to disappointing performances. Tragically, he was killed in action in 1944, aged 38.

In 1980 Javed Miandad scored 140 against Essex in his first match for the county and his batting, and that of his fellow Parkistani, Younis Ahmed (for whom Glamorgan was the third county he had played for), was usually decisive until their respective departures in 1986, Miandad's in unfortunate circumstances which did not say much for his loyalty to the county. In 1972, another exciting import, Roy Fredericks, was partnered by A. Jones in establishing a record opening partnership for the county of 330 against Northamptonshire.

It is not meant as any insult to Glamorgan that we leave St Helen's recalling the day in 1968 when they were comprehensively taken apart, in one over, by Gary Sobers. The bowler was Malcolm Nash and Ossie Wheatley, who was on the field, remembers the sequence of strokes.

The first six over long-on cleared the wall and smacked against a pub in Gorse Lane. The second went to mid-wicket, and apparently connected with another pub a little down the road. The third landed among the spectators at long-off, the fourth similarly at mid-wicket. The fifth was the one that Roger Davis caught at long-off before falling over the boundary line, and the last and biggest again flew over mid-wicket, down a side-street towards the town hall, and was not recovered until the next day.

NEATH

Neath may be only a few miles from Swansea but as you make the short journey, following the road which crosses the River Neath on its way up to the town, you feel the difference in the surroundings steadily unfolding. For a start you move away from the sea. More importantly you are moving into the valleys that are the heartland of South Wales.

As one would expect, the domination of rugby is almost absolute and the black shirts with white maltese crosses of 'The Mourners', as the Neath club are known, are among the most renowned in the country. Tony Lewis, Neath's favourite cricketing son, remembers

Neath, overpoweringly a rugby town

sending a pair of cricket boots to the cobbler in Neath for a set of new spikes. They came back with rugby studs fixed to the bottom. Lewis is one of the two captains of England to come from Neath, not a bad record for a rugby town. The other is C. F. Walters, who left Glamorgan to play for Worcestershire and who captained England in one match in 1934, against Australia at Trent Bridge.

Rugby dominates Neath and it also overshadows the actual cricket ground at the Gnoll, on the north-east side of the town where the road winds steeply away into the hills. The cricket ground's modest pavilion is no match for the neighbouring rugby pitch's floodlight towers, the grandstand stretching the length of the pitch and the shorter stand at one end, the front of whose roof is emblazoned with NEATH RFC in huge letters.

It is an interesting site, forming a plateau beneath the wooded hill, or gnoll from which it takes its name. On one side the hill stretches up to the peak of Cefn Morfydd at over 1,000 feet. It was once part of the Gnoll estate which passed through various hands until it ended up in the ownership of Neath borough council, who currently look after it. The estate originally centred on Gnoll House, home of the successive owners, which started life as a castle and was extended by an eighteenth-century owner. Sadly it was unoccupied from the 1930s, and by the 1950s had become so derelict that it was demolished in 1956.

The first recorded match at the Gnoll was in 1844 and four years later the Neath Cricket Club was formed. In 1868 the ground had its most illustrious visitor in W. G. Grace, admittedly as a young man of twenty, but, what a thing, the 'Champion' was out for nought in both innings 'ciphered by a professional called Howitt' as it was recorded. Grace was playing for a South of England XI against a XXII of Cadoxton (a local parish) for whom Howitt was the guest performer.

Glamorgan first played at the Gnoll, as a Minor County, in 1908. Their first first-class match there was in 1934 against Essex and the visit was largely as a result

of Neath town council, who had recently acquired the ground, spending a considerable amount of money to make it suitable for county cricket. The county continued to make an annual visit to Neath, except immediately after the Second World War, as the ground had suffered extensive damage, but by the 1960s one observer was commenting, 'There is a homely, if rather congested atmosphere at the Gnoll, but facilities for first-class cricket leave much to be desired for members, players and the press'. More critical were problems with the wicket. A high water-table and drainage off the hill onto the level cricket ground caused havoc in wet conditions. When a Benson and Hedges match against Gloucestershire in 1974 took three days to finish because of a water-logged pitch Glamorgan had had enough and they terminated their first-class visits to the ground. They did retain one important connexion, however, in the county's indoor school which had been built at the Gnoll in the 1950s and opened in 1954 by R. E. S. Wyatt. The school was improved and re-opened in the 1980s.

If the departure of Glamorgan was a sad blow for the Gnoll it did not deter the Neath club and borough council. In 1980–81 the present pavilion was built, on the top side of the ground, facing the wicket from square-leg, with a protective row of closely planted cypress trees and the wooded hill behind. Round the boundary, at the north – Llantwit Road – end is the scoreboard, built around the same time. After eleven years Neath CC got their reward and, as a result of Neath borough council offering Glamorgan a handsome sponsorship deal if they staged their match against the Australians at the Gnoll, the county returned in 1985. Part of the deal was a guarantee of various improvements many of which, such as new sight screens were prominently visible for the great occasion.

Despite the fact that the habitual curse of the weather brought it to an end after little more than one day, there was some splendid cricket as *Wisden* describes.

After a first day of record-breaking exploits by Glamorgan, there were only 95 minutes possible on the Sunday and the final day was washed out by heavy rain. However, the return of first-class cricket to the Gnoll after twelve years saw a multitude of records broken with brilliant strokeplay by Javed Miandad and Younis Ahmed. Their unfinished partnership of 306 was a fourth-wicket record for the county and the best for any wicket against a touring team. The county's total of 409 for three declared was the highest innings there. No player has scored more for Glamorgan against a touring team. Javed hit 30 fours and faced 225 deliveries in four and three-quarter hours in becoming the first man to score four double-centuries for the county. The previous highest score on the ground had been W. J. Stewart's 155 for Warwickshire in 1959. Younis, with his attractive 118, made it the first occasion for two Glamorgan players to register centuries in a match against a touring team.

As if this were not enough to celebrate the return to the Gnoll, the following year Javed's score was overhauled – albeit by a visitor, Graeme Hick of Worcestershire. Hick scored 219 not out off 146 deliveries in 172 minutes, including eight sixes and 25 fours. He scored even faster in the second innings – 52 from 22 balls, with three sixes and six fours. What's more, the match was finished, uninterrupted by rain.

A view of the Neath ground showing the old pavilion and, behind, the wooded gnoll, which gives the ground its name

ABERGAVENNY

Abergavenny is Glamorgan's most recent and most distant venue for county championship matches, and how different it is from the more traditional stages for the county's game. For a start it is not in Glamorgan, but neighbouring Gwent – once the old Marcher county of Monmouthshire. Abergavenny is a prosperous, bustling market town, and the cricket ground is situated in quiet leafy outskirts to the north, filled with detached houses with large gardens.

A fine row of mature plane and horse chestnut trees extends along the Avenue Road side of the ground, and the view away from the town is to friendly, rounded hills. The attractive, single-storey pavilion faces the wicket at right-angles and is filled inside with photographs of Abergavenny CC. After a disastrous fire in 1977 it had to be virtually rebuilt, but somehow the clock over the door survived, with its plaque noting that it was given by Mr and Mrs Harry Lyons in 1921. In front trim little clipped hedges around the benches give an impression of neatness and efficiency which the club's past bears out.

As at Sophia Gardens, Cardiff owes much to the family of the Marquess of Bute, so Abergavenny's cricket ground is similarly indebted to a Marquess who shares the town's name. Abergavenny cricket club was founded in 1834, but for the early part of its life led a somewhat nomadic existence, moving from one site in the town to another. In 1895 an approach was made to the then Marquess of Abergavenny, a keen supporter of cricket and one-time President of Kent CCC – a county with which his family also have strong connexions. He agreed to lease the club a four-and-a-half acre field and the new ground soon took its name

from the lane along one side called Pen-y-Pound. The Marquess gave further signs of his generosity in 1910, when he allowed the club to take in more land to extend the ground and in 1912 when he provided an enlarged pavilion. After his death in 1915 the club were fortunately able to obtain the freehold of the ground, thereby ensuring that it was not lost under buildings.

After the Minor County side of Monmouthshire

Above *Abergavenny, more rural than Neath but blessed with a similarly impressive backdrop of wooded hill*

amalgamated with Glamorgan in the 1930s the latter county took a keen interest in the ground at Pen-y-Pound. It was also in the 1930s that neighbouring Avenue Road was laid out with its houses, and this now provides the access to the ground and gives it its present name. In 1948 the first of a number of subsequent Second XI games were staged. During the 1950s Avenue Road also began to host benefit games, which always drew large crowds, none more so than that in 1972, for the Northamptonshire player, Dennis Brookes, when Frank Tyson was among the players.

The main step up came in 1981 when Glamorgan staged a Sunday game at Avenue Road against Worcestershire. Then, in 1983, came the first county championship game, also against Worcestershire. Since then the single first-class game has become an annual event – except in 1984 when the game against Cambridge University was moved to Fenner's. And even in the space of a few years Avenue Road can claim to have hosted a game with intriguing turns of fortune. Against Worcestershire, in 1985, the Glamorgan openers Hopkins and Holmes distinguished themselves to the extent of scoring 114 not out and 106 not out respect-

ively, enabling their side to declare at 250 for no wicket. But after Worcestershire had made a score of 294 in their first innings and were all set for another good knock in the second, it suddenly became a non-match. With six men struck down with a stomach bug and two others injured, Worcestershire were forced to bat on until saved by rain, as they were unable to declare and subsequently take the field, with only three men fit.

Abergavenny have supplied a number of players to the county, including Malcolm Nash. They are also a club who, by their good organization – such as raising the majority of the £20,000 necessary for the renovation after the 1977 fire – adventurous policies and high standards of maintenance, first attracted Glamorgan and now look likely to continue to play host to them annually. It must be about the only club ground in England to boast an electronic scoreboard, installed in the winter of 1984–85 at a cost of £1,500 (but retaining the memory of Bill McPherson, groundsman at Avenue Road for many years and in whose name the predecessor had been built in 1978). Players enjoy facilities as good as any at a club ground and the home-made teas are famous.

TOP Worcester: The delightful pavilion, framed by one of the ground's many fine trees and BOTTOM the classic cricket vista, a timeless scene

ABOVE *Edgbaston: Looking from the pavilion with the Thwaite scoreboard on the right*

TOP LEFT *Derby: The view to the grandstand with its idiosyncratic copper-domed cupola*

TOP MIDDLE Old Trafford: *Storm clouds gather ominously during the 1985 Test v Australia*

TOP RIGHT Old Trafford: *The pavilion full to overflowing for a Test Match*

131

*Headingley: The view towards the players' pavilion with
the spire of St Michael's church in the background. The
poplars to the left of the picture have, alas, since been felled*

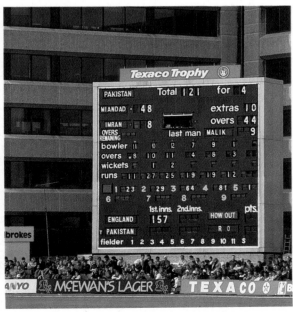

TOP *Trent Bridge: Looking down the wicket to the pavilion* and BOTTOM *the main scoreboard, overshadowed by Trent Bridge House immediately behind*

Northampton: A view from the pavilion framed by the floodlights of the 'Cobblers' football ground

*Leicester: Grace Road, looking towards the new pavilion
complex*

TOP *Fenner's: An early season game, before the trees are in leaf*

BOTTOM *The Parks: Secure in its tree-lined setting*

WORCESTERSHIRE

Worcester, 1905. H. K. Foster (right), one of the county's heroes, leaves the field with the visiting Australian, Syd Gregory

WORCESTER

Even on the most dismal of days, when unrelenting rain has ensured that there will be no play well before the umpires are due to walk out, Worcester does much to live up to its reputation. There is no question that the cathedral is the most impressive backdrop to any county ground and, even if it is not England's finest, it still provides the most celebrated of cricket pictures. The one bonus of a wet day is that it allows for an unhurried visit to the cathedral, to see the tombs of King John and Prince Arthur, Henry VIII's elder brother.

The view from the pavilion side of the New Road ground to the cathedral instills Worcester with a dignity which the club have been careful to retain. There has been nothing self-conscious about it for quite simply it would have been crassly stupid to do anything which might spoil the picture. And with the intervening land beyond the River Severn safely in the hands of the Dean and Chapter of the cathedral and the King's School there is no chance of some developer perpetrating any sort of horror on the landscape.

Worcestershire is anyway no county of developers, its rich farmland, fruit orchards and lack of industrial centres ensuring that it has remained essentially rural. It is also the smallest of the first-class counties and has been, for most of its history since acquiring first-class status in 1898, one of the juniors. For the majority of county opponents a visit to Worcester was an enjoyable excursion rather than a fixture of crucial importance.

The connexion between cricket ground and cathedral is not purely visual. Until 1976, when the county club were able to purchase the freehold for £30,000, the land was owned by the Dean and Chapter and the county club were tenants. Although, sadly, no member of the august group of clerics ever represented the county, the Dean and his assorted canons were benign and interested landlords. For Michael Vockins, Worcestershire's present secretary, their unassertive authority was somehow typified by the incumbent Dean's reaction to the club's request about the possibility of allowing betting tents on the ground in the early 1970s. 'We cannot condone it, but we will not object.'

Worcestershire came to their enviable site thanks to their honorary Secretary at the end of the nineteenth century, P. H. Foley. In 1898 he successfully negotiated with the Dean and Chapter for the lease of a piece of farmland across the river from the cathedral which at the time consisted of three fields with a hedge through the middle and a hayrick. Foley's next move was to entice Fred Hunt away from Kent, where he played for the county, to become groundsman, which he remained until the end of the Second World War. Hunt became one of the most famous of all groundsmen and there is a wonderful photograph of him taken at Worcester: cloth cap, moustache, waistcoat and huge leather boots; sitting on his horse-drawn roller flanked by his three assistants, all of whom look as though they have stepped straight off a threshing machine.

Hunt played for the county and for many years had his own farm next to the cricket ground, but in the early days it seems that one person who was not too happy was the tenant farmer who had lost a piece of his land, for the groundstaff had regularly to drive off horses, cattle and sheep before play could begin.

Nonetheless, the ground was ready for the inaugural game in 1899, by which time the pavilion had been built – just – and the opponents were no less a force than Yorkshire, reigning County Champions. One can hardly imagine the excitement when, as the Yorkshire openers Brown and Tunnicliffe – who only the season before had set their record of 554 at Chesterfield – opened the batting, only to be separated without a run being scored when Brown was dismissed by George Wilson. In the end Worcestershire did not win – that would have been too much to hope for – but they gave the champions, who included Hirst and Rhodes, a nasty fright, only going down by 11 runs.

That Worcestershire side was representative of one of the early playing forces behind the county, for it was captained by H. K. Foster and contained two of his six brothers, R. E. and W. L. For good reason did Worcestershire become dubbed 'Fostershire', for all seven sons of the Rev. H. Foster, a housemaster at Malvern College, played for Worcestershire. They were a sporting phenomenon such as only Victorian churchmen, schoolmasters and doctors appear to have been capable of producing. Three of them, H. K., R. E. 'Tip' and M. K. captained the county. 'Tip' Foster, without doubt the most talented cricketer of the brood, passed into history when, on the 1903–04 tour to Australia, he scored 287 at Sydney, which stood as a Test record for many years. Neville Cardus considered him, 'one of the three or four really great batsmen of the early 1900s'. It was a tragedy that he was never able to play regular first-class cricket and that he died of diabetes aged thirty-six.

Worcestershire would count themselves lucky to have had one such family to help set them on the road, but in the Lytteltons of Hagley Hall in the north of the county, they had a second. If the Lytteltons never made such an impact as players as the Fosters they were still

Schoolboys sailing on the flooded ground in the 1950s

devoted patrons. It seems that I will have to add to those churchmen, schoolmasters and doctors the occasional aristocrat, for the six sons of the fourth Lord Lyttelton were an amazingly talented collection. Four got blues, most played county cricket, one became a cabinet minister, another a bishop and a third headmaster of Eton – where they all went to school. Two of them: the Rev. the Hon. Edward and The Hon. George William Spencer, played for Worcestershire in the pre-first-class days.

Later, their kinsmen, The Rev. the Hon. Charles Frederick and the Hon. John Charles (later the ninth Viscount Cobham), played first-class cricket for Worcestershire, but the most renowned county cricketer from the family was the latter's son the Hon. Charles John, who became the tenth Viscount Cobham. A formidable presence and hard-hitting batsman, he played for the county during the 1930s and was captain from 1935–39. He was elected President of the county club six days before his death in 1977.

Like many cricket grounds Worcester is only blessed with an exceptional outlook in one direction – towards the cathedral and neighbouring areas of the city. In the opposite direction unattractive towers dominate the picture behind the pavilion. This is a pity for the pavilion, much as when originally built in 1898, has many delightful features and is totally in keeping with the reputation and character of Worcestershire CCC

and their ground. There are two large gables breaking the tiled roof, with, inside these, a pair of smaller ones for windows. It is the fifth, central, gable which is most worthy of mention, which one would scarcely be surprised to see adorning the roof of some house in cities such as Bruges or Amsterdam – although the weather-vane surmounted by a cricket ball would give it away. It contains the clock flanked by elegant green scroll-work and the date AD 1898.

Along the front of the pavilion are tubs and hanging baskets filled with flowers supplied by Webbs Nurseries – a number of other counties could take a leaf out of Worcester's book and drum up support of this kind from their local horticultural institution. The once open front of the pavilion now has large glass windows and inside is the long room and bar, between the committee room, and dressing-rooms in the adjacent building. Despite its exterior not everyone has been over-enamoured with Worcester's pavilion. On his first visit with Surrey, around 1920 Alan Peach asked in disgust whether 'eleven of them had to dress in that rabbit-hutch'.

Inside the pavilion is the evidence of one of Worcester's best-known and unusual properties, the almost annual flooding of the ground by water from the River Severn. On one wall is a brass plaque showing the height of the flood in 1947 – three and a half feet above the floor, itself some feet above the ground outside. The mark has not been attained since, but since Mike Vockins came to Worcester in 1971, there has been flooding every year bar one. The water does not actually come directly from the River Severn itself – as commonly believed – but from the backwaters feeding it from all sides of the ground. As the main river rises, so these are filled to overflowing – with the inevitable result. The flooding usually occurs around Christmas, although in 1987 it was just before the start of the season. Stories of salmon being caught and the heavy roller floating away are usually scoffed at with good reason, but it is quite true that the lower areas of all the buildings around Worcester's ground are uninhabitable for some weeks of the year. The flooding does seem to give unquestionable benefit to the turf, the smooth texture and healthy grass of which has been noted by many a visitor to the ground. Indeed, for many years, when stumps were drawn at the end of a day's cricket, out came wooden bowls and games were played in front of the pavilion. You cannot get a much better advertisement for smooth turf.

Other than the pavilion all of Worcester's buildings have been added since the 1950s. To one side of the pavilion is the Ladies' Pavilion, opened in 1956. Here, as with the main pavilion, the building is predominantly white, with a gable at each end and tiered open seats in front. It remained the ladies' exclusive domain until the mid-1970s and has long been famous among supporters for the quality of the home-made teas on offer.

Today a green and white striped marquee usually stands immediately beyond the Ladies' Pavilion for the use of sponsors. Close to the marquee is a horse chestnut tree which is one of a number planted around this side of the ground to mark specific occasions. As Mike Vockins explains, the arc round from the Ladies' Pavilion and marquee, which takes in the main scoreboard built in 1954 in a similar style to the Ladies' Pavilion, and continues in front of the cathedral, is sacrosanct as far as any plans for further development of the ground are concerned. As a result the seating remains simple open benches, the trees behind forming the boundary with the playing fields of the King's School. With Malvern and the Royal Grammar School, Worcester, the King's School is one of three with which the county have always maintained close contact. The Royal Grammar School have recently made a bit of a reputation for themselves by going independent, in protest at plans by Worcester County Council who wanted to make them into a comprehensive. This probably explained why the school has taken a prominent boundary advertising board.

There has been more development around the New Road boundary – in the opposite direction from the pavilion. Beyond the dressing-rooms and club offices next to the pavilion are the single-storey, covered New Road stand, built in the winter of 1973–74, the press box, and executive suite built in the winter of 1984–85 and the headquarters of the Supporters' Association.

Since their formation in 1951, the Supporters' Association have given continual, and at times crucial, support to the county club. They were the first county to operate a lottery or football pool – which has brought in large receipts. Most of the buildings added to the ground since the 1950s have benefited from financial assistance from the association.

Looking from the pavilion across the ground along the New Road side the main feature in the distance is the steeple of St Andrew's church, known locally as 'the Glover's Needle' not only because there was a glove-making factory next door, but also as a result of its extreme thinness – although the emphasis of its point was slightly blunted in 1987 by a case of steeplejack's scaffolding. To the left is the contrastingly squat tower of St Nicholas's.

In 1929 Worcester's identity took on a new importance in the national cricket calendar. The South African tourists played the first of their matches against the counties on the ground and established a tradition which was to last for many years. Worcester became synonymous with the start of the English season, an event to be awaited with anticipation. And what better way to celebrate it – in the popular imagination at least – than to make the journey through the county's fruit orchards in blossom to see the overseas visitors symbolically initiate a new season.

One year after the South Africans' visit, the Australians came and Worcester was treated to a display by Don Bradman which, taken with his subsequent efforts, are what really gave the tourists' visits to the ground their romance. Bradman scored 236, in 1934 he scored 206, in 1938 it was his highest – 258 – and finally, in 1948 he could only manage 107. The occasion of his third successive double-hundred brought the comment from Neville Cardus who, like every other cricket writer worth his salt, plus the television and a host of other supporting characters, was on the ground, that 'The flight of a bird and the flight of an aeroplane mark the difference between an innings by a Woolley and one by a Bradman'. The match also led him to comment that the crowd – 14,000 are meant to have squeezed in – was far too large. Considering that Mike Vockins reckons the present seating capacity is 3,500 which can be extended to 7,500 with temporary seats, one has to agree.

The idea of Bradman amassing his runs at Worcester in front of the cathedral gave the ground considerable prestige. Meanwhile the county's fortunes were not so buoyant and during the inter-war years it was rare for them to be far from the bottom of the table. During the 1920s they were often assisted on the field by the bowling of Fred Root, an import from Derbyshire whose salty humour added to his often highly spicy bowling of medium-paced in-swingers to a leg-side field. They owed more to their captain for some years, Maurice Jewell, who devoted himself to the club on and off the field. After his death, *Wisden* commented:

> Those whose memories start in 1946 or later have no conception how much some counties owed to certain amateurs, often only moderate players who could never have kept a place in a good county side, but who year after year gave up their summer to keeping their county going ... It was due largely to the devoted labours of such as these that no first-class county ever had to pack up, though some in those days came pretty near it.

Through the 1930s – and after the war, until 1955 – the backbone of the county's cricket was provided by the bowling of Reg Perks, an old-style professional whose consistency was shown by taking 100 wickets in his last season, aged forty-three, for the sixteenth year in succession. His total of 2,233 in his career remains a county record.

The first high-spot for Worcester came in 1964 when, under the captaincy of Don Kenyon, they won the County Championship. The next year they retained it – an unheard of feat by one of the 'lesser' counties. Kenyon's batting brought him the county's record of nearly 35,000 runs in his career and Worcestershire also had the benefit of Tom Graveney, who had moved from Gloucestershire in 1962.

If Perks and Kenyon are two of Worcester's most fondly remembered players, a third must be Basil D'Oliveira, now the county's coach. His graceful all-round performances were the perfect foil to the batting of Graveney during the same period, while his character and dignity were more than proven during the South African affair of 1968–69. Today his son, Damian, is one of the county's bright hopes.

From 1967–82 Worcester was home for the English season to the New Zealand batsman, Glenn Turner. During that time he compiled some formidable records – and seemed to do so with the minimum of fuss. In 1973, for his country who were touring, rather than for his county, he became the first and only batsman since the war to score 1,000 runs in May. At Worcester, in 1982, he played the outstanding innings of his career to reach his 100th hundred, scoring 100 before lunch and finishing with the county record of 311 not out.

In 1987 it seemed that cricket at Worcester might be taking a different direction and turning away from its traditional image of rural tranquillity when they took on Ian Botham – a move pressed for by the bat manufacturer, Duncan Fearnley, a power in Worcestershire CCC. Worcester's proximity to Birmingham worried many people that disruptive influences would be attracted to the ground. Fortunately, however, after the press had had a field-day at the beginning of the season which made the coverage of Bradman's exploits pale into insignificance, it seems that Worcester remains untarnished. There is no doubt that Botham's arrival focused attention on the club which had beneficial results. During the winter of 1986–87 the membership

The view back from the cathedral tower, across the River Severn to the cricket ground

141

doubled from 3,000 to 6,000, although Mike Vockins is certain that his arrival was one of three factors, the others being that Worcestershire were a young side and doing well and that England had been successful during their tour of Australia. Botham may have found the Severn somewhat further away than the Tone was at his old home of Taunton, but he continues to have a good go at reaching it.

KIDDERMINSTER

Worcester play the overwhelming majority of their games at the county ground and in 1987 only made one outing – to Kidderminster, bastion of the English carpet-making industry. In the past they have also visited Dudley and played in the middle of the racecourse at Hereford, but the best known ground will always be Stourbridge, as a result of the partnership between Frank Woolley and Arthur Fielder in 1909. For Kent against Worcestershire, they put on 235 for the last wicket, the twenty-two-year-old Woolley scoring 185 and Fielder 112 not out – his only hundred and the first by a number eleven in the county championship. Their partnership remains an English record and the third highest of all time for the tenth wicket.

The ground at Kidderminster cannot boast any such

Kidderminster in the 1950s

records and it is more modest in appearance than its West Midlands neighbour, whose entrance is through an imposing archway and whose pavilion would be large enough to satisfy most counties. Kidderminster's pavilion, however, is an attractive building, dating from 1925. Tiered seating in front leads up to a verandah; at either end of the tiled roof are gables in the black and white pattern familiar in this part of the world, in the centre a smaller gable with the clock, and on top the picture is set off by a louvred cupola and weather-vane.

The ground is situated on the A449 Chester Road North and was opened in 1870; Kidderminster CC bought it from the Earl of Dudley in 1919 and today they compete in the Birmingham League. Their most illustrious product has been Basil D'Oliveira, who played for the club in the league to qualify for Worcestershire. The first county game was played here against Glamorgan in 1921 and in 1973 the county temporarily deserted the ground – perhaps not surprisingly as in that year they were bowled out for 63 by Northamptonshire.

Among the most exciting games to have taken place at Kidderminster was the tied match against Somerset in 1939. Ten years later Somerset found themselves the losers, despite scoring 314 and 308, Worcestershire making 342 in the fourth innings – a total no doubt helped by the ground's small size. Rather than for any particular results, however, the ground is best remembered as a favourite haunt of Don Kenyon who scored nearly 1,500 runs here, including his highest score of 259, against Yorkshire in 1956.

WARWICKSHIRE

EDGBASTON

When weighing up the pros and cons of cricket grounds two equally over-used and often unsatisfactory words always seem to spring up: 'facilities' and 'character'. In Edgbaston's case they are particularly relevant, for while facilities are its forte, shortage of character is its main weakness. Perhaps it is a reflection on the city of Birmingham of which Edgbaston is one of the more prosperous suburbs: England's second city, so they say, and yet curiously lacking in identity compared to many lesser ones.

Of all English cricket grounds Edgbaston is the only one which gives the immediate feeling of being a stadium, an amphitheatre. I could not envisage 'Super-

bowl' at Lord's, or even Old Trafford, but Edgbaston, virtually enclosed with tier upon tier of seating, yes, I could see it here. Edgbaston seems to have as many plastic bucket seats as all the other county grounds – not including the Test Match ones – put together. When the Rea Stand which stretches right along the ground's east side has them, which will be in the near future, then it might even have more.

Approaching from the members' car park, the scale of Edgbaston is revealed before you are even inside the ground. The car park is enormous. In front lies the

Edgbaston, expansive and efficient, looking from the pavilion end to the pressbox stand and Thwaite scoreboard

143

rear view of Edgbaston's most monolithic building, the William Ansell Stand. As we shall see, William Ansell was the first key figure in Warwickshire and Edgbaston's history, but the back of the stand also contains the home of the goose who laid Edgbaston's golden egg, the Supporters' Club. In 1953 the club followed the example of neighbouring Worcestershire and set up a football pools scheme. It was hugely successful and provided the money to develop the ground into the modern Edgbaston. Within twenty years the pools scheme had produced enough money for £1 million to be spent on Edgbaston, £400,000 paid to the tax-man in betting duty and roughly the same amount invested or loaned to other needy county clubs.

In the early days Warwickshire cricket was hijacked out of its original stronghold in the shire around Leamington Spa and Warwick and forced into Birmingham where, it was argued, the necessary support and professional cricketers would come from. And yet the relationship has remained uneasy. Edgbaston is in Birmingham but one does not feel it has been as happy a marriage as those of Trent Bridge and Nottingham and Old Trafford and Manchester, for instance. The ground is cocooned by the leafy streets of well-off Edgbaston, and only over the tree-tops are the towers of the Bullring Centre and other Birmingham delights visible, at a reassuring distance. Support has often been hard to find; in 1972, the county's third Championship-winning year, when Warwickshire also did well in the two one-day

competitions, only 13,000 watched all the home games. If they had all come at once they would not have filled the ground.

The move to Birmingham was thanks to William Ansell, the club's first honorary secretary. He established a tradition of unusually long service in which he and two successors held the post for nearly one hundred years. They have also been to a remarkable degree the driving force behind the development of the club and ground.

Ansell was one of five men – and the only representative from Birmingham – who met in Leamington in 1882 and founded the Warwickshire County Cricket Club. His period as honorary secretary continued for another twenty years. During the two decades he had three major ambitions: a Birmingham headquarters for Warwickshire, first-class status for the county and, later, the staging of Test Matches on their ground. They were all realized.

After a prolonged search for a suitable site, in 1885 the county eventually accepted the offer from Lord Calthorpe of a 'meadow of rough grazing land in Edgbaston' which they could lease for twenty-one years. At the time Lord Calthorpe's family owned the whole of one side of Birmingham. Their connexion with Warwickshire CCC was particularly strong after the First World War when the son, The Hon. F. S. G. Calthorpe, played for the county, captaining between 1920–29.

Ten years later, in 1895, Warwickshire played their

Above *Edgbaston in 1894, the year Warwickshire secured first-class status*

Opposite *Edgbaston's second Test Match, in 1909. George Hirst bowling to Charlie Macartney*

first season as a first-class county after a series of triumphs and qualification – in the face of considerable opposition from other counties – the previous year. In two weeks in 1894 they trounced Nottinghamshire, Surrey and Kent – three of the strongest counties. There were bound to be reverses, however, and 1896 came the most ignominious, when Yorkshire ran up the not insignificant total of 887, which remains the highest in county cricket. Most people reckoned that Yorkshire only batted for so long to beat the record set by Lancashire the season before, with whom they were enjoying worse than usual relations at the time.

In 1902, came the first Test Match at Edgbaston to open that famous series against Australia. Many consider England's batting for this match to have been the strongest ever: A. C. MacLaren, C. B. Fry, K. S. Ranjitsinhji, F. S. Jackson, J. T. Tyldesley, A. A. Lilley (a Warwickshire player), G. H. Hirst, G. L. Jessop, L. C. Braund, W. H. Lockwood and W. Rhodes. They all scored first-class hundreds in their time.

Edgbaston seemed destined to produce memorable Test cricket, but was rarely given the opportunity. The next occasion did not come until 1909, when George Hirst and Colin Blythe took all 20 Australian wickets, bowling them out for 74 and 151 to give England victory. Then there was a long gap until 1924, when South Africa were bowled out for 30 and, like Hirst and Blythe before them, Arthur Gilligan the captain and Maurice Tate took all 20 wickets to give their side an innings victory. After a draw when South Africa next visited, in 1929, the game in which Duleepsinhji made his debut for England, Test cricket deserted Edgbaston,

tempted away by improvements at the midlands rival, Trent Bridge, and did not return for twenty-eight years.

Ansell resigned as secretary in 1902, and handed over to his assistant since 1895, R. V. Ryder. His spell in office lasted until 1944 when he in turn handed over to his assistant, Leslie Deakins. Deakins was to remain secretary until 1976, during which time he oversaw and on many occasions provided the initiative for the redevelopment of the ground. Like Ansell, Deakins had definite ambitions, the seeds of which had been sown during war-time service with the Royal Navy: to build up a side that would win the County Championship and to see Test cricket return to Edgbaston. Both were achieved, the first in 1951, the second in 1957. Deakins was fortunate in that in the early years he had a president who was equally ambitious and rich enough to make a sizeable contribution, Dr Harold Thwaite. The doctor has two monuments to his memory at Edgbaston, the Thwaite Gates, with piers surmounted by the county's bear and ragged staff, and the Thwaite Scoreboard – architecturally the best on any Test ground.

Other than the pavilion, which has been so altered and added to that its tiled roof and slender little pointed spire give the appearance of struggling to avoid being drowned by development, and the Thwaite scoreboard with its handsome tiled roof and clock, everything at Edgbaston is post-war. The most impressive sweep of concrete banking stretches round the west side from the William Ansell Stand, where the blocks of Priory and Raglan stands curve round to the Hill Bank. At the far end from the pavilion, which looks straight down the

wicket, is the Pressbox stand and scoreboard, then the Stanley Barnes Stand and along the east side, the Rea Bank named after the River Rea which runs along this side of the ground. Edgbaston's seating capacity is 17,500 and the total area owned by the club is nearly twenty acres.

Edgbaston's development and improvement has been almost continuous during the post-war period, but it is since the mid-1970s that it has acquired most of the impressive entertainment facilities which provide important commercial support during the cricket season and continued revenue from bookings throughout the year. No other ground can boast two ballrooms, and there are two equally expansive dining-rooms. There seem to be suites everywhere: the County Suite, the Pavilion Suite, the Executive Suite and the Club Suite.

Strategically sited around the ground are the executive boxes: twelve at the back of Raglan and Priory stands, three in the William Ansell and two in the Pressbox Stand – where two more are being added for the 1988 season. At the top of the William Ansell Stand is the Executive Suite, opened in 1975 and as successful as any of Edgbaston's ventures. One hundred companies pay £800 per annum for eight tickets to county matches and four for Test Matches. Below is the members' bar and dining-room. After a comprehensive tour one can see why David Heath, Warwickshire's current secretary, who has been involved with the club since the late-1940s, remarks that cricket is only one element of life at Edgbaston.

In the main pavilion the players have their dressing-rooms and dining-room and other modern necessities such as the physiotherapy room. The club offices are also here and, above, Edgbaston's one haven of the county's past, the Club Suite. Here is the club room, aptly named for it is a silent place with a most somniferous atmosphere. It is an inner sanctum for Warwickshire members – usually of senior age – who enjoy a first-class view of play from the comfort of deep armchairs. I feel that it is perhaps the only part of Edgbaston where P. G. Wodehouse would have felt at home. He was a Warwickshire member for many years and named his immortal butler after Percy Jeeves, the Warwickshire bowler, whom he watched at Cheltenham in 1913.

Here, in the club room, is Edgbaston's history. Team photographs of almost every year since the 1890s, a memorial tablet and role of honour for those Warwickshire players killed in the 1914–18 war, the England team who bowled South Africa out for 30 in 1924, and one of the county's most favoured players, Eric Hollies, leaving the field after his last match in 1957.

The Warwickshire stalwart Len Bates was actually born in the pavilion itself, in 1895. His father was groundsman and lived in what is now the committee room. Bates remembered one of his first jobs as a boy was putting leather shoes onto the horse who pulled the heavy roller. He played for the county between 1913–35, scored nearly 20,000 runs and was reputed to have once fallen asleep fielding in the deep. When he died his ashes were scattered over the ground.

Bates was still too young to play for the county during the triumphant year of 1911. It was the team of Frank Foster, the captain – an all-rounder full of inspiration whose career was finished by a motorcycle accident in 1915, W. G. Quaife who scored over 35,000 runs in his career and whose brother and son also played for the county, of the England wicket-keeper, A. F. A. Lilley, in his last season, and the man who succeeded him for Warwickshire, E. J. 'Tiger' Smith, and of Septimus Kinneir whose 268 not out in the Hampshire match was the highest score by a Warwickshire man at Edgbaston.

Between the wars Warwickshire were captained by two contrasting amateurs, the Hon. F. S. Gough-Calthorpe and R. E. S. Wyatt. Calthorpe played cricket for enjoyment and was almost unfailingly cheerful on and off the field. Wyatt was a knowledgeable tactician for whom cricket was a serious business and whose attitude was summed up when he explained why he enjoyed playing in Yorkshire. 'They played the type of game I liked to play myself . . . They gave nothing away'.

In 1922 Edgbaston witnessed one of the most extraordinary turn-arounds in cricket history. Having bowled Hampshire out for 15 in forty minutes, after scoring 223 themselves, Warwickshire were beaten by 155 runs. Hampshire scored 521 in their follow-on, their captain the Hon. L. H. Tennyson making 172 and his valet, the wicket-keeper, Walter Livsey scoring 110 at number ten. Set to score 314 to win, the stunned Warwickshire side were bowled out for 158. Calthorpe had planned a game of golf between the amateurs on the third day, so confident was he that the match would finish early, while his noble opponent, Lionel Tennyson made a handsome profit from the bets he wagered on a Hampshire win.

When Warwickshire won their second Championship in 1951 attendances for county cricket were at their zenith and nowhere was this more evident than at Edgbaston. The side had the county's first professional captain, Tom Dollery who, with Eric Hollies, was the backbone of the team and when they clinched the Championship by beating Yorkshire in July an aggregate of 43,000 attended the three days – a record for county cricket which broke the one of 32,091 set in Warwickshire's previous match at Edgbaston against Lancashire.

It was the combination of the ground's development, the county's success and the increased attendances which brought about the return of Test cricket in 1957 – and the match against the West Indies was more memorable than anyone could have possibly hoped. The delightful 'Collie' Smith, tragically killed two years later in a motor accident aged twenty-six, scored 161 in his first Test against England. Then, in England's second innings, the captain Peter May with 285 not out and Colin Cowdrey with 154, made 411 together – England's highest partnership for any wicket and a Test record for the fourth wicket. While they were amassing their runs poor 'Sonny' Ramadhin, who had taken seven wickets in the first innings, was notching up his own endurance record of 98 overs whose 588 balls were the most ever bowled in a first-class innings.

Colin Cowdrey will always have happy memories of Edgbaston, for eleven years later he celebrated his 100th Test appearance by scoring 104 on the ground. So too will David Gower, who has scored two delightful double-hundreds on the ground: 200 not out against India in 1979 and 215 against Australia in 1985. For elegance however, even David Gower is rivalled by Zaheer Abbas who, aged twenty-three in 1971, scored 274 for Pakistan to establish himself as a world-class player of the utmost style.

1957, when Test cricket returned to Edgbaston, also saw the captaincy of Warwickshire pass to one of the county's favourite players of recent decades, M.J.K. Smith. As well as a popular captain Smith was a prolific run-scorer and his total of just short of 40,000 in his career was a Warwickshire record until passed by Dennis Amiss. M.J.K. was succeeded as captain by another Smith – A.C. – who led the county to the Championship in 1972 and subsequently became Secretary of the club until his appointment as Chief Executive of the TCCB at the end of 1986.

There is no doubt that the single greatest event for Warwickshire at Edgbaston of recent years came in 1974, when John Jameson and Rohan Kanhai set a world record for the second wicket of 465, Jameson scoring 240 not out and Kanhai 213 not out. With Lance Gibbs and Alvin Kallicharran, Kanhai was one of a greatly talented trio of West Indians to play for Warwickshire, while more recently the main power of the county's bowling has been the Barbadian-born England player, Gladstone Small.

One hopes that Test cricket will never again desert Edgbaston, for it would be rendered somewhat dino-saur-like and quite out of proportion as just a home of the more humble county game. In the quest for improvement and modernity there has been little respite since the Second World War, both in the ground's policies and buildings, and on the field of play where for many years Bernard Flack, now the TCCB inspector of pitches, controlled a dazzling array of machinery. Most representative is the well-known 'Brumbrella', the enormous motorized cover, which lumbers out over the whole ground to keep off heavy rain. Nonetheless, if Edgbaston is a place where 'biggest is best' often seems to be the watchword, there are some reassuringly small and reticent features, one of which is the little arched wrought-iron gate in the ground's perimeter wall. It is the 'Sydney Barnes Wicket Gate', marking the spot where the legendary bowler entered the ground in 1894 to start his career playing for Warwickshire, and where his ashes have lain since his death in 1967.

The memorial plaque to Sydney Barnes

NUNEATON

Such has been Warwickshire's commitment to Edgbaston that they have made only minimal sorties to other grounds and since they deserted the county's second most populous city, Coventry, after the 1982 season, Nuneaton is the only ground to be visited for one county championship game a year.

Nuneaton lies in the extreme north-east of the county, within walking distance of Hinckley, Leicestershire's outpost just over the border. It is a coal-mining area and the Nuneaton ground was home for cricketers from the Griff and Coton collieries, members of the Griff and Coton CC.

Warwickshire played their first game on the ground in 1930 and *Wisden* commented that, 'the new departure was happily attended with pronounced success'. Even if continual rain made the event not quite so rosy as the Almanack would have one believe, the coal-mining crowd were treated to three hundreds, two for the visitors Leicestershire, by N. F. Armstrong and A. Shipman and one by Warwickshire's captain Mr R. E. S. Wyatt.

Nevertheless, it did not bring regular visits to Nuneaton. There was a long gap until 1960 and since then there have only been annual games since the late-1970s. In 1961 Bill Alley celebrated Somerset's visit to the ground with the highest score of his career, 221 not out with six sixes and 31 fours. More significant for the future of Nuneaton, the same year saw the closure of the collieries and the removal of the head-gear which had been the major feature of the ground's outlook.

The following year Tom Cartwright, the Warwickshire all-rounder, followed Alley's example by making 210, the highest score of his career. In 1964 he displayed the other half of his all-round ability, taking four for 3 and five for 37 when Nottinghamshire crashed to scores of 34 and 57.

Today Nuneaton is probably a cleaner and healthier place than in the old days and appears to have gained a regular place in Warwickshire's calendar. Alvin Kallicharran scored a lot of runs here and in 1982 Bob Willis reached his peak as a batsman: 62 not out against Gloucestershire, his highest first-class score. But I think I would have preferred the old days, with the colliery band playing under the bandstand, the wheels of the head-gear whirling and a lively crowd, sporting cloth caps, around the boundary.

Above *Nuneaton's colliery ground, looking towards the pavilion*

DERBYSHIRE

DERBY

The names of county cricket grounds frequently give an insight into their individual circumstances and provenance and, accordingly, are often to be cherished. They may tell of past history, the immediate surroundings or a generous benefactor. At Derby the ground is – or was called – the Racecourse Ground, and for good reason, as the present ground is on the site of the old racecourse. Derby has, however, suffered in the past from its reputation and this, as much as anything else, has made county officials anxious that it be known as the County Ground – a disappointingly anonymous title which sheds the air of jauntiness suggested by the old name.

Derby benefited from the boom in racing popularity towards the end of the nineteenth century. Equally important was its position as one of the great railway towns in the country, for it was the railways which partly brought about the dramatic expansion of racing at the time and the opening of numerous new courses.

Looking from the pavilion towards the elegant poplars of the Racecourse ground

Derby boasted a straight mile and an imposing grandstand complete with a copper-domed viewing cupola. Today the grandstand retains its proud stone tablet marking the building's construction – dated AD 1911 below the county's badge, the rose and crown. Certainly the flat, open and windswept site to the north-east of the city would not have worried the racing fraternity, who were used to even more inhospitable and bracing surroundings such as Newmarket Heath. In those days and, indeed, after the racing ceased during the 1930s, the cricket ground was inside the racecourse, to one side of its present position, a fairly stark affair with a small pavilion and some open wooden stands, and boundaries which stretched away into the wide expanses of the surrounding Racecourse Park. It was a place where players were constantly calling for an extra sweater. Too far away to be any use for players or spectators stood the obsolete racing grandstand, like a beached whale with, to one side, the old jockeys' quarters and enclosed area behind what had been the paddock.

In their book on county grounds, *Homes of Sport* (*Cricket*), published in 1952 Norman Yardley and Jim Kilburn commented with finality,

> Suggestions have been made for moving the Mahomet of the cricket 'square' nearer to the mountain of the stand, and turning the stand into a pavilion and members' enclosure, but the scheme has not yet passed beyond the stage of discussion. As the 'square' has just been re-laid, presumably the change is not imminent.

As things turned out they could not have been more wrong, for the move was made within a few years so that the new pitch stood in front of the grandstand. The conversion to pavilion did not take place – indeed, until 1982 there was no pavilion at all and the players' changing rooms and county club offices were in the old jockeys' quarters.

Stories about the discomfort of the players' changing rooms – as well as the lack of a pavilion and the ground's other shortcomings – were legion. On one occasion, Dennis Lillee was attempting to find somewhere for a satisfactory wash after a gruelling spell of bowling for the Australian tourists against the county. Of the two showers he was directed towards the first produced nothing at all, the second a mingy dose of rusty water. Eventually he settled for the only available bath, one

leg of which was supported on a brick which gave way, depositing the luckless Lillee and his bath-water onto the shower-room floor!

These were not the only problems. The ground's low-lying position combined with poor drainage to bring about a surfeit of slow, dull wickets. Of a different nature was the tendency for the ground at Derby to be compared with the county's other main one, Queen's Park, Chesterfield, snugly enclosed with its gardens, crooked spire and well-deserved reputation as one of the most picturesque grounds in the country. Finally, it should be said that football is probably the sport which is of primary interest to the vast majority of Derby men and therefore enthusiasm for cricket has often been difficult to encourage – a situation which the performance of the county side has rarely done much to improve.

By the 1970s the general situation had reached such a low ebb that there was even talk of closing the ground. (It was no coincidence that from 1971 the county's position in the championship was as follows: last, last, second from last, last, third from last, and third from last – about as dismal a run as any county has ever aspired to.) Happily closure was averted, for it is a sad county which does not have cricket at its county town, or at the place where its club was founded, as it was in the Guildhall in Derby in 1870.

Whether it was the threat of extinction or just the

The old ground at Derby, before the move to the Racecourse grandstand

emergence of a determination by the county's committee to do something definite which provided the impetus, since then things have undeniably improved. Certainly a major uplift was provided by victory in the NatWest Trophy in 1981, when Northants were beaten in a thrilling final, Derbyshire winning the tied match by virtue of having lost fewer wickets. If Derby has not yet completely shaken off its unenviable reputation among county grounds it has certainly spruced itself up and gone a long way towards securing its future.

The starting-point for improvement was the purchase of a lease on the ground of 125 years from Derby City Council, who own all of Racecourse Park. The money to buy the lease was generously loaned by the local authority and, with security of tenure, development of the ground could begin. Between 1982 and 1984 there was a flurry of activity. The new scoreboard was built – on the far side of the ground from the grandstand – close to the old one which has been retained and houses a broadcasting room giving a grand view down the wicket.

The major addition was – at last – a respectable pavilion, whose front looks onto the wicket at an angle as it extends from the quaint signal box (originally the racecourse judges' box), which stands at one end of the grandstand. The back of the pavilion conveniently faces the new county club offices – built onto the front of the corrugated-iron indoor school which was refurbished at the same time, and is close to the car park inside the ground's main entrance.

In its own unassuming way the Lund pavilion (named after Harry Lund, a committee member at the time and one of the benefactors of the pavilion development) is an elegant and certainly inoffensive building, long and low, with a simple roof broken only by two slit-like gables, one of which houses the pavilion clock. (In fact a second, more striking clock surmounts the new scoreboard.) The pavilion's best feature is the balcony which extends the whole length of the upper storey, although, knowing that Robert Bakewell – England's greatest wrought-iron craftsman, who lived in the early eighteenth-century – was a Derby man, makes one hanker for a more ornamental balustrade.

Now the players have changing-rooms which are a considerable improvement on the old ones in the run-down jockeys' quarters. The ground floor also contains the committee room and – taking up most of the space – the Moss Room (named after John Moss, another committee member who gave financial assistance to the building of the pavilion), which contains a bar and the players' dining room. Above is a sponsor's box and the Strutt Room, the latter a smart 'function' room, named after a family of local industrialists and landowners and staunch club supporters, containing its own bar and dining-room.

On round the boundary from the pavilion, to the west side of the ground, is the area of most recent development. In the wake of the Bradford disaster the ground's mobile wooden seating was dispensed with and replaced by a pair of neat, open stands, with bright red brick backs and sides containing rows of tiered, fixed blue plastic seats. Called the Steetley and Butterley stands, they are named after the two Derby companies who sponsored their construction. The two new stands have increased the ground's seating capacity to around 2,000 although, with open spaces around all the boundary the total capacity is more like 10–12,000.

It is likely that the Butterley Company provided the bricks for the two stands, as well as for the building which houses the Derbyshire Sports Club, between them. In addition to the cricket, the Sports Club caters for the four hockey pitches which appear in winter, on the site behind the club building and two stands. It seemed characteristic of the club's new, thoughtful approach towards their ground that there is a generous space for cars with disabled drivers between the Sports

Club and the Butterley Stand.

If the various recent developments have dramatically improved the ground at Derby, the old grandstand remains the most impressive feature. At one end is a members' enclosure – although this is normally limited by the sightscreens – and along the whole of the grandstand the seating is still simple wooden benches. Behind the enclosure is the press box. Prominently displayed on the copper dome of the old viewing box is 'Banks's Ales' – and why not, as they provide the beer in the bar at the back of the public seats in the grandstand. In fact, another brewery, Bass, from nearby Burton-on-Trent have been one of the club's major benefactors in recent years.

The bar is part of the Grandstand Hotel, whose entrance is on the far side from the cricket ground and which takes up much of the building. Of all unlikely occupants, the rest of the enclosed part of the grandstand, behind the tiered seats of the members' enclosure and the press box, consists of the offices of the Ministry of Agriculture. If their presence is characteristically low-key it is a depressing thought that the theatrical viewing-dome has been denigrated to becoming one of their store-rooms.

If the present occupants of the old judges' box are quite different from the top-hatted gents who would have adjudicated over the jockeys and horses they are equally important. One room houses the scorers, while next door is the public address system, operated on most match days by Ken Roe, chairman of the ground committee and stalwart of the club for as long as most people can remember. As if to confirm the signal box's integral role, the heavy innings bell hangs from the eaves of its roof.

As much as anything else, the planting of protective rows of poplar trees around two sides of the ground – to the north and east where the most penetrating winds come from – has helped to give a more sheltered and friendly atmosphere. Fortunately, as a result of the abundant space, the trees do not crowd in on the boundary but are set well back across mown grass. In addition a long mound has been raised along the east side, adding further protection and breaking up the monotonous flatness of the site. Inevitably, the mound supports prominent advertising boards during matches.

Probably the best view of the ground is from the scoreboard end, across to the long range of buildings – old and new – on the far boundary, where on a sunny day the light flashes and gleams off the copper dome in a most arresting manner. Looking the other way, from the grandstand terraces, one sees the city skyline, now partly obscured by the poplars, dominated by the tower

of Derby Cathedral (originally All Saints Church and only elevated to cathedral status in 1927). It is a pleasant surprise to learn that much of the cathedral is the work of the eighteenth-century architect, James Gibbs, best known for St Martin-in-the-Fields in London.

If recent years have seen a great improvement in the facilities and appearance of the ground at Derby one can only hope that an accompanying elevation in the playing fortunes will not be long in following. The NatWest victory in 1981 was the sole success in one-day competitions and the only real achievement since the Second World War. Certainly it is now only the most senior supporters who can remember the treasured winning of the Championship in 1936 – sadly not achieved at home at Derby, but against Somerset in the cathedral city of Wells. Derbyshire lost the match, but they secured enough first innings points to set up an unassailable lead in the competition. Their captain was A. W. Richardson, the only amateur among ten professionals, who remarked after the game at Wells that what pleased him most was the boost the Championship victory would give to his professionals' winter pay – usually a meagre retainer. Like many amateur captains Richardson, a Wykehamist who once put on 117 in a second-wicket stand of 295 for his school against Harrow, was never a great player, but his main quality was as a warm and loyal leader of his men.

Richardson may have led Derby in their finest hour, but he should not be confused with another of the same name, Samuel Richardson, who defrauded the club of most of their money during the 1890s, when they were struggling to re-establish themselves after the ignominy of having had their first-class status removed for seven years in 1887. Richardson's dishonest activities were discovered by perhaps the county's most illustrious visitor, F. R. Spofforth, 'The Demon', who, having emigrated to England in 1888, found a wife in the village of Breadsall – a couple of miles from the county ground – and played for Derbyshire for three seasons. How ironic that arguably the two most fearsome bowlers for Australia and England – Spofforth and Larwood – both emigrated to live in the country of their main opponents.

If 'The Demon' was the county's foremost visitor from overseas another, Eddie Barlow, the dynamic South African all-rounder, did a great deal to repair their flagging fortunes during his two years of captaincy in 1977 and 1978. However it is home-grown men who have dominated the county's sides and shown their talents over the years. Batsmen like H. Storer, T. S. Worthington and L. F. Townsend were all capable all-rounders, all of whom played in the Championship-

winning side. Of the bowlers, W. H. Copson, who took 160 wickets in the Championship season, including dismissing five or more batsmen in an innings thirteen times, only took up cricket because during the General Strike of 1926 fellow miners persuaded him to play cricket to fill in the enforced absence from work. What a start his first-class career enjoyed – he bowled Andrew Sandham with his very first ball. After the Second World War the formidable opening pair, H. L. Jackson and C. Gladwin, confounded many a county batsman during the late-1940s and 1950s.

In more recent years the trio of Derbyshire players, M. Hendrick, G. Miller and R. W. Taylor all played together for England (although, admittedly, Taylor came from nearby Stoke-on-Trent). In addition to his personal records, Taylor shares one that must be unique, in being the last of only three full-time wicket-keepers for the county between the First World War and the 1980s. The other two were G. O. Dawkes and H. Elliott and between them the trio notched up a total of over 1,400 appearances for Derbyshire.

One important connexion that has persisted throughout most of Derbyshire's first-class history is with Repton, not surprisingly as the school is only a few miles south of Derby towards Burton-on-Trent. And what better school could a county hope to have on the doorstep, for Repton's cricketing history is second to none? Unfortunately the county did not secure either the services of J. N. Crawford, the foremost schoolboy cricketer of all time, or of C. B. Fry, the school's most gifted all-round product. Two Richard Sale's – father

and son – went on to play for the county though, and for twelve consecutive seasons, from 1951–62, the county was captained by Reptonians, first G. L. Willatt and second, D. B. Carr – the only Derbyshire man to score 2,000 runs in a season. A master, J. D. Eggar, also gets himself into the Derbyshire record books, having scored 219 in the county's record second-wicket partnership of 349, made with C. S. Elliott in 1947.

All this has not, however, made for an abundance of success at Derbyshire CC and troughs have been notably more evident than peaks throughout the county's history. Today, with a membership of around 1,500, Derbyshire is one of the smallest clubs, but at least the members now have a county ground which is far from being the butt of the county circuit that it used to be. If Derby will never be beautiful, its position to the northeast of the city, on the Nottingham Road, is spacious, unlike so many grounds hemmed in by rows of houses or spoilt by modern buildings in their immediate vicinity. And if plenty of grounds share stands with football or rugby grounds none other boasts one that belonged to a racecourse. Also, with the new pavilion and other buildings, it is an up-to-date ground well suited to the modern county game.

It there is one thing the Derby ground does lack which would certainly add tone and gravity, it is a pair of fine entrance gates; surely there must be a local man following in the footsteps of the great Robert Bakewell?

Above *Derby, showing the grandstand with its viewing cupola and the new pavilion to the right*

CHESTERFIELD

If Derby is the county's headquarters, Queen's Park, Chesterfield is its showpiece. More than that it has character few county grounds can rival. One feels it to be completely just that this tough, dour, industrial town only a few miles south of the Yorkshire border, and built predominently of now blackened local stone, should sport a cricket ground whose delights far outstrip what other softer, more attractive towns can offer.

Ever since it was first laid out, in 1897, to celebrate Queen Victoria's Diamond Jubilee, as were many other parks around the country, Queen's Park has remained what it was first intended to be – a place for recreation for the inhabitants of Chesterfield. The park lies on the south-west side of the town, across the River Hipper and busy Markham Road but linked by an elegant arched footbridge which spans both. The almost circular cricket ground takes up the eastern half of the park, the rest of which is an open area of recreation used as a car park when county matches are on. On the far side from the cricket ground an enormous new sports centre is being built on Boythorpe Road.

If the forms of recreation have changed a bit over ninety-odd years the friendly atmosphere of relaxation has not. This as much as anything else gives the ground its charm. Equally importantly Queen's Park has a series of delightful features – the bandstand, the boating lake and the gardens – foremost and best known of which is the view across the ground to the crooked spire of All Saints Church, rising an elegant if eccentric 238 feet, its height accentuated by the fact that the fourteenth-century church, and surrounding town centre, are on a hill. Legend has it that the devil twisted his tail around the spire in a fit of rage, hence causing the famous crook. Whatever the story, stretching up from the square tower which supports it, the spire presents as fine a vista as any county ground can offer.

It is quite clear that not only do Chesterfield Corporation – who own Queen's Park – maintain the whole park to a high standard, they also employ some expert gardeners. Throughout the summer they produce displays of bulbs and bright-coloured annuals totally in character wih their setting and reminiscent of much late-Victorian and Edwardian gardening. Some of the ornamental beds greet the visitor as he arrives over the footbridge from the town, but by far the best of the gardens are at the far end, to the side of the pavilion.

Previous page *Queen's Park Chesterfield: Few grounds can boast such a setting*

It is from this side, from the Boythorpe Avenue entrance, that the first-time visitor is best advised to approach the cricket ground. Opposite the entrance is the elegant green and white bandstand and along one side of the path leading down to the cricket ground is an impressive herbaceous border, backed by a wooden trellis covered with roses. Here many a gardening wife lingers while her husband presses on so as not to miss any cricket action. On the other side of the path the lawn is studded with circular flower beds and at the end, far enough from the boundary to be out of danger from big-hitters is the gardeners' *tour de force* – a white-painted conservatory filled with purple-flowered bougainvillea and other exotic plants. On a raised bank in front of the conservatory was a special display for 1987, with 'St John's Ambulance Brigade Centenary 1887–1987' encircling a floral picture of the St John's Maltese Cross. No doubt 1997 – the centenary of Queen's Park – will see a similarly skilful and pleasing celebration.

The visitor should not allow the horticultural delights to distract him for too long, however. Moving on to where the path reaches the cricket ground, with rockeries on either side, he is greeted with the view to the church spire stretching above the trees on the far boundary. The trees which surround the ground on all sides – mainly well-grown limes and horse chestnuts, except for the line of younger limes along the recreation ground side – are an integral part of Queen's Park and give it a feeling of protected seclusion.

The pavilion faces straight down the wicket from the south end with, on both sides, permanent terraces with green benches which form the members' enclosure. It is a striking building with gables at either end, one of which contains the clock. In between the gables is an upper balcony where an umbrella is a sensible precaution – as it is on all the seating around the ground, none of which is covered. On the wall of the pavilion a stalwart of the cricket club is remembered by a neat plaque saying: 'This balcony was extended in 1936 in commemoration of a legacy bequeathed to the club by the late George A. Eastwood JP, a former vice-president and generous supporter.' If the pavilion facilities are limited, one hopes that there are not plans for extension or modernization. Queen's Park is a ground where this would undoubtedly be detrimental. As it is the players eat in one of the marquees erected along the top of the embankment along the west side of the ground.

When the county are playing temporary tiered seating is erected at the far end – or lake end as it is known – one block to the left of the sightscreen and a larger one stretching round the boundary to the green

wooden score box tucked under the trees on the Park Road side. Refreshment marquees along the embankment on the recreation side of the ground complete the picture.

The ground itself has a pronounced slope from the pavilion end down to the lake end. Its relatively small size has encouraged adventurous hitting and big scores, but often this has been countered by the wicket which, if not unpredictable, is certainly testing for batsmen after rain.

Derbyshire first played at Queen's Park in 1898 and, although the arrival of county cricket was certainly to be celebrated, the first season was somewhat overshadowed by the performance of the neighbours and arch-rivals, Yorkshire, and in particular of their openers J. T. Brown and J. Tunnicliffe. In a Yorkshire total of 662 – still the highest score against Derbyshire by any county – Brown and Tunnicliffe scored 554 for the first wicket, a record which stood until 1932, when their Yorkshire successors, Holmes and Sufcliffe, bettered it by one run at Leyton. Because of Chesterfield's proximity to the county boundary Yorkshire have always been the club's primary opponents and the home fixtures have almost invariably been played at Queen's Park.

Without doubt the most memorable – and extraordinary – match to have been played at Queen's Park, and one which Derbyshire men are happy to remember, was against Essex in 1904. On the first day the visitors

Chesterfield's handsome pavilion, with the clock mounted in the right-hand gable

ran up a total of 597 – in less than six hours – with P. A. Perrin scoring 343 not out, including 68 fours which is still the world record for boundaries in a single innings. On the second day Derbyshire replied with 548, largely thanks to C. A. Ollivierre, the first black West Indian to play for an English county, who scored 229. On the last day the variable nature of the wicket came into play and Essex were bowled out for 97, leaving Derbyshire the relatively easy task of making 147, which they did for the loss of one wicket, Ollivierre again being the hero, scoring 92 of the total needed. Certainly no batsman has scored as many as poor Perrin and ended up on the losing side.

Another notable victory for Derbyshire took place in 1947 when Somerset were beaten by an innings on the first day. George Pope, the Derbyshire fast-medium bowler and one of three brothers to play for the county, returned six for 34 in the first innings and seven for 16 in the second and Somerset only managed totals of 68 and 38.

In the past Chesterfield crowds have had a reputation for being free with their comments, and in particular their criticisms. In *Homes of Sport* Norman Yardley and Jim Kilburn described it as 'a crowd with a reputation for unambiguous expression of opinion. The

Chesterfield spectators are sometimes noisy, and they can be rude, but they are rarely indifferent to the cricket being set before them'. One must remember that Yardley and Kilburn were Yorkshiremen and, if there were instances of rudeness, they were most likely to be directed against fellow members of their county.

Today, rather than the derisive call of barrackers, one is more likely to hear the high-pitched and high-spirited cries of children who have been deposited by their parents on either the boating lake or the miniature railway at one end of the ground. How convenient and agreeable to have ready-made entertainment for the children so that peaceful spectating can be enjoyed uninterrupted. And when there is no play the lake corner of the ground is a regular meeting-spot for mothers and children, prior to pushing the prams around the ready-made circuit of the hard-surfaced cycle-track which forms the perimeter of the cricket ground.

Until recent years, or more exactly the improvement of the county ground at Derby, Chesterfield hosted the largest number of the home county championship matches. The balance has now been redressed and in 1987 seven matches were played at Derby and four at Chesterfield. Certainly it would have been a tragedy if the suggestion that all home championship matches – raised in the early 1980s – should be played at Derby had ever been carried out, for Queen's Park is a ground which few cricketers have not enjoyed playing on and which all spectators find delightful.

HEANOR

In 1987 Derbyshire deserted the Peak District's famous spa town of Buxton to play their only county championship match away from Derby or Chesterfield in the very different surroundings of Heanor, which is, to date, the newest ground to host a county championship match. The small town is a few miles north-east of Derby, close to Ilkeston where the county also played, and just over the border from Nottinghamshire. Buxton, where first-class matches had been played – albeit not every year – since 1923, had the distinction of being the highest first-class ground in England, but by the 1980s its wicket and the general facilities were being criticized and all too often the situation was worsened by the intervention of rain.

In contrast to Buxton's Georgian elegance, Heanor

The scorers keeping cool during Heanor's inaugural County Championship match in 1987

Heanor, the church tower appearing between floodlight pylons for the adjacent football ground

is a dour, no-nonsense mining town perched on a hill just over the county boundary from Eastwood – the birthplace of D. H. Lawrence, whose books are full of vivid descriptions of his early life in this mining community. The cricket ground at Heanor is well disguised by rows of squat houses and if you cannot actually see the head-gear of a colliery anywhere in the immediate vicinity the dank smell of coal is normally pervasively present and in one direction the blackened stone of the square tower of the town's church tells of the place's main livelihood.

As if to overcome the unprepossessing surroundings, the weather behaved itself for one of the rare spells of warmth in 1987 and Heanor's inaugural county match, against Hampshire, was played in blazing sunshine. Nor were the local crowd disappointed by the cricket. In three days over 1,200 runs were amassed – the small size of the ground assisting to some extent – and three hundreds scored; by Mark Nicholas and David Turner for Hampshire and by Bruce Roberts for Derbyshire. Derbyshire's captain Kim Barnett just missed his century, being out for 91 and as was fitting for a first match, an exciting chase by the home team, set to score 298 in 59 overs, ended in victory with two balls to spare.

Facilities are, not surprisingly, limited on the small ground used to club cricket. There is a marked slope in one direction down the wicket, but the main problem for cricket of first-class standard is the area shared with Heanor Town Football Club whose pitch is next door on the top side of the ground. All the same, Heanor's residents strongly hope that they will enjoy future visits from the county.

LANCASHIRE

OLD TRAFFORD

If the cricket world in general is prepared to doff its cap to Lord's as the premier ground, one can be sure that no Lancastrian would give the MCC's headquarters precedence over Old Trafford. The esteem in which the men of the north-west hold their ground may be tinted with partisanship, but, brought up as they are on tough, competitive league cricket they are uncompromising in their demands for high standards and the qualities of Old Trafford have been acknowledged and recorded by scores of others – players, commentators and spectators alike.

What better verdict can a ground boast than that of an MCC committee, set up in 1931 to inspect and report on the Test Match grounds, particularly with reference to their ability to cope with rapidly increasing crowds: 'Old Trafford was in every respect most desirable, and in fact the only ground they had visited where no improvement could be suggested'. H. D. Davies described it as, 'that perfect stretch of cricketing turf within its chaplet of dignified masonry which men know and revere the wide world over'. Even a Yorkshireman, Jim Kilburn, was moved to write,

From this acquisition has grown the extensive headquarters of Lancashire cricket, superb stage for Test Matches since 1884, a ground of delight in its playing characteristic and splendour in its accommodation; a palace of cricket, scarred by war and enshrined by tradition; a name to be respected and an experience to be enjoyed.

Praise indeed.

As a result the first-time visitor can be forgiven a slight feeling of trepidation as he approaches Old Trafford. Arriving by car he is likely to pass the four modern office blocks which announce the destination to be near: Statham House, MacLaren House, Duckworth House and Washbrook House. They are on the right as one drives along Talbot Road before turning into Warwick Road to find the public car park and main entrance. By train the visitor should take care not to alight at Old Trafford station – one stop further out from Manchester's centre is Warwick Road, with its own turnstiles leading straight into the ground.

This station entrance is the best vantage-point for an initial view of Old Trafford. Opposite is the pavilion, facing the wicket at right-angles, which immediately invests the ground with a feeling of establishment and authority. Its appearance would be slightly brooding without the twin copper domes on either side, surmounted with flagpoles, which offset perfectly the dark tiled roof, blackened stone and deep red brick of the building. Instead it is a building which personifies Lancashire cricket and has a presence few other than Lord's can rival.

To the right generous open terraces, supporting smart new bucket seating, curve round to Old Trafford's newest building, which looks down the wicket, the Red Rose Suite and Neville Cardus Gallery opened in 1987. To the left more open terraces (with the important distinction that on this side they are part of the members' enclosure), where the new buff-coloured plastic seats have not completely replaced the more colourful old blue, wooden benches, stretch round to the Ladies Stand, the Board of Control Stand and the Executive Suite. It is an impressive sweep which, taken all the way round, provides seating for 20,000 spectators.

It was in 1856 that the Manchester CC was evicted from its ground on the Chester Road and, on looking for new quarters, found less than a mile away a site reported by *Bells Life* a year later as consisting of, 'eight acres of good, level, sandy ground'. The paper also noted that 'The pavilion is erected on the north side; and while it is a great ornament to the ground, it is well adapted for the purposes for which it will be used. It consists of a centre compartment (intended for a dining hall) and two wings, a turret surmounting the centre'. Finally, not the least consideration, 'Underneath the building is an excellent wine cellar, no unimportant acquisition in a cricket pavilion'.

The newspaper's mention of both the quality of the

ground and the facilities of the pavilion highlights what have been maintained ever since at an almost invariably high standard. Perhaps because of the mild, damp conditions due to Manchester's north-westerly position, the grass at Old Trafford is enviably soft and green, and it is this, combined with the unusually clear light, which many players remember. Off the field of play, there have been few complaints about conditions and facilities for either players or spectators.

The 'new' pavilion was built in 1894, four years before the Manchester club were able to buy the ground (a total area of eighteen acres), from Sir Humphrey de Trafford for £24,082. Since then the pavilion has been used as a hospital during the First World War, bombed during the Blitz of the Second and seen continuous change on all sides. Nonetheless it has retained much of its original appearance.

If changes and improvements have regularly taken place during the ground's history, it is in the last few years that they have been most extensive and dramatic. The leading light behind the modernization of the ground was Cedric Rhoades, Chairman of Lancashire CCC from 1969–86. Rhoades was one of a number of figures in English cricket at that time who were con-

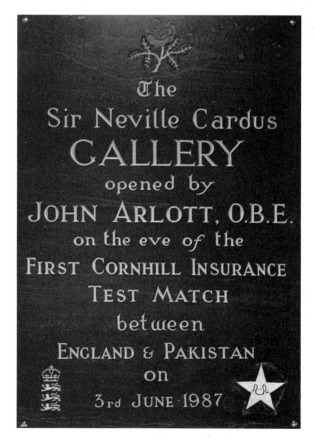

vinced that cricket grounds had to make themselves financially independent of attendance income – which was steadily falling away. The way to do this was to offer year-round facilities of a sufficient standard which would attract commercial support and sponsorship.

In 1982 a Ground Development Appeal produced over £200,000 and in 1984 a Test Centenary Appeal produced a further £47,000. The catering enterprise (run by Greenall Whitley, a local brewery) and cluster of dining-rooms of various sizes at the back of the pavilion were extended. The modernization of the seating around the ground was begun. In 1984 the Executive Suite with its twenty boxes was opened, as were the shop and museum. Finally – for the moment at least – the Red Rose Suite and Neville Cardus Gallery above were opened in 1987.

The list of commercial packages on offer at Old Trafford is almost limitless. At one extreme are the executive boxes, let on an annual basis for £6,000 per

The plaque for the new press box at Old Trafford, given the only possible name

Above *Old Trafford before modern development, full, as usual, for a Test Match*

annum or from day to day, and from here prices drop through the range and depending where you (or more likely, your company) opt for on the ground. The Neville Cardus Gallery houses the new press box. Its opening by John Arlott silences what had been one of the few dissenting voices over the Old Trafford facilities, that of the gentlemen of the fourth estate. The old press box, on top of the Ladies Stand on the far side of the ground was once described by R. C. Robertson-Glasgow: 'at the other, at a quaint angle, the press box, which suggests that it might have been designed by Einstein immediately after a reunion dinner of mathematicians'.

Sponsors, commercial hosts and advertisers may be well looked after at Old Trafford but so is the more humble spectator. For the real enthusiast, schoolboy or old stager, the new museum is the best possible place to while away the lunch interval, or one of the frequent stoppages which rain inflicts on the ground. Everything is presented to the highest standard, from the carpeted floor to the glass-fronted wooden display cases and green plush seats. Paintings, photographs, bats and china figures recall the great figures and events of Lancashire's history and, in one place, a letter from the Keeper of the Privy Purse, Buckingham Palace, dated 1951, records the club's royal patronage.

I am commanded by the King to inform you that his Majesty has been graciously pleased to grant his patronage to the Lancashire County Cricket Club. It will be in order for the words 'Patron – His Majesty the King' to appear in future under the name of your club on all correspondence.

Those wondering what connexion the monarch may have with the county forget that he – or she – counts among their titles the Dukedom of Lancaster.

A rather less grand exhibit is a red paper handkerchief returned to Old Trafford by John Arlott after he had opened the Neville Cardus Suite, with an accompanying letter explaining that in his absent-mindedness he was often prone to pick up 'hankies' for temporary use, mopping his brow and ending up pocketing them.

For the members there is the pavilion with its large bar and, along the front, the Long Room with tall arched windows. Here are paintings of A. N. 'Monkey' Hornby, A. C. MacLaren, Neville Cardus and a glamorous photograph of the young Queen Elizabeth II – the present patron.

Ladies are not allowed into the pavilion but they have their own stronghold of the Ladies Stand next to the Members' Enclosure where they may take one male guest (and a junior) but unattended men are not permitted. Here proper propriety is observed: at one entrance to the Ladies Stand is a prominent sign requesting, 'No Bare Torsos Please'.

In Old Trafford's history, Lancashire's story is interwoven with Test cricket. Before the turn of the century the legendary Hornby and Barlow were the first heroes. Immortalized by the poet Francis Thompson, the diminutive amateur captain and his professional all-rounder henchman are also depicted, flanking their wicketkeeper, Richard Pilling, in the stained glass window which now hangs in the entrance of Old Trafford's Executive Suite. The window has a curious story: it was presented to the county club by Barlow's illegitimate son, whose mother was the book-keeper of the Imperial Hotel in Blackpool – Barlow's home town – and with whom the cricketer lived after his wife died until his own death in 1919. Originally the window had hung in the vestibule of Barlow's house, but after his death it was moved by the only child of his marriage, Alice, and installed in a summer-house in her garden. Her half-brother – whom she refused to recognize – only gained possession of the treasured heirloom when she died and he was able to buy it from the new owners of her house.

From Hornby and Barlow the mantle passed to A. C. MacLaren and J. T. Tyldesley, the former Cardus's 'noblest Roman of them all', the latter one of England's greatest professional batsmen. When Lancashire's innings began with MacLaren, Spooner and Tyldesley Cardus wrote, 'No county has had an innings opened with so much mingled grandeur, graciousness and sword-like brilliance as these three cricketers spread over the field day by day'. Sadly for Old Trafford MacLaren scored his record 424 away at Taunton, but Johnny Tyldesley made his highest score of 295 not out at home in 1906. His 3,041 runs in the 1901 season remain a Lancashire record – but only just – for his younger brother Ernest came within 17 runs with 3,024 in 1928. It is a suitable coincidence that the achievements of the two brothers are highlighted in *Wisden*'s distinguished list of batsmen with 25,000 runs in a career by being next to each other – Ernest's 38,874 just pipping his older brother's 37,897.

Opposite above *The Old Trafford Pavilion, imposing and full of character*

Opposite below *Lancashire players using the members' dining room for net practice in 1928*

These early years also saw outstanding performances in the Old Trafford Tests. In 1896 Ranjitsinhji scored 154 not out against Australia and in doing so he 'stroked and turned the crimson rambler to the confines with oriental splendour' according to one eye-witness account. His innings made him only the second England player (after W.G.) to score a hundred on his debut and the first man to score a hundred runs before lunch in a Test. This record did not stand for long – six years later in the great match of 1902 Victor Trumper scored his hundred before lunch on the first day – and became the first of only four men in history to do so – and one of the closest of Tests ended with Australia winning by three runs.

But there have been some bizarre – as well as heroic – deeds done at Old Trafford. In 1912 T. J. Matthews, an Australian leg-break bowler who only took 16 wickets in his Test career, got six of them when he created the unique record of a hat-trick in each innings of a Test Match, bowling against South Africa in the Triangular Tournament. Both on the same day as well. No bowling feat, however, has of course compared with Laker's nineteen Australian wickets in 1956.

In 1934 poor Gubby Allen bowled 13 balls in his first over against Australia and no one is certain whether it was because of the intense heat, the huge hole left by the outsize boot of the Australian bowler Bill O'Reilly which Allen had to try and avoid, or because he had a whisky-and-soda before going out to field having exhausted himself batting shortly before – the only time in his career he drank before the close of play. Gubby Allen's embarrassment was however minimized, he always maintains, by the good-humoured reception he got from the Old Trafford crowd, and the fact that there were two chances, both missed because the England fielders were laughing too much!

The same year also witnessed a moment of great nostalgia. Jack Hobbs, in what was to be his last season and in his fifty-second year, had promised his friend George Duckworth he would play in his Benefit Match. Hobbs scored 116 – his first hundred of the season and the last of his record 197. Jim Kilburn described the scene:

He was given an ovation all the way from the wicket to the boundary edge. As the gate of the pavilion enclosure was opened for the departing 'Master' the thunder of applause turned spontaneously to song and Jack Hobbs climbed the pavilion steps through the ranks of standing members to the strains of Auld Lang Syne as a chorus was taken up all round the ground.

In days gone by Lancashire's county schedule was dominated by the rivalry with Yorkshire and the two 'Roses Matches' held over the Whitsun and August Bank Holidays. These games, which alternated annually at Old Trafford, invariably drew the largest of non-Test crowds to Lancashire's headquarters and if they rarely produced a result it was because of the grim determination of both sides not to lose. Everyone at Old Trafford – and, indeed, Headingley – would admit today that the competition has lost its edge and gone are games such as the first post-war Roses Match at Old Trafford, in 1946, when over 37,000 packed into the ground on the first day and on the second the captains agreed to shorten the boundary to give more space. On this occasion a typically gritty partnership between the Yorkshiremen Maurice Leyland who scored 41 not out in his last Roses Match and A.B. Sellers (53 not out) saved the game for their county.

In more recent times one-day cricket has superseded the Roses Match as the major crowd-puller at Old Trafford. Certainly there was good reason in the early years of the limited-overs competitions when Lancashire's record was supreme among the counties. It was in 1971 that Old Trafford witnessed one of the few one-day games which has already passed into folklore: the Gillette Cup semi-final against Gloucestershire which began at 11 o'clock and ended in virtual darkness at 8.50 p.m. David Hughes, having said to his captain Jackie Bond, 'If I can see 'em, skipper, I think I can hit 'em', proceeded to take John Mortimer for 4, 6, 2, 2, 4, 6 in an over. The 'Lamplight Match' as it has become known ended with the jubilant crowd of over 23,000 flooding onto the pitch.

In 1899 Neville Cardus made his first visit to Old Trafford as a small boy which he remembered for a startling welcome as he attempted to purchase a ha'penny bun. 'As I stretched up to the counter to pay an explosion happened; glass splinters flew about. I was terrified until a kindly Lancashire voice said, 'It's alright sonny, it's only Jessop just coom in'. Nearly a hundred years later, in 1981, the man who some have called the modern Jessop, Ian Botham, played one of the most explosive innings the ground has witnessed when he demolished an Australian attack to score 118, reaching his hundred in 86 minutes and scoring six sixes and thirteen fours. In between times there has been a wealth of cricket days for the Lancashire crowds to remember and there is no reason to doubt that they will continue in the future.

Above *Liverpool's ground at Aigburth, packed for the county's game against New Zealand in 1949*

LIVERPOOL

All Lancashire grounds pale beside Old Trafford, so firmly is the county's cricket rooted in its headquarters. In the early years of Lancashire's cricket, however, the Liverpool club maintained a fierce rivalry with the Manchester club from their ground at Aigburth and if, in the end, they conceded superiority to Old Trafford, Aigburth has witnessed league cricket of the highest standard and indeed many memorable games involving the county.

The ground at Aigburth was first used in 1881 and could hardly have had a better game for the opening than that between Lancashire and an outstanding Cambridge University side, who won with one day to spare. Later in the season, the match against Yorkshire scheduled for Aigburth was moved to Old Trafford after a written request from Hornby, the Lancashire captain,

which seems to have overtones of the above-mentioned rivalry. In a letter to the committee Hornby requested:

> I write to you on behalf of the County Eleven (and in the interest of cricket) to allow the match, Lancashire v Yorkshire, which is advertised to take place at Liverpool on July 28 to be transferred to Manchester as we all think the ground is in such a dangerous state, and not fit to play a bona fide County match on at present.

Whether Hornby's complaints were justified or not, things have definitely improved and today, David Hughes, Lancashire's veteran player and current captain, considers Aigburth to be 'the best wicket in England'. Whether other players would agree with him or not, it is a ground of considerable stature, thanks largely to its impressive pavilion at the Aigburth Road end, whose architecture of red brick and tiles, with large

gables and patterns of green and white woodwork is matched by the smaller building further round the boundary.

Inside the pavilion boasts some of the largest dressing rooms in the country and along the front of the rows of terraced green benches beds of roses are in flower when Lancashire visit for their one county championship game and Sunday league game – in late June or the first week of July. From the upper levels of the pavilion is the view straight down the wicket to ships passing up and down the River Mersey beyond, or on across to the Wirral on the far side.

Of all the elegant batsmen of the Golden Age, few could rival R. H. Spooner, who was a Liverpool man. After serving in the Boer War in South Africa he returned to Lancashire cricket and, against Gloucestershire in 1903, delighted his home crowd at Aigburth by sharing in a first-wicket partnership of 324 with his captain A. C. MacLaren which remains a record for the

county. At the other extreme, the record tenth wicket partnership for Lancashire, 173 by J. Briggs and R. Pilling was also made at Liverpool, as early as 1885.

On a number of occasions in the past Lancashire's games against the visiting tourists were played at Liverpool. Perhaps none was awaited more keenly than that of 1930, against the Australians, for it was to be the only occasion that Lancashire's veteran Australian fast bowler, E. A. McDonald, was to bowl at the new Australian star – Don Bradman. It was a confrontation which 'Ted' McDonald would indeed have relished. He was someone who bowled his best in response to a challenge rather than being interested in amassing wickets for the record books. Bradman had made nine runs when his erstwhile compatriot, with what was always one of the quietest, most balanced and fluid fast-bowling actions in history, brought his innings to an abrupt end by shattering his stumps.

Cecil Parkin, Lancashire's other best-known bowler to join the county from outside, albeit only Durham, rather than Australia, would also have had fond memories of the Aigburth ground. On his first match for the county in 1914 he exploited a damp wicket to take 14 for 99 against Leicestershire. A man of often irrepressible humour, the moment in a match which most delighted Parkin was the wicket of C. J. B. Wood, the Leicestershire captain who was so enraged that he turned and

flattened the stumps with his bat. Parkin once told Neville Cardus that, 'when the day comes when I can't play cricket I'll do as them Roman emperors did – I'll get into a hot bath and cut mi ruddy throat'.

Parkin could have been justly proud of his performance but as an aggregate it did not rival that of Harry Dean who one year earlier took 17 for 91 against Yorkshire. Dean's performance took place in a specially arranged match to mark the visit of King George V to Liverpool and it remains Lancashire's best match aggregate and the best by either county in Roses matches.

As he did on a number of grounds, Walter Hammond made the largest score in Liverpool's history, when he scored 264 for Gloucestershire in 1932, although Lancashire men are more likely to savour the 248 made by J. T. Tyldesley against Worcestershire in 1903.

In recent years it has often been the batsmen from visiting counties who have taken advantage of Liverpool's wicket to amass large scores. In 1983 the Hampshire opener, Gordon Greenidge performed the remarkable feat of scoring a hundred in each innings of the county championship match (104 and 100 not out) as well as 162 on the Sunday of his county's visit to Liverpool, giving him an aggregate for the four days of 366 runs.

Above *The Aigburth pavilion, which boasts some of the largest dressing rooms in the country*

Opposite *Southport, during one of the intervals in 1987*

SOUTHPORT

It was not until 1959 that Lancashire made their first excursion to the ground at Trafalgar Road, Southport, home of the Southport and Birkdale Cricket Club. The prosperous seaside town lies to the north of the county's great conurbations – in the heart of Lancashire's golfing country with Royal Lytham St Anne's opposite, just across the estuary of the River Ribble.

Various clubs had been thriving in Southport and next-door Birkdale since the middle of the nineteenth century and eventually, in 1902, there was a marriage of the surviving Southport and Birkdale clubs who became based at the latter's Trafalgar Road home. Trafalgar Road had already showed itself to be by far the best appointed cricket ground in Southport and in 1881 had been upgraded by the addition of what was obviously a pretty impressive pavilion, according to one local paper.

> The building is in the Queen Anne style with quaint windows and over the central doors the initials of the Club are worked out in stained glass. The interior comprises dressing rooms, a large and lofty main apartment fitted with a refreshment bar, beneath which is a capital cellar. A verandah runs in front of the pavilion and completes one of the best buildings of the kind we have ever seen.

Cellars were obviously an important consideration in Lancashire pavilions.

In 1948 the Trafalgar Road club achieved a long-standing ambition when they were admitted as one of sixteen fully accredited members of the Liverpool and District Competition. From now on the move towards hosting county cricket gathered pace and improvements such as tiered terracing to accommodate 2,000, and a new score box made a visit from the county increasingly likely.

After the inaugural county match – against Worcestershire – in 1959, the first real occasion at Trafalgar Road was a benefit match played for Brian Statham against Oxford University (captained by the Nawab of Pataudi). It was this match which revealed the potential of the Southport ground for attracting large crowds of holiday-makers. Four years later it was clear that the size and facilities of the pavilion were no longer satisfactory, particularly for the annual county visits, and in July 1965 the Earl of Derby – whose family seat is at Knowsley, Liverpool – opened the new building.

In 1969 Southport had its first taste of big-time cricket when Lancashire played Glamorgan there in the first year of the John Player League Sunday competition. The game was in July, up till when Lancashire (the eventual winners of the competition) were unbeaten. The game at Southport was televised and the crowds poured in. Half an hour after the start of play the gates were closed with 10,500 inside and many hundreds more queuing down the road outside. The attendance was – briefly – a record for the Sunday competition.

In 1979 David Lloyd scored a hundred in each innings of the match against Worcestershire (116 and 104 not out) to give Lancashire victory. Three years later, in 1982, Graeme Fowler performed the same feat against Warwickshire – but his effort was only one feature of one of the most extraordinary county championship matches ever played.

Warwickshire batted first and on the first day ran up the massive total of 523 for four declared. After their openers had been out cheaply Alvin Kallicharran and Geoffrey Humpage scored 234 not out and 254 respectively to put on 470 for the fourth wicket. In doing so they broke a fistful of records: their partnership was the highest for the fourth wicket in England (beating that of Hayward and Abel set up in 1899), the highest for any wicket except the first, and the record for any partnership by Warwickshire. In his career-best 254 Humpage hit 13 sixes, the most ever by an Englishman and a total in England only equalled by Majid Khan and Gordon Greenidge.

The second day, with Warwickshire in the field, saw the records shift from the enormous to the unusual. David Brown, Warwickshire's manager, took to the field in place of Gladstone Small, who was standing by for England and yet back in his county's match in the afternoon. In his spell on the field Brown became the first substitute in county cricket to take a wicket.

It must have seemed that Warwickshire were faced with the simple task of bowling Lancashire out twice in two days. In a bizarre reversal of fortune things turned out rather differently, in a manner which must have reminded Warwickshire of the unhappy day in 1921 when Hampshire beat them, having been bowled out for 15 in their first innings but managing to run up 521 in their second.

Having scored 414 for six declared, Lancashire managed to bowl out Warwickshire for 111, largely thanks to their opening bowler, Leslie McFarlane taking six for 59. Scenting the most unlikely of victories, they scored the necessary 226 runs without loss. The batting hero was Graeme Fowler, who set up a unique record of his own. Having been injured in the field on the first day, he batted with a runner during both his innings of 126 and 128 not out.

Southport has not again witnessed such stirring events but, by any standards, it was a match for the record books and one which has given the seaside town its place in English cricket history.

LYTHAM

It was only as a result of a dispute in 1984 with the local club at Blackpool, who staged a joint benefit match for Ian Botham and Geoffrey Boycott without first consulting the county, that Lancashire decided to leave the holiday town where they had played since 1889 and move a few miles down the coast to Lytham, who play in the Liverpool and District Competition. The ground of the Lytham Cricket and Sports Club may be typical of a club ground, but, as is usually the case where visits from the county are a recent privilege, the facilities are, in the circumstances, first rate.

Unfortunately, the first county championship game at Lytham, played in 1985, was spoilt by rain, although the young Lancashire number ten, David Makinson, did manage to delight the crowd by hitting seven sixes off the Northamptonshire bowler, Richard Williams, in his innings of 58.

Lancashire have continued to visit the ground for one championship match each season and, although it looks likely that the county may return to Blackpool for one-day games, at present Lytham's fixture is secure.

An aerial view of Lytham

YORKSHIRE

HEADINGLEY

There is nothing fancy about Headingley; it is reassuringly Yorkshire. One native of the county, Jim Kilburn, commented drily, 'The touch of sentiment so strongly impressed upon other great grounds has seldom fallen significantly upon the Headingley atmosphere'. This is perhaps being a bit harsh, for although Yorkshiremen are not given to flights of fancy few people are more deeply stirred by great cricket deeds – however depreciative they may try to remain. Donald Bradman certainly felt this and always maintained that the Yorkshiremen gave him the best reception of his life.

Mind you, Bradman earned the acclaim. On his first appearance on the ground, for the Third Test in 1930, he was twenty-one. He scored 334, including 105 before lunch on the first day and 309 in the day, a Test record. On his next appearance, in 1934, it was 304; in 1938 only 103. Then, on his last appearance in 1948, it was 173 not out in Australia's second innings to help them towards the 404 they needed to win. It was Bradman's last Test hundred and his figures for four Tests on the ground were an aggregate of 963 and average of 192.6. In a gesture of thanks the Yorkshiremen made him an honorary Life Member of their club, of which there are only a dozen or so.

Headingley remains what it has always been, a place for the playing and watching of cricket. Yorkshire's membership of over 12,000 is the largest of any county and only Lancashire has consistently come anywhere near its figure. They do not need to be enticed to watch cricket by the promise of plush bars and restaurants, or slick commercial packages. There is a White Rose Executive Club and there are boxes, but nothing like what they get up to at Old Trafford. Crowds for county games have diminished – as they have everywhere – but Headingley Tests are more consistently full than any others bar those at Lord's: 158,000 attended the five days of the 1948 Test, the most ever to watch a game of cricket in England.

Leeds has not always been the headquarters of Yorkshire cricket. In the early days after the formation of the county club in 1863 this was vested in Bramall Lane,

Sheffield and the influential figures were all Sheffield men. The first step towards the shift of power came in 1888 when a group of well-off sportsmen banded together to buy lot 17A in a sale of land by the Cardigan estate. They formed the Leeds Cricket, Football and Athletic Co. Ltd and, most significantly, their chairman was Lord Hawke. Two years later Yorkshire played their first game on the new ground and in 1899, when the number of Test Matches was expanded from three to five, Headingley was chosen with Trent Bridge as one of the two grounds to be added.

This was the major step towards Yorkshire cricket being based in Leeds. Sheffield did host one Test, in 1902, but it was the only one and the next year the Yorkshire CCC office moved to Leeds. Strangely enough, as with all the grounds in the county, Yorkshire CCC still do not own Headingley, but remain tenants of the Cricket, Football and Athletic Company. One feels, however, that their security of tenure is guaranteed.

At the end of the nineteenth century Headingley was still a quiet suburb of Leeds, enclosed by the rows of terraced homes of workers in the woollen industry and passed by lanes such as Kirkstall Lane which still gives its name to the north end of the ground. The development of Headingley into the ground of today was primarily the work of Sir Edwin Airey, who became chairman of his family's construction company in 1932 and devoted himself to the improvement of Headingley. One incentive was the destruction of the old main stand by fire on Good Friday in 1932. Airey's company built the new one at the cost of £20,000.

It is this stand which reminds the visitor to Headingley of the site's joint use and to many Yorkshiremen – particularly those who live in the rugby league stronghold of West Yorkshire – Headingley is the home of Leeds Rugby League Club, where the game is regularly played at international level. The Athletic part of the original company's name is represented by the cycle track around the cricket boundary. The football pitch is an impressive affair with its enor-

FRESHMENTS

HIRE A CUSHION FOR COMFORT
only 6 D
LEAVE ON SEAT AFTER USE

mous stands on either side and made even more so by the knowledge that it has a system of underground heating which ensures that play is possible in the most Arctic of conditions.

On the cricket side, Airey's new building forms the main stand, Grandstand or New Stand as it has been variously known. It is large and featureless, its grey roof extending low over the upper storey, whence the press enjoy a good vantage-point and where the Leeds Taverners Club have their slightly more luxurious quarters. Below is the Len Hutton bar, with tiered seating stretching down to the ground's perimeter.

One definite shortcoming about Headingley is that the normal functions of a pavilion are divided between two quite separate buildings. Next to the main stand is what was the pavilion, which seems to have been a place of some character. The centre block has been completely altered, however, losing its wide balcony in front of the upper storey of seating, the tiled roof and cupola. Now the front is glassed in on the upper levels and only the wings of the building retain tiled roofs. The most important difference is that it is no longer used by the players, but only Yorkshire members.

The players share a building round on the northeast side of the ground with the offices of the Yorkshire secretary, Joe Lister. It is an unattractive and dull brick

Headingley, when the Australians visited in 1930 and the Yorkshiremen first witnessed the Bradman magic

box, its only decoration the white railings of the outside steps and balcony. One feels that it is hardly a building of sufficient calibre to send out players in a Test Match, and it also has the disadvantage of doing so in an anonymous fashion, from a curious angle.

At the Kirkstall Lane end is the Winter Shed, which has a spruced-up top level containing a dozen executive boxes. Shed remains an apt description of the larger, ground floor which in the summer serves as the public bar and eating area. It is very much as it was when Yardley and Kilburn wrote in the 1950s that 'the refreshment arrangements are decidely utilitarian', and when visiting Headingley you are best off following John Arlott's advice and taking a picnic.

Immediately round from the Winter Shed is Headingley's one gesture to modernity, the electronic scoreboard. As well as details of the actual score it is able to flash up a comprehensive variety of messages, from the vital statistics of a bowler or batsman to views on the playing conditions such as 'fine weather is expected' as appeared when I visited the ground and the players were forced off for an early tea by bad light.

Above *The ground in 1935, showing the new grandstand*

Below *The electronic scoreboard, full of varied information*

From the scoreboard Headingley's largest area of seating stretches round the west side of the ground to the main stand: deep tiers of uncovered grey bucket seats. It is these grey seats which predominate around the ground and, except when the ground is full for a Test Match, are primarily responsible for Headingley's somewhat mournful appearance.

From the west side of the ground the view is dominated by the tall, blackened spire of Headingley's parish church of St Michael's, stretching above the red-brick houses immediately outside the ground. Some years ago these houses were a cause of controversy, a number of the less generous-spirited members of the cricket club complaining about the outstanding – and free – view of play which they afforded. As a result a screen of poplar trees were planted which certainly helped to soften the appearance of this part of the ground but, whether through sabotage or ill-suitedness to the conditions, they are no longer there.

One disadvantage for the visitor wishing to give Headingley a thorough exploration is the spectator's inability to circumnavigate the ground completely unless you are a Yorkshire member, there being no passage around the members' enclosure. This was explained to me by the attendant on the public turnstiles off Kirkstall Lane, who like all the others on the ground was an immaculately uniformed member of the Corps of Commissionaires – a rather unlikely appearance at Headingley. He had all the cheerful warmth that his place of work lacks, letting me in without charge as I was late and the prospects of a finished game were slim. He spent much of the afternoon directing me to various parts of Headingley which he was certain I should not overlook in my research.

The Winter Shed used to serve as the Indoor School but now there is an impressive new one, just across St Michael's Lane from the main entrance to the ground. Next door to the main gates are one of the ground's few ornamental features, the Herbert Sutcliffe gates, a handsome affair of wrought iron and gold-leaf decoration. They are well deserved for the immaculate opening batsman produced unrivalled consistency for Yorkshire between the wars – for example, his 74 opening partnerships of a 100 or more with Percy Holmes – and he still holds most of the county's batting records.

Almost from the day that Lord Hawke took over the captaincy of Yorkshire in 1883 the county enjoyed a position of unprecedented and unchallenged ascendancy in the championship, at least until the most recent decades. They have won over thirty times; only two other counties have got into double-figures and the nearest is Surrey with 18. It has been said that Lord Hawke took over a team of drunks and one parson (in fact a Methodist preacher). Certainly the all-rounder Bobby Peel was sacked for appearing drunk for a game, but whatever the original circumstances, Hawke moulded a team which launched the roll-call of great Yorkshire names and the county's successes.

Among the batsmen in Hawke's side none rivalled Stanley Jackson for charisma. Many people regarded 'Jacker' as the epitome of the Golden Age and if his most famous deeds were performed for England he indulged his own Yorkshire crowd during 'Jackson's Year' in 1905, scoring 144 not out as England's captain in the Test Match against Australia – the first Test hundred at Headingley.

Peel's dismissal opened the way for Wilfred Rhodes who, with George Hirst, dominates all bowling and all-round records. They were two unparalleled cricketers, who played 883 and 718 matches, respectively, for Yorkshire and whose careers linked the Hawke era with the inter-war years of Holmes and Sutcliffe, Maurice Leyland and Hedley Verity. Verity died from wounds in 1944 and remains perhaps the most cherished of Yorkshire's cricketers. It was at Headingley, in 1932, that the slow left-armer achieved the best bowling analysis of all time – 10 for 10, including the hat-trick,

against Warwickshire. After the war the flow of success continued, with only occasional setbacks, until the end of the 1960s. So did the individual performances: Hutton's majestic batting and Trueman's fiery bowling, the latter becoming a personification of Yorkshire in the popular image.

As far as Len Hutton was concerned, he had to wait a long time to play in his first Test Match on Yorkshire soil – until the South African tour of 1947. Pudsey – Hutton's home town – lies between Leeds and Bradford, only a few miles from Headingley and his supporters turned up in their thousands. They were not disappointed as Hutton scored 100 on a testing wicket. He was to score two more in his subsequent five Test appearances on the ground.

At the same time there crept in the vein of dissent, controversy and infighting which has plagued modern Yorkshire. The Wardle affair in 1958 was followed by the departure of Ray Illingworth to Leicestershire, Brian Close to Somerset, and later Chris Old to Warwickshire and Bill Athey to Gloucestershire. They were all Yorkshiremen, at heart, whom the county could ill afford to lose.

In terms of personalities the modern period has been dominated by Geoffrey Boycott. In 1977 Boycott achieved the zenith of his career, when, in front of his home crowd at Headingley he became the first man in history to score his 100th hundred in a Test Match. By the time of his eventual retirement only Sutcliffe still rivalled his batting records for the county and, year after year, his consistency in the national batting averages was phenomenal. In the meantime he had aroused stronger and more divisive feelings in Yorkshire – and outside – than virtually any other player. When I visited Headingley I invited the opinion of my neighbour at one point, a veteran who had done thirty years down the mines and who had spent most of his life cycling or walking the twelve miles from Featherstone to Headingley to watch Yorkshire. I was treated to a twenty-minute homily on the qualities of 'our Geoffrey'. I felt afterwards that it had been an even chance of my getting the exactly opposite opinion.

Personalities have not brought the only controversy to Headingley. In 1961 there was a storm over the wicket when Trueman took 11 for 88 against the unfortunate Australians and Ray Lindwall declared that the wicket 'was not fit for any cricket above beach level'. In 1972, again against Australia, Derek Underwood exploited a rain-affected wicket, also suffering from the turf disease, fuserium, to take 10 for 82 in the match and in 1987 there were rumblings after Pakistan gained the victory over England which later gave them the Test rubber. In

1975 the problem was one no groundsman could have countered: the wicket was dug up by vandals protesting about the imprisonment of a certain George Davis.

If these have been the unhappier episodes in Headingley's career as a Test ground they are greatly outnumbered by historic occasions. For C. B. Fry the Headingley Test of 1907 against South Africa was 'the game of a lifetime' when, on a wet wicket, England struggled against the googly-bowling quartet of Vogler, Schwartz, Faulkner and White, but won thanks to Colin Blythe taking 15 for 99. When Australia came in 1926 Charlie Macartney, who had scored a hundred at Headingley on his last visit in 1921, this time scored 112 before lunch and went on to 151. Then came the Bradman era.

In 1966 Sobers produced one of his most sparkling all-round performances, making his highest Test score in England of 174 and taking eight for 80 in the match which West Indies won by an innings and 55 runs. None of these, however, can match the Test Match against Australia in 1981 when, as *Wisden* reported, 'A match which had initially produced all the wet and tedious traits of recent Leeds Tests finally ended in a way to stretch the bounds of logic and belief. England's victory, achieved under the gaze of a spellbound nation, was the first this century by a team following on, and only the second such result in the history of Test cricket'. The great turn-about came in England's follow-on when Ian Botham scored 149 not out to save England from the possible innings defeat and leave Australia needing 130

to win. His innings was matched by the bowling of Willis who took eight for 43 and Australia went down by 18 runs.

Today it seems that Yorkshire may have put most of their troubles behind them and, with a talented and, to a large extent, young side are once again in serious contention for the county spoils. In 1987 I witnessed their victory over Essex, nearly prevented by rain, which took them to the top of the County Championship, albeit temporarily – a position they have become quite unaccustomed to in recent years. The day also presented a reminder of the old spark of rivalry with Lancashire. Shortly after Yorkshire had gained victory the scoreboard flashed up the news that Kent had held Lancashire to a draw, which brought as loud a cheer as the home win.

While some things have changed others have not. They are all still Yorkshiremen – even if only one is called Sidebottom – born and bred in the county and if this policy can induce an insular outlook it has served them well in the past. It remains unthinkable that Yorkshire should not have a Test Match ground and if Headingley comes in for occasional criticism and is unfortunately a place of neither charm nor beauty, it is the citadel of Yorkshire cricket and as such commands considerable respect.

Above *Looking across the ground from the members' pavilion, towards the wintershed, its row of boxes supporting a packed open terrace*

SHEFFIELD

Until the mid-1970s Sheffield meant Bramall Lane, first home of Yorkshire CCC and a cricket ground since it was leased from the Duke of Norfolk in 1855. It was always, likewise, the home of Sheffield United Football Club and it was the determination of the combined cricket and football club who owned the site to convert Bramall Lane into a football arena suitable for the First Division side Sheffield United were at the time, which determined that the cricketers should leave.

As a result they now play at Abbeydale Park, out of the city – as Bramall Lane was in its younger days – and with beckoning hills giving an unexpectedly attractive background. Abbeydale Park has the distinction of being the only ground in England to have been home for two first-class counties. At one time Derbyshire, whose border is within virtual walking distance, played some matches there.

Description of Bramall Lane should be left to a

Yorkshireman, such as Jim Kilburn, writing in *The World of Cricket*.

The Lane giving approach from the town ran southwards to Bramall's file factory and separated the new sports ground from a much bigger area of cultivation we should now call allotments were they not long buried beneath the sprawl of housing. An ultimate irony lies in one reason for the original selection of site: 'It had the advantage of being free from smoke'. As Sheffield grew the fields retreated until Bramall Lane was left in its present isolation, treeless, enclosed, begrimed. It remains as a reminder of the older age, a treasure in the new, an anachronism. Only its purpose now justifies continued existence. There is nothing of beauty to please the eye or stir the spirit in the Bramall Lane of today. Its outline is harsh, its colours are drab, its air is filthy. It has nothing to commend it to cricket beyond its situation, its history and its smooth turf where the footballers fear to tread.

Above *Abbeydale Park, Sheffield, with its pleasant hilly vista in the background*

Opposite *Bramall Lane in 1901, the year before the ground's only Test Match*

Tough and dirty though it may have been, Bramall Lane was steeped in cricket and the departure to Abbeydale Park ended a major chapter for Yorkshire. Although it only staged one Test Match Bramall Lane witnessed numerous historic games – notably in the Roses matches and in games against visiting Australian sides. The crowds were, almost without exception, enormous and tolerated often fearsome discomfort. The members and players had the pavilion at one end, which was large but with many shortcomings, and the members' enclosure continued around the open embankment on the southeast corner. From here there was open concrete terracing along the east side – standing room for football supporters and at times backside-numbing seating for cricket crowds. At the far end from the pavilion was the main covered stand, serving the football pitch some distance from play but with a view down the wicket.

The concrete terraces along the west side were the heartland of Bramall Lane. The crowd here were known as the Grinders and their comment and criticism was the most renowned in the country. Few players escaped their attention and it was a lucky man whom they applauded. As Kilburn said, 'From these uncomfortable seats a warmth of affection flowed out to favourites and a chilling tide of disparagement surged across the unfortunate ... To be praised at Bramall Lane was a cricketing accolade; to be condemned was a memorable and devastating experience'.

1872 was one of the first times that the crowds came in their droves to Bramall Lane; the attraction was to see W. G. Grace in his first county game on the ground. He did not disappoint them, scoring 122. Just over a century later, in Bramall Lane's last season of 1973, Phil Sharpe, one of Yorkshire's favourite players of modern times, delighted the Sheffield crowd by scoring 133 not out. The last match was, fittingly, the Roses match of that year and it ended as so many had before it, in a gruelling draw. It was perhaps no coincidence that Wilfred Rhodes had died only days before, and at the start of the game the Bishop of Wakefield held a service of remembrance. For all its warts, the kind of loyalty which Bramall Lane inspired was illustrated by one of the great figures of Yorkshire's early years, Ephraim Lockwood, when, on a tour to North America he was asked what he thought of the Niagara Falls which the side were visiting. 'Nowt. If this is Niagara give me Sheffield any day'.

One quality for which Bramall Lane was always renowned was its wicket and whether the new ground at Abbeydale Park would be able to compare was a major consideration when Yorkshire first played there in 1974. At first it was most encouraging and in the second game on the ground Boycott made the most of things by scoring 149 not out against the neighbours, Derbyshire, the first of five hundreds he made there.

For a time, however, the pitches were criticized and in 1978 the Middlesex fast bowler, Wayne Daniel gave the Yorkshire batsmen a most uncomfortable time, forcing two to retire hurt and injuring three others. The following year when the wicket was affected by rain, Warwickshire were bowled out for 35, no batsman reaching double-figures. In 1983 the pitch was reported as sub-standard when, for once, Derbyshire had the better of things against their neighbours, beating Yorkshire for the first time for twenty-five years.

Abbeydale Park is a world away from Bramall Lane, whose history it will never rival. It is essentially a club ground, home of the Sheffield Amateur Sports Club and has most of the attendant pleasures and shortcomings. Certainly the air is cleaner than at Bramall Lane and the prospect beyond the ground distinctly more agreeable. Yorkshire continue to play two county championship matches in Sheffield and indeed it would be a sad day if the county ever deserted their original home.

MIDDLESBROUGH

Acklam Park, Middlesbrough is the youngest of York-shire's grounds and today is not actually in Yorkshire, belonging to newly-created Cleveland. The ground has only hosted first-class games since 1956 when Gla-morgan were the first visitors. The annual game at this, the most northerly ground to stage county cham-pionship matches in England, exemplifies Yorkshire's strongly held tradition of distributing their cricket to supporters all over their far-flung county, rather than always expecting them to make the journey to their headquarters at Headingley.

Rugby union is played next to the cricket ground so that, until the departure from Bramall Lane and Park Avenue, Bradford, Yorkshire had the unusual dis-tinction of grounds next to football, rugby union and rugby league pitches. Fortunately there is no overlap at the Middlesbrough ground – just as well in view of the ground's reputation for difficult and often lively wickets.

When Yorkshire visit Acklam Park, the small pavilion, used by both cricketers and rugby players, is added to by scaffolding stands and marquees. The most regularly used position for viewing is the embankment which, as Kilburn commented, 'has the backless seating that becomes a trial in a full day's watching'.

More often than not bowlers have enjoyed playing at Acklam Park more than batsmen. Yorkshiremen would prefer to forget 1965, when Hampshire bowled them out for 23, the lowest total in their history. The pitch was always lively and 22 wickets fell on the first day – a typically belligerent Trueman playing the only innings

of note, 55, including 26 off one over by Shackleton. The next day disaster struck; no Yorkshire batsman made double figures and Hampshire's fast bowler, 'Butch' White had six for 10, at one stage having taken five wickets for no runs. Similar conditions in 1969 enabled Yorkshire to bowl out Gloucestershire twice in a day. The visitors were all out for 41 in their first innings, no batsman scoring double figures and Chris Old, who comes from Middlesbrough, delighted his home crowd by taking seven for 20.

As he has done on most Yorkshire grounds, Boycott has scored a large quantity of runs at Acklam Park. In his last season of 1986 he had the satisfaction of making his 150th hundred on the ground which made him Yorkshire's leading century-maker in front of Herbert Sutcliffe's 149.

HARROGATE

As Yorkshire's visits to Middlesbrough take the county game to the northern outpost and to the populous area of Teesside, so their visits to Harrogate are for the benefit of the Dales and for the inhabitants of and visitors to the famous spa town. The ground enjoys a relaxed, almost rural atmosphere which is not to be found on any other of Yorkshire's grounds.

The resident Harrogate club have a distinguished and long-established history and have been leading members of the Yorkshire League for many years. It is partly thanks to them that their ground, with its limited facilities of one small wooden covered stand and an equally small pavilion, provides such an enjoyable setting for the county's games.

In recent years Yorkshire have only played one annual county championship game at Harrogate, in June, but the cricket is augmented into a Festival week by the one-day matches of the Tilcon Trophy, which have been played since the late-1970s.

There is no doubt that Harrogate's hey-day as a host for Yorkshire cricket came during the 1960s when, out of the county's six championship wins in the decade, four of them were achieved at Harrogate. In 1960 Worcestershire were beaten and the title retained. In 1966 they just achieved the necessary victory over Kent while the following year, again needing victory to ensure the championship, they overwhelmed Gloucestershire with an innings victory in two days, Illingworth taking 14 wickets in the match, including seven for six in the second innings.

Of the four years it was 1962 which witnessed the most memorable scenes, in September, right at the end of the season. On the first day Glamorgan were put in on a drying wicket and were bowled out for 65, Don Wilson taking six for 24. On the same day Yorkshire fared little better, managing only 101 of which Ken Taylor, who opened their innings and was last out, made 67. The second day was washed out by rain and on the final day Glamorgan were again bowled out – this time for 101 – leaving Yorkshire needing 66, which they made for the loss of three wickets. It seems scarcely credible, but 10,000 squeezed in for two days' play.

Opposite *Acklam Park, Middlesbrough, with the rugby ground at one end*

SCARBOROUGH

Scarborough completes the diverse picture of Yorkshire's cricket grounds and as well as being quite unlike any other in the county, has carved for itself a unique niche in English cricket. Yorkshire have played county championship matches at Scarborough since 1896 but it is for its Festival, begun twenty years earlier and which traditionally closes the English season in the first days of September, that Scarborough is uniquely famous. The elegant seaside town, always the most fashionable away from the south coast when seaside towns were fashionable, the attractions of the ground and quality of the pitch and, not least, the quality of the cricket, all made for an occasion no other cricket ground has been able to boast. It was, as Jim Kilburn wrote, 'first-class cricket on holiday'.

I should not give the impression that the Festival has stopped, for it still continues and in 1986 the hundredth was held. It has, however, changed: as a result of alterations in the first-class programme, the greater quantity of cricket through the summer making players less interested in prolonging the season, and as a result of the tourists no longer appearing.

In the Festival's great years the three traditional fixtures were: Yorkshire v MCC; Gents v Players and an Invitation XI against the Tourists. The MCC and

Above *India playing Pakistan, sponsored by 'Help the Aged', at Harrogate in 1986*

179

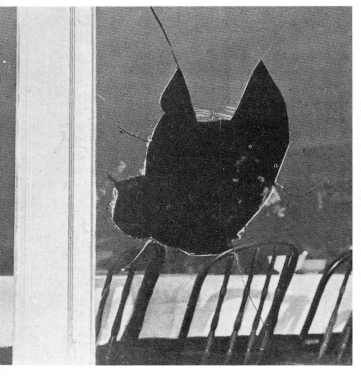

Above *One of the pavilion balcony windows at Scarborough, destroyed by a hit from J.N. Crawford in 1908*

Right *Scarborough in 1913, the last of the festival's halcyon years*

Invitation XIs were chosen first by C.I. Thornton, organizer of the Festival, then by H. D. G. Leveson-Gower and finally by T. N. Pearce. Gents and Players finished in the 1960s and the last tourists visited at the end of the 1970s. The last Yorkshire v MCC match had been in 1970, until the fixture was revived at the end of the 1987 season. Since 1971 the major feature has been a one-day knock-out competition – the Fenner Trophy until 1981 and subsequently the Asda Trophy.

One sketch of the early years of the Festival has passed into English literature. Sir Osbert Sitwell's grandfather was the 1st Earl of Londesborough, the Festival's first patron and in his autobiography, *Left Hand Right Hand!*, Sir Osbert recalls a visit to Scarborough when he was four, the year being 1897.

Chief of the treats (though never, alas, for me) was the Cricket Week, when Scarborough broke out into its greatest display, and there was feasting in the hot tents of the rich at the ground's edge. My grand-father, the founder and president, delighted to entertain – I was going to write 'the hungry', but though he loved, too, to do this on other occasions . . . here it would be more correct to say that he fed those who possessed a regular and recurrent appetite. The tents blazed with the ties of the cricketing clubs and the port-wine coloured faces of the *aficionados*, and between the rounds of cold salmon and cold chicken that were dispensed, we would have to sit solemnly and watch the progression – if such it can be called – of this, to me, always unattractive and lengthy game. But my grandfather loved it and, guided by intuition, had formed, from the first moment of my appearing, extravagant expectations of my future prowess at it. In myself, out of all the family, he had divined the cricketer, and so had arranged with 'W.G.' to enter my name for the MCC on the very day of my birth.

These were the days when C. I. 'Buns' Thornton was the leading figure at Scarborough. He was regarded as

the greatest hitter of the day and once hit a straight drive over the tall Victorian houses at the south end and into Trafalgar Square behind – a distance of over 120 yards. The sides he raised were consistently top-class and in 1921 they became only the second team to beat the Australians after A. C. MacLaren's side had done so at Eastbourne.

Close to the centre of Scarborough, the ground lies off the North Marine Road which gives it its name, and beyond which lies the sea only a few hundred yards away. The red-brick pavilion, which faces the ground from one corner and was built in 1895 has not changed substantially. It retains its attractive arched facade behind which are the dressing rooms on the ground floor and above a narrow balcony in front of the dining-room and club offices. These belong to the Scarborough CC, founded in 1849, when they played on Castle Hill, who habitually have been one of the strongest clubs in England.

To celebrate the golden jubilee of the Festival in 1926 the main open concrete stand along the north side, between the pavilion and scoreboard, was built. This is interrupted (roughly behind the bowler's arm) by the scorer's and press box, whose elevated position gives a fine view of play and which was decorated in 1972 by a weather-vane complete with stumps and cricketers. Along the west side there used to be a rather inferior covered wooden stand known as 'the Cowshed' which was replaced in 1956 with the present terraced stand. Next to this, in the opposite corner to the pavilion is the most decorative quarter of the ground where, for the Festival, the marquees of the Scarborough President and the town's mayor are put up and the band play under their bandstand. The seating along the south – Trafalgar Square – side is partially covered and stretches up to the open embankment enclosing the North Marine side of the ground.

For many years virtually all the leading English players would appear at Scarborough at some point in their career and their appearance usually guaranteed

Scarborough's elegant pavilion

the ground – whose capacity is 14,000 – being full. Most often the favourites were the Yorkshire heroes, but many others have left their mark, not least Jack Hobbs who scored 266 not out for the Players against the Gents in 1925.

For many Yorkshiremen, holiday-makers and other cricket lovers Scarborough is an annual pilgrimage and they come year after year. The ground has never hosted a Test Match as Patsy Hendren thought it deserved to do, although it has seen one Prudential Trophy match in 1978 against New Zealand. However the Festival may have changed Scarborough retains strong links with Yorkshire, who play two county championship games there each year. It also retains the relaxed holiday atmosphere one might expect in such a long-established and still prosperous resort, the bright, refreshing air of the seaside and – during the Festival at least – a feeling that the cricket is still played for enjoyment as much as competition.

NOTTINGHAMSHIRE

TRENT BRIDGE

The early history of Trent Bridge is part of cricket folk-lore. William Clarke, sometime bricklayer, keeper of the Bell Inn in Nottingham, lob-bowler and cricket enthusiast of rare initiative, crossed the River Trent, took up with and, in 1837, married, the widow Mary Chapman who ran the Trent Bridge Inn; he subsequently laid out a cricket ground in the fields at the back of the inn. From here Clarke set out with his All England XI, touring the country and spreading the cricket gospel. In 1855 they played a West Gloucestershire team – more likely to have been an XVIII or a XXII than an XI. W. G. Grace, aged seven watched his brother, E.M., aged thirteen, play for the home side. The young lad impressed Clarke to the extent that he gave their mother a book of cricket instruction. It seemed, however, that the matriarch already knew her ducklings. While she admitted that E.M. was good, she assured Clarke that she had another boy who was more promising.

Since the first match on 'Clarke's new ground' in July 1838 Trent Bridge has never looked back. Nottinghamshire, for whom it was the obvious home

after the formation of the county club in 1841, were always strong in these early years and virtually invincible for much of the second half of the century. When the Test grounds were extended from three to five in 1899 Trent Bridge and Headingley joined Lord's, The Oval and Old Trafford. The Midlands ground, strategically positioned on the traditional boundary of north and south, assumed a position of national importance it has never lost. Today modernity and the need to provide accommodation and facilities on a suitable scale have not been allowed to intrude to an unwarranted degree and Trent Bridge remains friendly, spacious and quietly proud of its well-displayed history.

The spaciousness of Trent Bridge is no illusion – its six acres of grass are unusually expansive. In the old days this meant there was ample space on the grass

Below *William Clarke's original ground at Trent Bridge, with the inn in the far left corner*

Overleaf *An aerial view of Trent Bridge in the 1920s, with the inn outside the enclosed ground*

outside the boundary rope, favourite haunt of school-boys, but advertising boards put an end to that. In addition, Trent Bridge appears to have avoided the temptation of vast, stadium-like seating which has rendered other Test grounds somewhat characterless.

As at most grounds the capacity of Trent Bridge has diminished – not only because of the loss of the areas of grass, but also as fixed seating has replaced benches or standing space. If the 30,000 who watched one day of the 1948 Test Match against the Australians all turned up today probably only half of them would get in, as the current seating capacity is only 10,500, though this can be extended to about 15,000 for Test Matches.

One says that modernity has been kept in check at Trent Bridge, but today one corner at the far end from the pavilion – the Radcliffe Road end – is dominated by the L-shaped tower of Trent Bridge House, head-quarters of Nottinghamshire county council. Compared to many modern buildings its bland uniformity is inoffensive but it has radically altered the appearance of the ground. The main scoreboard immediately in front, always reckoned to be impressively large, is positively dwarfed. Anyway, at the expense of its over-powering presence, the sale of the land for Trent Bridge House produced valuable money for the cricket club and cricket-loving county workers are in clover.

On the opposite side of the ground is Trent Bridge's pavilion – a delightful contrast and one of the most satisfying – in appearance and facilities – in the country. It is only a shame that alterations in 1953 to the centre block did away with the elegant canopy over the ground floor, the first-floor verandah above and the arched wrought-iron colonnade on top. In place of the canopy and verandah is a sort of suspended portakabin, housing scorers, radio and television commentators and the public address operator's room, occasional base of Mr Harry Dalling, the Ground Superintendent whose family are almost part of the fabric at Trent Bridge. In place of the colonnade huge glass windows afford an excellent view of play for visitors to the 1980s executive suite.

Otherwise the pavilion has remained remarkably unscathed since it was built in 1886, replacing one of 1872 on the same site. Not surprisingly the original had been on the far corner of the ground, immediately behind the Trent Bridge Inn. The tiled, gabled roofscape of the pavilion presents an almost domestic picture which would be completed by columns of smoke rising from one of the numerous brick chimney-stacks. In fact this is not being too fanciful, for until 1955 the pavilion

Opposite *Modern Trent Bridge*

contained a flat occupied for many years by Walter Marshall – from 1897 until 1935 chief coach and then head-groundsman – and subsequently by the Dalling's: Harry's father, Frank, was head-groundsman, so was his brother – also Frank – and his nephew is on the groundstaff today.

In the centre of the main roof is the clock, set in a dormer and topped by its weather-vane. The pair of arched doorways giving access to the ground on either side of the main block remain from the days when the amateurs had their dressing-room on the east side and the professionals theirs on the west. In 1898 a new dressing-room was built over the professionals' and the old amateurs' became the present committee room. All these rooms have spacious covered balconies brightened up during match days with hanging baskets of flowers.

The two best recent additions to the pavilion are the library, opened in 1979 and the museum, opened in 1987. The former, named after Frank Ernest Gregory, President from 1971–74, is the domain of Peter Wynne-Thomas, the librarian and leading light of the Association of Cricket Statisticians, who sports the most impressive of walrus moustaches.

Wynne-Thomas's enthusiasm about cricket in general and Nottinghamshire in particular is boundless, whether he is explaining how the shelves in the library were courtesy of Boots the chemists, one of Nottingham's leading companies or how Trent Bridge remains a ground where schoolchildren are most definitely welcome. My visit in 1987 coincided with 600 children from various Nottinghamshire schools whom he was taking on an exhaustive tour of the ground and the delights of the pavilion. He had had a larger party the week before. The juniors were more attentive than most adults would have been, and many of them agreed with me that the best things in the pavilion are the door-handles – magnificent brass cricket balls – fifty in all, added as part of general improvements in 1979. The children's presence gave the ground a bit of life and was, I thought, one in the eye for the old fogeys who cannot stop droning on about how much better it was in their schooldays.

Peter Wynne-Thomas also had a measure of influence in the museum upstairs, specifically in the ingenious map of the county he has produced. It shows the birth-place of all Nottinghamshire players, and emphatically disproves the idea that the connexion between the county cricket and the collieries is a myth. The huge concentration is in the coal-mining west half of the county, focusing on places such as Sutton-in-Ashfield, Kirkby-in-Ashfield, Eastwood and Hucknall Tarkard. Pride of place probably goes to Nuncargate, birthplace

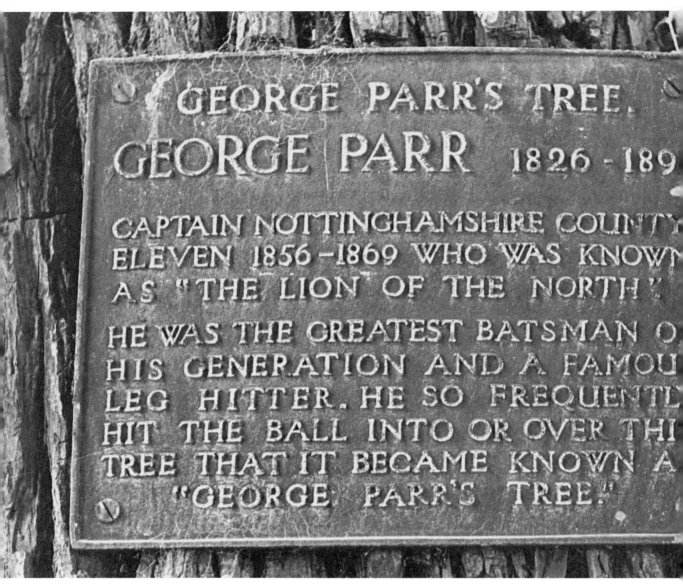

GEORGE PARR'S TREE.
GEORGE PARR 1826 - 189

CAPTAIN NOTTINGHAMSHIRE COUNTY
ELEVEN 1856 - 1869 WHO WAS KNOWN
AS "THE LION OF THE NORTH".

HE WAS THE GREATEST BATSMAN O
HIS GENERATION AND A FAMOU
LEG HITTER. HE SO FREQUENTL
HIT THE BALL INTO OR OVER THI
TREE THAT IT BECAME KNOWN A
"GEORGE PARR'S TREE."

of Harold Larwood and Joe Hardstaff junior.

The other main building at Trent Bridge stands to one side of the pavilion. Built towards the end of the nineteenth century it was originally called the Ladies' Pavilion. About the same time as discrimination in the stand came to an end it was largely converted, in 1970, into the Century Restaurant and the whole building was renamed the Cyril Lowater Suite in thanks to the benefactor. The restaurant is open all year round and extremely popular.

Elsewhere around the ground most of the stands are now two-tiered with the top storey open – and have been built since the end of the nineteenth century. The oldest surviving one is the Bridgeford Road stand dating from 1899, but it was thanks to one of Nottinghamshire's most generous supporters, Sir Julien Cahn, that the largest stretches were built in the late-1920s and early-1930s, including the first concrete stand, on the Hound Road side vacated a few years before by Notts County Football Club, and the present Radcliffe Road and West Wing stands, the latter to one side of the pavilion in the members' enclosure.

Although ostracized in some circles because he was Jewish, Sir Julien Cahn was one of cricket's most colourful patrons. As well as his support for Nottinghamshire, he laid out two cricket grounds of his own, one at West Bridgeford on the edge of Nottingham and the other at his home, Stanford Hall. Here cricketers

in temporary quarters next to the pavilion. By far the most ambitious project was the Larwood and Voce stand, opened for the England v Australia Test Match in 1985 on the site of the old Hound Road stand. With the bar immediately behind the cost of the new stand was £450,000, although much of this will no doubt be recouped by the bar which has public access from Hound Road and is open all year.

In the progress there have been inevitable losses and one hankers for the tea-garden, with shaded tables beneath apple trees, which was swept away in 1974 to make room for the squash club and cricket club offices. This is near the main entrance with its wrought-iron gates remembering J. A. Dixon, captain from 1889–99, unveiled by Sir Stanley Jackson in 1933. In 1975 came one loss which no one could have done anything about: Parr's Tree, an old elm on the west side of the ground, blew down in a gale. It was named after George Parr, 'the Lion of the North', who succeeded Clarke as captain of the All-England XI and Fuller Pilch as England's best batsman. Such was the power of the Nottinghamshire man that he regularly dispatched the ball into the branches of the tree and at his funeral a branch was added to the wreaths on his coffin. Now the spot is marked by a plaque next to the Parr stand. The wood was put to good use, being made into miniature bats and sold by the county club.

It would have amused old William Clarke that Mrs Grace's promising boy scored the first hundred on his ground at Trent Bridge. What did not amuse W.G. himself was the occasion of the first Test Match there in 1899. Captain of the England team, the great man was aged nearly fifty-one and knew his limitations. As he walked out to open the innings with C. B. Fry he said, 'Now steady, Charlie, I'm not a sprinter like you'. His considerable size was not so serious a problem when batting as when in the field when, on his own admission, 'the ground was too far away', and the Nottingham crowd barracked him for being so slow. It was a sad occasion and W.G. had had enough. 'That's it Jacker,' he said to Stanley Jackson after the game. 'I shan't play again'. It was a watershed in English Test cricket, for as W.G. bowed out Wilfred Rhodes, the only man to have played Test cricket at a greater age than Grace, played in his first Test.

Ever since that first encounter, Test Matches at Trent Bridge have produced a feast of interest and, as often as not, a feast of runs. Perhaps the most remarkable was the 1938 England v Australia Test, a game which seems to have been crammed with records. England batted first and in their only innings scored 658, including four hundreds. The opener, Charles Barnett, missed

from Test class downwards played in luxurious surroundings and Sir Julien himself went out to bat in a pair of inflatable pads. A millionaire thanks to the furniture empire he inherited from his father and continued to expand, he is estimated to have spent £20,000 a year on cricket.

The last few years have seen developments at Trent Bridge continue apace. The press box at the Radcliffe Road end has been replaced with executive boxes, all suitably named: Butler, Carr, Hardstaff, Keeton, Simpson, Whysall and Voce. The press are at present

Above *George Parr's tree, the leaves on the right revealing its identity as an elm*

becoming the first – and only – Englishman to score a hundred before lunch on the first day by two runs. His partner, Hutton, also scored a hundred, Paynter a double-hundred and the twenty-year-old Compton became, and remains, England's youngest century-maker. Compton developed a penchant for Trent Bridge, scoring a total of five Test hundreds here including the ground's highest Test score of 278 against Pakistan in 1954.

In reply Australia in 1938 scored 411, in which McCabe's rallying 232 was, in Bradman's opinion, the greatest innings he ever saw. In Australia's follow-on Bradman himself and W. A. Brown saved the day with hundreds giving the game an aggregate of seven individual centuries.

If there have been Test innings at Trent Bridge to compare with McCabe's they were played by Frank Worrell and Graeme Pollock. In 1950 the West Indies came to Nottingham fresh from their first Test victory in England, at Lord's. Harry Dalling remembers going into the West Indian dressing-room on the morning of the second day to find Worrell having a nap. It obviously stood him in good stead. Going in to bat at 12.30, he returned at the close of play with 239, having mastered the bowling with consummate ease. The next morning he went on to 261.

In 1965 South Africa made what was to be their last visit to England and at Trent Bridge Graeme Pollock marked their swan-song by playing one of the classic innings of modern Tests, scoring 125 off 145 balls out of a total of 160. His brother Peter completed the family double by taking 10 wickets: South Africa's victory gave them the rubber.

All innings by visitors to Trent Bridge must, however, take second place to C. G. Macartney's performance against Nottinghamshire in 1921. On a sweltering June day he savaged the county's attack to score 345 in just under four hours – the most runs ever scored in one day. It must have been a similar occasion to one which Cardus recalled when Macartney looked out of his hotel window one morning and remarked, 'Lovely day. Cripes, I feel sorry for any cove who's got to bowl to me today'!

Trent Bridge's reputation for runs needs no doubting, particularly when one sees that over 80 double-hundreds have been scored on the ground. The tradition of flawless wickets was a long-established one which started in 1877 with the appointment of 'Fiddler' Walker as the groundsman. Walker's nickname was not a suggestion of devious practice but recognition of his skill with the violin. He was the first man to use marl in the preparation of wickets, calling his mixture 'hair-oil' and for nearly twenty years he produced wickets as flawless and conducive to run-scoring as any in the country.

Whatever the triumphs of visitors to Trent Bridge and the highlights that Test Matches have brought it has always been famous to a greater degree than any of the other Test grounds except perhaps Old Trafford, as the home of its county. There is no doubt that the sight that those who witnessed it will remember longest, and that those who missed it most wished they had seen, was Harold Larwood bowling from the Radcliffe Road end. Larwood's bowling combined for the spectator the fascination of real speed with the most perfect of actions. He took over 1,000 wickets for Notts as did his henchman, the left-armer Bill Voce. They were members of the 1929 side who, under their tough and uncompromising captain, A. W. Carr, won the County Championship.

Also in the 1929 side were two of Nottinghamshire's foremost cricketing family, the Gunns. George Gunn was by this time aged fifty and nearing the end of his career, while his son, G.V. was in his second season for the county. Two years later, in George's penultimate year they established a unique record by both scoring a hundred in the same innings. George Gunn's eccentricity was famous and the reason for his appearances for England in England being limited to one. No one appreciated it more than Neville Cardus, to whom Gunn once remarked, 'Batsmen make two big mistakes, they have always made same two mistakes. They take too much notice of the wicket, pattin' it and looking at it. Then they make a worse mistake – they take too much notice of the bowling'. No bowler intimidated George Gunn, not even E. A. McDonald to whom he once bantered, when McDonald had threatened to knock his head off, 'Ted, you couldn't knock the skin off a rice pudding'.

For seventy years, between 1880 and 1950 there was always one Gunn playing for Nottinghamshire and sometimes more. The first was William, followed by his two nephews George and John, last came G.V. William was a contemporary of Arthur Shrewsbury, W.G.'s favourite and a Nottinghamshire character second to none. Shrewsbury was for many years the outstanding professional batsman in England. He made two scores of 267 at Trent Bridge and, in the course of the second, against Sussex in 1890, he put on 398 for the second wicket with William Gunn, a first-class record that stood for nearly fifty years. It has only been bettered once in a county match.

Second to the Gunns among Nottinghamshire cricketing families are the Hardstaffs. Father and son, both

called Joseph and known as Joe senior and Joe junior, played for the county and so would Joe minimus have done if his father had not stopped him joining the county staff with the argument that the job of a professional cricketer was no livelihood. Joe junior was acknowledged as among the most elegant of English batsmen during the years either side of the Second World War. In 1937 he scored over 2,500 runs in the season, including an innings of 243 at Trent Bridge against Middlesex.

In 1981 Trent Bridge celebrated as it had not done for over half a century when Nottinghamshire won the County Championship for the first time in fifty-two years and it is most recently that the county have come closest to the successes of their illustrious past. The Championship was clinched on the home ground with a crushing defeat of Glamorgan. This and many of the county's subsequent successes have been immeasurably assisted by two overseas players, the South African Clive Rice who was one of the outstanding county captains of modern times, as well as being a high-class all-rounder, and the New Zealand all-rounder Richard Hadlee, whose phenomenal talents were illustrated by his achievement of the 'double' in 1984.

There is no question, however, that Trent Bridge's favourite player for many years has been the home-bred Derek Randall. His own extraordinary brand of fidget, humour and brilliance perhaps in some ways recalls George Gunn and certainly he has been one of the major draws for spectators. In 1979 he treated his supporters to one of the great batting displays of his career when, against Middlesex, he scored 209 and 146 in his two innings of the match.

In 1988 Nottinghamshire achieves its 150th anniversary. There will be great celebrations and an appeal to raise money for, among other things, the rebuilding of the Bridgeford Stand. Going into the season as they do, as County Champions and holders of the NatWest Trophy, and given the well-charted history the ground has so far enjoyed, there is every chance that all expectations will be realized. It would be richly deserved.

WORKSOP

Trent Bridge has dominated Nottinghamshire's history to such an extent that the ground at Central Avenue in Worksop, the only other in the county to have been

Above *The old pavilion at Worksop with, to the left, the new building under construction*

granted any number of county games, has seen less than forty matches since the first in 1921 (compared to over a thousand games played by Nottinghamshire at Trent Bridge). Today Worksop is the only place Nottinghamshire visit away from their headquarters.

The ground, which is home to Worksop CC, is within easy walking distance of the town centre – Central Avenue is the street leading from the main shopping street past the turning to the ground's entrance – and, equally conveniently, within fifty yards of the main bus station. Next to the cricket ground is the pitch of Worksop Town Football Club, bringing the usual problem in such instances of the shared ground producing a rough outfield.

The land for the cricket ground was originally given in 1901 by William Allen, a local brewer, who also presented the first pavilion. This was replaced in 1972 with a new building which served both cricketers and squash players, whose new court was built at the same time. By the 1980s the cricket club had decided that it was time they had their own pavilion, and the new addition, to one side of the squash court, was first used in 1987. Neat and functional, with shallow steps along its front, the pavilion contains a tea-room, kitchen, two changing-rooms, an umpires' room, and shower-rooms.

Otherwise, the facilities at this club ground are understandably limited and in the past they have always welcomed the two caravans, one for ladies, the other for the umpires, which have been thoughtfully provided by the county from its Trent Bridge headquarters. The best viewing position for spectators is from the raised bank on either side of the sightscreen at one end of the ground – the pavilion and other buildings are all on one side.

As Worksop is only a few miles from the county boundary the traditional opponents have always been neighbouring Yorkshire. If there have been occasional mutterings from the visitors as to why they should consistently be denied playing at Trent Bridge, some Yorkshiremen will remember Worksop with affection: Fred Trueman, who took eight for 84 in 1962 and, more especially, Geoffery Boycott who scored over 900 runs on the ground at an average of well over 100, his highest score being 214 not out in 1983. His last visit to the ground, in 1986, was overshadowed by the first three Nottinghamshire batsmen all scoring hundreds: Broad 122, Robinson 105, and Johnson 105 not out, to give their side a total of 404 for three declared, but in characteristic style Geoffrey batted out three and a half defiant hours for 56.

LEICESTERSHIRE

LEICESTER

Leicestershire play the South Africans at Aylestone Road in 1907

Grace Road, Leicester may be a cricket ground, but it is also a place which celebrates the county's foremost sporting opponent – the fox. 'Old Charlie' provides the County Cricket Club's badge and he is on display all over Grace Road. Most prominent is the gleaming gold running fox on the weather-vane which surmounts the new scoreboard and clock-tower. One mask – woe betide the man who calls it a head – hangs over the front door of the pavilion. There is a stuffed fox in the inevitably named Fox Bar for members and another one next door in the indoor school – which doubles up as the members' and players' dining room in the season. He was presented by the President, William Bentley, in 1973, having been caught on the Rushley Fields Manor

Estate. The oldest covered building on the ground is called 'the Meet' and the two plush entertainment suites are the Fernie and the Quorn, named after two famous Leicestershire hunts.

We should not, however, be diverted by Grace Road's connexion with the chase, for behind the masks and brushes is a county ground which has achieved a spectacular face-lift in the last twenty-odd years. This has left it with the impressive reputation of being the best appointed of all non-Test grounds. In fact Grace Road came within a whisker of hosting a one-day international in 1981, but the TCCB were nervous of far more than the 12,000 capacity trying to get in, and moved the match to one of the established grounds.

In the process of its transformation Grace Road has shrugged off most of the reputation with which it was blighted – along with its Midland neighbours, Derby and Northampton – from the resumption of cricket after the Second World War until the mid-1960s when improvements began.

In the old days, few people other than county die-hards relished a visit to Grace Road. For a start it is as difficult to find as any county ground – this problem has not actually disappeared, only being alleviated by the liberal use of yellow 'County Cricket' signs – and the attitude of most players was summed up by the laconic Jim Laker, for whom on one visit Grace Road, 'looked its usual broken-down shambles and it seemed quite incredible that those rickety, worn-out old steps which led into darkness to the leaky, spasmodic cold shower had not yet completely disintegrated. The changing-rooms remained indescribable'.

Part of the problem was the lack of continuity in Grace Road's history. The ground was first played on in 1878. One of the first matches was against D. W. Gregory's Australian side, when Alec Bannerman scored the maiden hundred by an Australian in England and 'The Demon' Spofforth warned what was to come in future Test-playing tours when he took nine wickets in the match.

In 1895 Leicestershire were accorded first-class status, but shortly afterwards it became clear that the ground's inaccessibility – the only mode of transport from the city centre two miles away was a horse tram – was a major problem and, in 1901, the county moved citywards, to new quarters at Aylestone Road. Here they remained until 1939, but building developments during the Second World War made return impossible; therefore, in 1946, Leicestershire were back at Grace Road.

The sixteen-acre site at Grace Road, originally purchased by the Leicestershire Cricket Ground Company in 1877, was enclosed on three sides by Grace, Milligan and Hawkesbury Roads. (Herein lies the origin of the name – nothing to do with W. G. who never played here, only at Aylestone Road, but after the man of property who built the houses of the adjoining street.) Today the fourth side is enclosed by Park Hill Drive. The land had originally belonged to the Duke of Rutland whose family have retained a spasmodic connexion with the club, the ninth Duke serving as President in 1932–33. In 1900, the last season before Grace Road was abandoned for Aylestone Road, Leicester-

shire were involved in an unusually high-scoring match against Sussex, when the home team scored 609 for eight declared and the visitors replied with 686 for eight, Ranjitsinhji scoring 275.

Aylestone Road was home for many of the county's outstanding players: W. E. Astill, their best all-rounder and George Geary, Leicestershire's most fondly remembered professional, L. G. Berry, the county's most prolific batsman – both in one season and in his career – and not least, the great New Zealand batsman, C. S. Dempster, who delighted Leicester crowds during his short stay with the county between 1935 and 1939. It was also the scene of many of the great moments in the county's history; some for the county such as S. Coe's innings of 252 not out against Northamptonshire in 1914 which remains the highest score for Leicestershire, others against, notably George Hirst's innings of 341 in 1905 for Yorkshire, which was the highest score of Hirst's career and remains the fourth highest in county cricket.

In the inter-war years spectators and players alike were less fussy about comfort and facilities than they are today. All the same, there developed a problem at Aylestone Road as a result of the electricity works which was built next door, as described by Kilburn and Yardley.

There was, however, one inescapable discomfort after the adjoining electricity works had been built. The cooling towers dominated the cricket scene and insisted upon catching the eye, and clouds of fine ash spread over the field and into buildings and clothes and food, and were also apt to catch the eye. Sandwiches were egg, tomato and grit, and it was impossible for players or spectators to keep fresh and clean through the day. In the press box pens and pencils scraped their way across the paper, no doubt to the detriment of smooth and kindly criticism.

One feels it would have been the death of many a typewriter as well.

In the end it was not the smut, but building works by the Electricity Board, which ended the Aylestone Road era and in 1946 Leicestershire returned to Grace Road after an absence of nearly fifty years. By this time ownership of the ground had passed to Leicester Education Authority. Any aspirations the county club may have had for improvements were stifled and at the same time they could only play on the ground when it was not being used by the City of Leicester School. As a result the old Victorian pavilion remained unchanged and Leicestershire were forced to visit a selection of

Opposite *Grace Road's new scoreboard, topped by clock and gilded fox*

other grounds around the county, including Ashby-de-la-Zouch, Loughborough and Hinckley. Finally, in 1966, the ground was purchased for £24,000 and almost immediately the improvements began which have effected such a transformation during the last twenty years.

Most people would agree that the architect of Grace Road's rejuvenation, as well as of the county's rising fortunes during the 1970s, has been Mike Turner, who became Leicestershire's Secretary in 1960 and has been the club's Secretary-Manager since 1969. When Leicestershire paid him the unprecedented honour of giving him a benefit after he had served twenty-five years as Secretary, John Arlott wrote that, 'the cricket historians of the future will salute him as the man who lifted Leicestershire from a minor to a major cricketing power'. Born in Leicester, Turner started his career on the playing staff for Leicestershire and appeared for the county ten times between 1954–59. He would be the first to admit that he was well-advised to turn his atten-

tion from playing cricket for the county to organizing it for them.

Mike Turner came to be recognized as the prototype modern cricket administrator: someone who appreciated that running county cricket would inevitably become increasingly expensive and that the capacity crowds that were the norm in the early post-war years would not always be there. To counter this the county clubs needed to be given a sound financial basis, while both the cricket that they played and the surroundings it was played in had to be of sufficient standard to attract members, casual spectators, sponsors and commercial hosts. If Turner became the driving force at Grace Road his efforts were by no means single-handed and he had the support of a sympathetic committee and, not least, of C. H. Palmer who had been both captain and secretary of the county from 1950–57.

Above *The Meet, Grace Road's stand which came from Aylestone Road*

The face-lift at Grace Road began with the new pavilion, opened by the Bishop of Leicester on June 25 1966 – only six months after the ground had been purchased. While it is certainly not a thing of beauty the Grace Road pavilion provides the modern facilities so conspicuously lacking in its Victorian predecessor. Obvious effort to help the pavilion's appearance as much as possible is shown by retaining wooden benches in front and the welcome colour of beds of roses.

The pavilion was followed by lesser trimmings: new gates at the ground's various entrances, a white railing boundary fence and, not least, some sympathetic tree planting. To some extent this was enforced by the much lamented loss of elm trees along two sides of the ground to Dutch Elm disease. Now the Milligan Road side is lined with a fairly unusual variety of lime – *Tilia euchlora* – with beds of jolly roses underneath. Along the opposite, Park Hill Drive, side are whitebeams and plane trees. At the far end from the pavilion, the main car park contains a variety of trees – mainly sorbus and

silver birch – all given and planted by members and behind here a bank of one hundred rhododendrons provides a splash of colour during the early part of the season. One nice connexion was maintained by the present Earl of Lanesborough when he planted a group of nine trees (he is the ninth Earl) in front of the groundsmen's building, for his great-grandfather had been the club's original President from 1879–85.

More important that any of the architectural or horticultural additions which were appearing at Grace Road was the arrival, in 1969, of Raymond Illingworth from Yorkshire, which proved to be the greatest coup Leicestershire's new regime were to make. During his ten seasons as captain Leicestershire not only broke their duck but ended up with five titles under their belt. Best of all was the 1975 season when they did the double

Above *Grace Road's pavilion complex, with the two executive suites, Quorn and Fernie, on either side of the first floor*

of their first County Championship and second Benson and Hedges Cup. No county had previously won two competitions in one season.

In 1978 an appeal to mark the centenary of cricket at Grace Road provided money for concrete terracing and fixed seating – instead of old wooden benches – in most of the uncovered parts of the ground and for the development of the Pavilion Suite. This is the block to the left of the pavilion as you look from the playing area, where on the ground floor is the Indoor School/Dining Room with the Fox Bar next door. Above is the 'Fernie' sponsors' suite, a new press box and, on one end, the open Butler Stand which provides the best view of play for those members who do not mind a somewhat eyrie-like vantage-point.

1978 also saw the introduction of the club's Lottery Club which has made a substantial contribution to the finances. The improvement is revealed in comparing the figures for 1972, the first year of success when the Benson and Hedges Cup was won, when the club's total income was £45,000 (including a contribution of £4,000 from the TCCB) with 1986 when the total income was £499,000 (including £145,000 from the TCCB).

The pavilion complex was completed in 1982 with the addition of a further building on the other side of the now sandwiched pavilion, which contains a second sponsor's suite – 'Quorn' – above new club offices. It is in the entrance lobby to these offices that one gets a good insight into what a conspicuously successful and prosperous modern club Leicestershire has become. Instead of the usual aerial photos of the ground, or inevitable team groups there is a set of portraits of many of the Leicestershire players by the most contemporary of fashionable portrait-painters, Bryan Organ, who leapt to prominence with his pictures of the Prince and Princess of Wales. Mind you, the choice of artist is hardly surprising because before taking up his brushes Organ played for the Leicestershire Second XI during the 1950s and has remained a devoted supporter ever since. The only slight headache for Mike Turner is the pictures' insurance value!

Bryan Organ was also involved in Grace Road's latest addition – and without question the ground's only really elegant one – the new scoreboard and clock cupola, used for the first time in 1987. The committee had decided that they would spend a bequest of £3,000 from the late Lord Bishop's wife on a new scoreboard and clock when they were offered the clock by a Leicestershire company who had had a cancellation for

one which measured five feet by five feet. Some clock. As a result they decided to do things properly and called in Bryan Organ and an architect friend of his who together designed the striking edifice – and provided the gold leaf for the fox which surmounts the weather-vane. The new addition is positioned between Grace Road's two covered stands, the one for members is the George Geary Stand, on the Milligan Road side of the ground.

Not everything is new at Grace Road. 'The Meet', which was an open stand at Aylestone Road and was moved to Grace Road, since when it has been given a curved roof in the style of some farm buildings and a public bar which now takes up the ground floor, still stands in one corner of the ground. If the walls of the corridors and club offices are hung with the successful sides of the past few years, the Fox Bar and Indoor School have many a reminder of the old days: bats and caps, a huge collection of many Leicestershire club ties, George Geary's enormous boots – only Maurice Tate's can have been bigger – and, outstanding among the pictures, a complete set of Albert Chevallier-Taylor's 'The Empire's Cricketers'.

There are unexpected touches such as the illuminated scroll to mark John Arlott's retirement from the Grace Road Taverners. I particularly liked the telegram sent by the ninth Duke of Rutland – obviously interested, if not involved in the club before his spell as President – to C. J. B. Wood in 1911. Wood had just created a unique world record by carrying his bat through both innings of a match – against Yorkshire at Bradford, and scoring a hundred in both. His Grace, however, was obviously not blinded by the occasion. '"Many congratulations to you on your wonderful achievement. I hope the rest of the eleven will put their backs into the game and help to win a match soon." Duke of Rutland. 16 Arlington Street.'

In David Gower Grace Road has produced the most elegant English batsman of recent years and in 1987 Leicestershire gave him a well-deserved benefit. If his appearances for the county have all too often been interrupted by the demands of Test cricket his importance to the club – both as player and personality – would appear to be immeasurable judging by the comments of many people at Grace Road. David is also my closest link with cricketing fame, for we both played in our prep school eleven, at which stage he was already proving himself something of a prodigy.

Opposite *Hinckley's first county match, against neighbouring Warwickshire in 1911*

Overleaf *Hinckley's present ground, with the pavilion boasting its own Father Time weather-vane*

HINCKLEY

Hinckley is the only place Leicestershire now takes its championship cricket to, away from Grace Road. The town is tucked into the county's south-west corner a stone's-throw from the border with Warwickshire and only a few miles north of Coventry. The county had previously used two diffrent grounds at Hinckley, leaving the second in 1964. The present ground, just off the busy A47 Leicester road, was opened in 1968, although the county did not make their first visit until 1981.

The ground belongs to the Leicester Road Sports Club. As well as the cricket ground there are rugby and football pitches and tennis courts. Roughly two miles from the centre of Hinckley the ground is far enough out to be enclosed by trees and hedges rather than rows of houses. The pavilion at one end, to one side of the sightscreen, also serves the rugby club and despite having the cobbled-together and mournful appearance of so many pavilions it is easily able to cope with the county's annual visits.

The pavilion does boast two elevating features: a Father Time weather-vane, with the old reaper in the same pose as he strikes over the Grandstand at Lord's, and a shiny innings bell. The origin of both is revealed in a plaque on the pavilion wall. 'These were donated in memory of Malcolm Paris by his many friends at the Leicester Road Sports Club, May 1976'.

From the pavilion a line of young lime trees curves around the ground, parallel to the boundary, passing the neat brick scorebox and continuing around the far end. Although still small the trees help give the ground a feeling of enclosure, although long before they reach full maturity some people will wish that they had planted them less close together and further from the boundary.

Looking towards the far end of the ground from the pavilion one's eye is carried to a landmark on a slight hill a couple of miles away, which tells of Hinckley's most significant cricket connexion. This is the squat tower of the church at Barwell, the village where George Geary was born. Although Leicestershire did play one or two games at Barwell itself immediately after the Second World War, this was after Geary's retirement,

and for his second benefit, in 1936, he chose Hinckley for his benefit match, it being the closest ground to his home. Although he served his county well on this occasion, Geary hardly swelled the coffers of his benefit fund. On a helpful wicket he took 13 for 43 in the match and went home with £10, the game having only lasted two days.

George Geary was probably the most fondly remembered cricketer in Leicestershire's history. He played for the county between 1912–38 and although his bowling was often of decisive quality, including at Test level, as when he dismissed Bradman in the First Test at Trent Bridge in 1934, caught by Hammond at slip, he was also someone who would quite happily bowl all day for little return, because he considered it to be his job. He took over 2,000 wickets in his career – as well as scoring over 13,000 runs – and his 16 for 96 against Glamorgan in 1929 is a county record. When he left the county he became the coach at Charterhouse and was for many years as renowned for his youthful products as he was popular with the boys. One colleague remembered visiting Geary at Charterhouse when the latter said, 'come over here, I'll show you an England cricketer'. It was a fourteen-year-old called Peter May.

Since their return to Hinckley Leicestershire have found it a productive ground. They have won the single county championship match in the majority of years and have yet to lose there. They marked their return in 1981 with probably the best game to date, when they beat Nottinghamshire – the eventual County Champions – by four wickets. In Leicestershire's first innings of 431 for eight declared three players, the openers Balderstone and Steele (100 and 116 respectively with a partnership of 206), and the hard-hitting Brian Davison (123) all made hundreds. Nottinghamshire, forced to follow on, appeared to have saved the game when Derek Randall and Neil Weightman – the latter in only his second first-class game – scored 101 and 105 respectively, but Leicestershire managed to bowl them out and score the final run off the penultimate ball of the game.

Hinckley: the old ground in the 1960s

NORTHAMPTONSHIRE

NORTHAMPTON

There are not many people you can find to extol the virtues of the county ground at Wantage Road, Northampton, or even, for that matter, of the history of Northamptonshire CCC. Most of those who do – like Matthew Engel of *The Guardian* – are Northamptonshire natives and do so in a guarded, self-effacing manner. The present Secretary/Manager, Stephen Coverdale, has no doubt that in the early 1970s when he was playing for Yorkshire, Northampton was the worst ground to visit. All of them would admit that, for the majority of their lives, both ground and county club have struggled for recognition and praise.

An early post-war view of Northampton: looking across the pavilion from the football pitch side of the ground

In 1885, when the land for the ground was originally purchased, H. H. Stephenson – a man of some stature in the cricket world, who played for Surrey and took the first English team to Australia – was asked to inspect the site and pass judgement. His verdict was succinct and confident. 'This would make one of the finest grounds in England'. Sadly, the potential has never been realized.

In the early days the new ground was most welcome because it brought to an end the unsatisfactory previous arrangement of the club playing on Northampton Racecourse. Here their efforts to 'enclose' the ground for games were objected to by Northampton burghers and deemed to be illegal by the mayor. As a result games were constantly interrupted and on one occasion the groundsman, Alfred Stockwin, came to blows with the driver of a brewer's dray when the latter insisted

on steering his horses and heavy load straight over a freshly-prepared wicket.

It was also at this time, admittedly before the county achieved first-class status, that Northamptonshire established a record not even the Fosters of Worcestershire could rival. The Founder and Principal of Abington House School was a certain Mr William Kingston of whose nine sons eight played for the county between 1874 and 1909, one, J.P., being the county's first captain. They were sporting and God-fearing in the best Victorian tradition, three of their number becoming clergymen.

The new ground was 'Ten acres in the parish of Abington', today part of Northampton and easily accessible from the city centre via the Wellingborough road. Approaching the ground one passes attractive, tree-lined Abington Park and spirits are temporarily raised that the surroundings of the cricket ground are similar. Alas not. The ground is largely enclosed by uniform rows of terraced houses, mainly built towards the end of the nineteenth century for the workers at the neighbouring Manfield shoe factory, their deep red brick not ugly, but very monotonous. One cannot help reflecting that Northamptonshire is a county of lovely countryside, filled with houses and church spires built of the matchless local stone, but of unlovely towns – Northampton, Kettering and Corby – and it is the cricket ground's inevitable misfortune to be in urban surroundings.

But it is unfair to blame a cricket club and their ground for their surroundings which – in the great majority of cases – they are powerless to influence. More pressing problems arose within the ground, partly as a result of the joint nature of the original venture. The ground was not purchased by a cricket club, but by the Northamptonshire County Cricket and Recreation Grounds Company Limited. Within a few years the result was the Victorian equivalent of the modern sports and leisure centre: as well as cricket there was football (association and rugby), tennis, bowls, bicycling and tricycling and athletics. One is relieved to hear that the local archery club were turned down – the mind boggles at the thought of cricketers, cyclists and sprinters avoiding hails of arrows as well as each other – as were, nor surprisingly in those pre-suffragette days, the lady cricketers.

Today, as well as the cricket, the survivors are soccer and bowls. One of the main shortcomings of the Northampton ground is the area of overlap between cricket and football on one side of the ground. The football pitch, home of fourth division Northampton Town Football Club – The Cobblers to their supporters – runs at right-angles to the wicket and the shared space ensures a rough outfield on this side of the ground. In addition the football season makes cricket impossible

Above *Modern Northampton, a view from the old pavilion back across the ground*

in April and September, when the county has either to play away or to visit another ground of their own.

The bowls club, by contrast, has often been more popular – at least in the past when, because of the limitations of the original pavilion, the players were forced to go to the bowls clubhouse in one corner of the ground for their meals. Prior to then they had eaten at the County Hotel on another corner, beyond the football pitch, and more than one Northamptonshire cricketer retired to become landlord – not least C. J. T. Pool, their leading batsmen in the early years of first-class status, who gave his name to the gates at the cricket ground's main entrance.

Northamptonshire has the smallest population of any of the first-class counties and today only just manages to maintain a membership of 2,000. Support has always been difficult to drum up and this has often combined with shaky management to put great pressure on the financial health of the club. As a result they have frequently relied upon the generosity and goodwill of individual benefactors, none of whom was more important than Alfred Cockerill, who guaranteed the cricket club possession of their ground in perpetuity – something they would have been most unlikely to manage by themselves.

Cockerill progressed from market-gardening to something of a mercantile and property-based empire, but all the while he was devotedly interested in the fledgling Northamptonshire cricket club. In the year of the ground's purchase he had offered to 'fork, plough and seed it'. He was taken on and it is significant that he asked for his nominal fee to be in the form of shares in the company. He appears to have sensed that the club would possibly be unable to guarantee their own security of tenure so over the years he spent £10,000 acquiring shares until eventually he owned the ground. Finally, at a meeting in 1923 when the company was liquidated, he handed over the ground to the cricket club's trustees at a peppercorn rent for one thousand years. When, a few years later, the pavilion was extended and a balcony added, they were named after Cockerill and today you will find a picture of him in the pavilion, wearing a rakish hat and an entrepreneurial grin. His son, Harold, who remembers watching his first game in 1919 and has been mayor of Northampton, is still to be seen on the ground.

Northamptonshire seem never to have been able to shake off the label of 'lesser' – or at least they have only done so sporadically during most of their history and for any length of time during recent years. Despite a number of outstanding and delightful individual players the team's fortunes have at times plumbed depths no other county would ever hope to rival. First-class status, which came in 1905, was only achieved thanks to the formidable all-round prowess of one player, George Thompson. When *Wisden* made him one of their 'Five Cricketers of the Year' in 1906 the Editor commented, 'But for his bowling it is quite safe to say that Northamptonshire in 1905 would not have been given a place among the first-class teams ... Thompson to a greater extent than all the other members of the team put together, rendered the promotion possible'.

Thompson, who went on to become the first Northamptonshire cricketer to play for England, was known as the 'Northamptonshire Nugget' partly because of his value as a cricketer, but also because he was Jewish. About this he always remained quite unmoved, once remarking, 'They say I am a Jew, but I am not sorry to be one. At least I have four thousand of the best tucked away in the bank, unlike yon bloke [another Northamptonshire professional] who will be buried by the parish'.

In 1912 the county attained the dizzy heights of second place in the county championship – to general astonishment – but the success was short-lived. The inter-war years were a period of almost unrelenting failure, reaching its nadir during the 1930s. Between 1930 and 1939 the county were bottom of the table seven times, second-bottom twice and only struggled to thirteenth place in the other year. From May 1935 to May 1939 they did not win a single match. If there were highlights, all too often they were provided by visiting teams. Kent's Colin Blythe had already, in 1907, achieved his record-breaking bowling feat of 17 for 48 in a day, but in 1920 came Northampton's most historic match, when Percy Fender scored a hundred in thirty-five minutes and the match aggregate was 1,475 runs for 27 wickets. A few years later Hammond made one majestic hit clean over the pavilion.

All too often, Northamptonshire's fortunes have been affected by cruel fate. Thompson's career was brought to a premature end by ill-health. R. P. Nelson, who took on the daunting task of the captaincy in 1938, was killed in action with the Royal Marines in 1940, aged twenty-eight. As well as his talents as a player, he had shown every sign of being the leader the county desperately needed, as recorded by a former captain, W. C. Brown. 'At the end of 1937 the Northamptonshire side were a disorganized rabble. In two seasons he quietly and imperceptibly moulded them into a team which it was impossible to recognize as the same lot who had done duty before he took over the captaincy'.

Most poignant, however, has been the premature end to the careers of the county's two most exciting batsmen as a result of motor accidents. In 1928 the nineteen-year-old A. H. Bakewell was the most exciting prospect Northamptonshire had had for years. In 1933 he played the best innings ever seen on the county ground, scoring 246 off Nottinghamshire when, as R. C. Robertson-Glasgow remembered, 'Sam Staples set the field for his accurate off-breaks and Bakewell again and again drove him from the leg stump crack against the rails through vacant extra-cover'. In 1936 he scored 241 not out at Chesterfield and it was on the return journey from this game that his car overturned, killing his companion, R. P. Northway and so damaging the twenty-eight-year-old Bakewell's arm that he never played cricket again.

Just over thirty years later, in 1969, the career of Colin Milburn was effectively ended when he lost an eye in a motor accident. Milburn was aged twenty-seven and since his appearance in 1960 had thrilled both Northampton and England spectators with his big-hitting. In the grim days of declining crowds during the 1960s there was no more assured crowd-puller than 'Ollie' Milburn.

If Milburn was one of the most colourful characters to arrive at Northampton during the post-war years another was certainly F. R. Brown, who took on the captaincy in 1949 and embarked upon a glorious Indian summer of his career which also saw him captain England. Brown injected a sense of purpose into Northamptonshire it had not had before and by the time he gave up the captaincy a near-revolution had been effected. His arrival also coincided with the beginning of a period of prosperity such as the club had never enjoyed before, largely thanks to a thriving Supporters' Club and football lottery. In 1958 they were able to spend £40,000 on the present Indoor School with a stand seating 600 above, positioned next to the old pavilion.

It was a period when many players from outside the county made great contributions. Dennis Brookes, a Yorkshireman, continued amassing the runs which have made him the county's leading run-scorer, both in one season and a career; Frank Tyson arrived from Lancashire and, although some people said that he was limited by the Northampton wickets, his meteoric career for England did the county's prestige no end of good. In addition there were three Australians: J. S. Manning, a left-arm bowler, George Tribe, an outstanding all-rounder and Jock Livingston, a left-hand bat who delighted in hitting leg-spinners into the bowls club at Northampton. In 1958 Raman Subba Row – like Brown,

a product of Surrey – took over the captaincy from Brookes and in the same year made the county's record score of 300 against his old county at The Oval.

Brown's captaincy may have ushered in a period when, at last, it seemed that Northamptonshire had found some identity as a first-class county, but it is in the last decade or so that they have achieved concrete success and, at the same time, that the ground has benefited from substantial improvements. In 1979 a new pavilion was built, next to the indoor school, so that now the main range extends from the old pavilion and indoor school, both of which provide excellent views of play straight down the wicket, to the new building across one corner of the ground.

If it is architecturally uninteresting, the new two-storey building has anyway greatly improved facilities with its dining-room and bar, dressing-rooms and offices. Further round the boundary is 'The Mound', the smallest building at Northampton but the one with easily the most character. The two-storey building, with its black and white facade is often compared to a signal-box. It has had a varied history, serving press and scorers, housing the printing-press for scorecards and

Right *The old pavilion at Northampton*

the groundsman's equipment. In 1975 it became a club shop and, finally, in 1986 it graduated to being a 'hospitality' room with its own bar.

Unfortunately Northampton cannot escape from the football pitch at the far end, which has the rather rundown appearance of most non-first division clubs. If anything the picture was improved by the disappearance of the main football stand which faced the cricket pitch, and whose demise was brought about by inspections after the Bradford disaster. These inspections also sounded the death-knell for the cricket ground's old west stand which, single-handed, had done more for Northampton's unfortunate appearance than any other building. Facing the wicket from square-leg, the uncomfortable wooden stand had got steadily more decrepid and, 'every time it got hit you were surprised it did not fall down'. It was also a hot-bed of barracking – on one occasion in 1907 Jessop was forced to interrupt an innings and cross the pitch to remonstrate with one assailant. No one was sad to see it go and in its place is a spanking new stand with room for 270 people in bright orange plastic seats, put up at a cost of £30,000.

Much of the credit for the improvements was due to Ken Turner, secretary from 1958 until 1985. A man of unending enthusiasm and resourcefulness, Turner was not above organizing pop concerts and discotheques in the indoor school to help the club's finances. More important was his role in the recruitment of overseas players such as Bishen Bedi and Mushtaq Mohammad, decisive in 1976, when, under Mushtaq, the county won their first competition – the Gillette Cup – and came second in the county championship.

It seems, however, that the county may never shake off the hint of ill-fortune which has always dogged them. In 1981 they lost the NatWest final to Derbyshire when the scores were equal but Derbyshire had lost fewer wickets and in 1987 they lost in the finals of both the Benson and Hedges Cup and the NatWest Cup, as well as falling away from a potentially winning position in the championship. All the same, they have become as powerful a force as any in county cricket at the moment, and if their county ground will only ever be a place of pilgrimage for any but the most ardent Northamptonshire supporters, it is at least recognized and respected and – in recent years – greatly improved.

WELLING-BOROUGH SCHOOL

Wellingborough School shares with Cheltenham College the distinction of being one of only two school grounds to host first-class county cricket. As one would expect, Northamptonshire's visit is delayed until the end of term. Whereas Cheltenham has its famous festival of three county championship games, Wellingborough hosts only one.

If its history does not compare with that of the Gloucestershire school – Northamptonshire have only played at Wellingborough since 1946, as opposed to the 100-plus years at Cheltenham – it certainly provides an enjoyable excursion for the county, players and supporters alike, and the ground boasts some real surprises.

The lowest step from the pavilion out to the ground was originally the doorstep of W. G. Grace's Bristol home. It was collected by a Wellingborough master and cricket fanatic, E. Murray Wytham – by all accounts the 'Mr Chips' of Wellingborough – who heard that the house was being demolished, and drove through the dead of night to collect some memento to bring back to Wellingborough. It is traditionally necessary to step

firmly onto the stone en route to the wicket to ensure scoring any runs, although at the moment this is impossible as the valuable item is being restored.

It was Murray Wytham who was also responsible for Wellingborough's other individual feature, which must rank among the most extraordinary cricket customs anywhere. For many years after Northamptonshire started visiting the school there was an annual ritual each Halloween when the signatures of those players who had appeared in the county's match, along with a scorecard, were ceremoniously buried in a bottle on one corner of the square. One hopes that it was not the interference of the assembled company which forced Northamptonshire to abandon the ground for one year in 1982 because of the poor wicket, but happily the absence proved only temporary.

The London road runs past one end of the ground while at the other the rest of the school's playing fields stretch away. During county matches marquees at this end help to enclose the ground and round from the sightscreen, roughly at third-man while bowling is from the London road end, is the pavilion, in itself a delightful oddity as the only thatched pavilion on the county circuit, built originally with funds raised from the school tuck-shop.

If the facilities are limited the atmosphere certainly is not; the main room and tea-room are lined with oak panels bearing the school XIs down the years. Over

Opposite *The signal-box, which is the most characterful of Northampton's buildings*

Above *The thatched pavilion at Wellingborough School*

Above *WG's doorstep – a famous feature of the pavilion*

Right *A good crowd at the picturesque Wellingborough ground*

thirty pupils have subsequently played for Northamptonshire, six becoming captain, while a number of others played first-class cricket elsewhere. The first to join Nothamptonshire was Arthur Henfrey, but the most distinguished was George Thompson. Between the wars another Wellingburian, J. E. Timms, was more often than not the mainstay of the county's shaky batting. Unusually, both he and Thompson were amateurs who subsequently turned professional.

The name which dominates those Wellingburians who played for Northamptonshire is Wright. Around the First World War years the school produced nine Wrights who played for Northamptonshire. They consisted of three sets of brothers, two of whom were cousins, the other pair unrelated: Albert, Ernest, Richard and Stephen; cousins of Bertie, Nicholas and Philip; no relations to Alan and Ronald. The only two to play regularly for the county were P. A. 'Bill' – an outstanding bowler – and R. L. 'Dick', but in 1922 or 1923 there could have been five Wrights of one sort or another in the team.

As was the case in many schools, Wellingborough's most talented prospect, Sydney Askham, was killed in action in 1916, aged nineteen. Askham had already played for the county in 1914 – a year before he was due to leave school.

When Yorkshire came to Wellingborough for the first time in 1949 Len Hutton must have put both feet firmly on W. G.'s doorstep, for in Yorkshire's total of 523 he scored 269 not out. In the three days of the match over 1,000 runs were scored and in Northamptonshire's second innings Dennis Brookes and Norman Oldfield saved the game with an unbroken opening stand of 208.

No doubt the relatively short boundaries played

their part in this high scoring game as they did in 1986 when a record Sunday league crowd for Northamptonshire watched Ian Botham hit a typically belligerent 175 off twenty-seven overs. Botham's score was one run short of the record for the competition, but his 13 sixes was a record, and outstripped his tally of only 12 fours.

Despite the excitement, Northamptonshire supporters would prefer to remember the guileful Indian Bishen Bedi enjoying his swan-song on the ground against Middlesex in 1977. Bedi exploited a spinner's wicket to the full to take five for 24 and six for 83 in Middlesex's two innings and he and Willey were the only wicket-takers.

LUTON

Since 1986 Northamptonshire have taken one county championship match each season outside their boundary to Wardown Park, Luton in neighbouring Bedfordshire, having previously visited for Sunday league games since 1973. As a ground used by Bedfordshire Luton has hosted Minor Counties cricket for many years.

Wardown Park is the home of Luton Town CC and their energetic committee ensure that the county's visits have been notable occasions. Northamptonshire support in Bedfordshire is strong, as it is in neighbouring Buckinghamshire which similarly encourages games at Milton Keynes – although not, as yet, county championship ones. For Northamptonshire, as with the other smaller first-class counties, any amount of support is important, particularly if it will swell the membership or bring in business interest and sponsorship. At Luton willing sponsors have filled the marquees erected around the ground.

To one side of the pavilion, which contains a well-appointed clubhouse and bar filled with photographs of past highlights on the ground, is a grassy bank favoured by many spectators. Perhaps most significant, the Luton wickets have been universally praised and the most prized recent addition in the pavilion is the framed report from *The Times*, by Richard Streeton, giving a highly complimentary account of the first championship game.

It was, indeed, as good an inaugural match as Wardown Park could have hoped for. Yorkshire were the visitors and in Northamptonshire's first innings Robert Bailey scored his maiden double-hundred, while for Yorkshire Ashley Metcalfe's 151 was his second hundred in consecutive innings. Although the match did not produce a result the three days saw over 1,100 runs scored and universal enjoyment for players and spectators alike.

Above *Wardown Park, Luton, a ground to which Northamptonshire have made many popular visits*

OXFORD

THE PARKS

To read R. C. Robertson-Glasgow writing about the Parks is one of the supremely nostalgic experiences of cricket literature. 'Crusoe', who was a blue for four years, 1920–23, loved the Parks. For him it was a place where 'all the geese were swans'. It was a 'refuge for the connoisseur of the beloved game'. It was also the place where he gained his nick-name, courtesy of the Essex batsman, C. P. McGahey. Returning to the pavilion a victim of Robertson-Glasgow's bowling, McGahey was asked by his captain how he was out and replied, 'I was bowled by an old ... who I thought was dead two thousand years ago, called Robinson Crusoe'.

Life at Oxford has changed dramatically in the last few decades and the University's cricket has changed accordingly. The 'gilded youth' element has virtually gone while the spirit of amateurism is pursued self-consciously rather than instinctively. Much has been said about the declining standards of Oxford and Cambridge cricket and whether their matches still deserve to be first-class. A lot of the blame has been levelled at admissions tutors. Today one would be astonished to see the figure of Zuleika Dobson wandering towards the boundary of the Parks: when Fry, Foster and Palairet were batting it might not have been at all surprising.

Despite all this the Parks remains one of the most evocative of cricket grounds for two reasons; its setting, and the fact that it has been, with Cambridge, the great nursery of English amateur cricket. Elegant batsmen – and, less often, outstanding bowlers – county captains, Test players, and the game's leading administrators have emerged from the Parks in an almost unbroken flow since the University first played there, in 1881. The flow may have become a trickle in recent years but, against the odds, Oxford and Cambridge still regularly dispatch players to the counties and occasionally to Test level.

In whatever ways the University's cricket has changed the beauty of its ground has remained unspoilt. It is quite unlike any other first-class ground in atmosphere – in fact it has more affinity with the first XI ground of a school's playing-fields: no boundary advertising boards, cars or permanent seating, no marquees or entrance fee; the boundary is marked by a rope and lined by benches – in some places scattered – for the often fleeting spectator and all around are the trees and grass of the University Parks.

It is the trees that are the Parks' great quality and contribute most to the setting. Past Oxford men knew about tree-planting, as they did about most things, and looking from the pavilion to the far end of the ground the view is enclosed by a protective belt of trees of wonderful richness and variety along the Parks' perimeter; green beech, copper beech and weeping beech, horse chestnut, cedar and pine with, in front, cherries, malus and other smaller ornamental varieties. Stretching from here along the east side of the ground, beyond which flows the River Cherwell, young flowering thorn trees line the path. It is a setting at its best during the weeks of the University term around early June and which helps one to forget that on a grey, windy April or May day the Parks can be one of the coldest grounds in England.

The density of the trees along the Parks' northern perimeter has suffered in the past from Dutch Elm disease. Now gabled buildings can just be seen through the occasional gap but it hardly detracts from the scene. The most prominent buildings are in the opposite direction, looking back to the main part of the city. Fortunately they are some distance away, for the various modern ones which predominate have little, if any, architectural merit and would certainly intrude disastrously if any closer. The only one which was probably there when the University first played is Keble College chapel which, if not up to the standard of most of Oxford's University buildings, is at least bold Victorian.

The pavilion, looking down the wicket towards the trees, has all the character one would hope for. It remains virtually unchanged from when it was built in the first year the University played in the Parks, and retains many of the features one associates with the period: the tiled roof is broken by three bold gables,

each with a window and white woodwork, the central one containing the clock; beneath these a sloping tiled roof is supported by decorative wooden arches and covers the pavilion's verandah, one end of which contains the press box. The roof is surmounted by a cupola of almost absurd height and, on top, a weather-vane complete with gleaming cockerel.

Inside the pavilion is even better. The one main room has as many beams as a Jacobean hall and a fireplace as well. The walls are covered – literally, and alternative space will shortly have to be found – with oak boards whose gold lettering proclaims every University side since 1827, including 1839 when only ten players turned up for the University Match at Lord's. It is historic, warm and friendly. The batting side usually watch play from here as the dressing rooms are down below and the players have lunch happily cheek-by-jowl with an assortment of other characters, either officiating or involved with OUCC.

It is the roll-call of teams which evokes the glories of Oxford cricket. Some players reached their peak as University cricketers – often not having either the time or inclination for county cricket thereafter – while others went on to become leading figures of their generation. Typical of the former group was R. A. H. Mit-

chell, blue for four years from 1862–65, and who led Oxford to successive victories in the last three. The *Who's Who of Cricketers* comments that 'his appearances in first-class cricket were very limited, though he was regarded as one of the best batsmen of his day'.

Virtually every decade contains examples of the latter: Lord Harris and A. J. Webbe from the 1870s, L. C. H. Palairet, R. E. Foster, Plum Warner from the 1890s, as well as Oxford's most complete academic and sporting all-rounder, Charles Fry. Between the wars there were many, not least D. R. Jardine, Ian Peebles, Errol Holmes and Greville Stevens. Since the war have come D. B. Carr, Colin Cowdrey, M. J. K. Smith, A. C. Smith and Vic Marks.

One outstanding thread through Oxford's history has been the contribution of overseas players – many of them visitors to the University as Rhodes Scholars. The Nawabs of Pataudi senior and junior were among the best father and son duos ever to play for Oxford, Alan Melville later captained South Africa, Martin Donnelly, for many people the best of all Oxford batsmen, A. H. Kardar and Imran Khan – these are a selection who went on to play Test cricket.

As well as the individual players one should remember the deeds of some of the teams. That of 1884, captained by M. C. Kemp is usually considered to be the best of all time. They won seven out of eight matches – only losing to the Gentlemen – and beat Cambridge and the Australians – no other Oxford side

Above The pavilion at the Parks, with beech and poplars to one side and a small, but discerning attendance on the seats in front

has done this – when the Australians included Spofforth and Boyle, Murdoch and Bannerman. In 1900 Oxford was undefeated for the last time in a season – for either University, in fact – and R. E. Foster scored nearly 1,000 runs, including 169 v London County in the Parks when, of all impudent things, he hit W. G. for four consecutive sixes. In 1920 they were nearly as strong as the great Cambridge side, in 1959 A. C. Smith led a revival of the University's fortunes and in 1976 Vic Marks led them to their first win against Cambridge for ten years.

The pavilion is no longer the only permanent building and next to it is a characterless modern square, fortunately low enough not to obtrude, which contains – among other things – the OUCC office, usual base of Dr Simon Porter. He is Senior Treasurer and Fixture Secretary for the club and an indefatigable supporter of the University cricket, deploring the trends which harass the admission and careers of potential blues. I thought it was totally suitable that, until 1983, the club's President was the distinguished historian and cricket enthusiast, Lord Blake – the Provost of Queen's College. Since then it has been M. J. K. Smith.

On the pavilion's other side the scorers' quarters and scorebox are almost obscured by the overhanging branches of a beech tree. In contrast to the tree's rounded shape are three tall poplars farther round, in front of which is my favourite corner of the Parks, the refreshment tent. One feels it could have been there when 'Crusoe' was bowling. It is a military-style, khaki affair and inside the fare is simple to a degree: sandwiches – a limited selection – crisps, bitter or lager. The only complicated note concerns the serving of drinks; there is a 50p deposit on glass mugs, so unusually the beer is carefully measured out of the glass 'halves' into plastic pint containers.

It is not the only thing that has remained largely unchanged. Just next door a Land Rover which could have served with the Long Range Desert Group during World War Two was being loaded with grass cuttings by the groundsmen. No admission is charged; as a result

spectators just seem to appear across the meadows from any direction, and the scorecards are more expensive than usual – 30p in 1987. Indeed the scorecard reveals that the University has entered the spirit of modern cricket to the degree of having sponsors, although I was reassured to see that one was Blackwell's the bookshop.

If many of the spectators around the boundary are essentially itinerant, the stalwarts of the OUCC sit on the white benches in front of the pavilion. Many are recognizable as dons, some live locally, one or two may have sons playing. However little it spoils the picture, there is no escaping the fact that crowds are pitifully small and there is no use pretending that the cricket, like the University's other sporting activities, is of any more than minimal interest to all others than those directly involved.

However poorly supported games may be, and however many times the University may struggle to bowl out county sides who all too often run up scores of over 300 in a day, there is a certain inevitability about Oxford's cricket in the Parks – as there is about the dons' tennis which follows at the end of the summer term. It will lose neither its beauty nor its illustrious past, nor the spirit captured by Geoffrey Bolton writing about Martin Donnelly in the *World of Cricket*.

Bare figures can give no idea of the electric atmosphere in the Parks when that short, sturdy figure went in to bat. A lucky spectator might have half an hour to spare between, say, a lecture at Keble and a tutorial in Parks Road. In that half-hour he might see Donnelly hit nine boundaries, each from a different stroke . . . If Oxford were fielding the spectator's eyes would turn to cover-point. There have been great covers in cricket's history – Royle, Jessop, S. E. Gregory, Hobbs, John Gunn – but few greater than Donnelly . . . Equable of temper, modest, friendly and possessing a great gift of fun, Martin Donnelly was as popular off the field as on it. His cricket career was short: memories of it will endure.

Overleaf *The final preparations are made to the invariably excellent Parks wicket*

CAMBRIDGE

FENNER'S

Fenner's is the only first-class ground in England to emulate Lord's in taking its name from the man who initiated cricket on its turf. In 1846 F. P. Fenner leased a field to one side of Parker's Piece – where the undergraduates regularly played their cricket – from Gonville and Caius College. Two, no doubt, languid young aristocrats, their lordships Stamford and Darnley decided that they would like somewhere more private than Parker's Piece for their cricket and Fenner was approached. In 1848 he granted a sub-lease on the ground to the University club and it has been their home ever since. Although more obviously in the confines of the city than Oxford's expansive Parks, it was long admired as one of the most delightful first-class grounds.

In recent years it has lost some of its charm. The old pavilion, at the Gresham Road end of the ground, was replaced in 1972 by the present building, which was designed by a Cambridge blue, Colin Stansfield Smith. It stands at the opposite end and sadly lacks its predecessor's ornamental facade, being instead distinctly functional, built of wood and ugly modern brick.

Inside it is, however, unquestionably better appointed, for by the time of the old pavilion's demolition – it had already been badly shaken about by wartime bombs – its facilities were universally acknowledged to be little more than primitive. In the Long Room of the new one is a bar and dining-room, whose

Cricket on Parker's Piece, a 19th-century view

walls are hung – as at Oxford – with past teams of blues. Below are changing-rooms. Behind where the old pavilion stood is a low range of modern flats, only partially screened by horse chestnuts. To one side the tower and spire of Cambridge's Roman Catholic Church maintain one familiar view from the ground.

It is along the west side of the ground, behind the scorebox and press box that the most dramatic change has been imposed. Originally this was partially open, across busy Gonville Place to Parker's Piece. On this open common, where Tom Hayward and Jack Hobbs both learnt their cricket, there can be as many as eight games of cricket in progress at any one time and Hubert Doggart, blessed with a voice of stentorian power, was reputed to have once sent back his partner on Fenner's, with the result that two men were run out on Parker's Piece. Now even he would not be heard, the monolithic Kelsey Kerridge Sports Hall and a multi-storey car park having been erected in between.

While the appearance of Fenner's may have suffered a little it remains, like its Oxford counterpart, strongly charged with a sense of history. And if the leisurely glamour has gone from the cricket as it has from most aspects of university life, Fenner's continues its long-established tradition of preparing players for the counties. As recently as 1982 the University was able to boast, in Derek Pringle, an England player who was still an undergraduate. One wonders whether any of his predecessors, given the opportunity, would not have preferred to captain Cambridge in the University Match, rather than appear for England as he did. For the 1987 season two counties, Somerset and Surrey, had ex-Cambridge captains, in Peter Roebuck and Ian Greig.

From very early days the cricketers shared Fenner's with the University's athletes who, until the late 1950s used the cinder track around the boundary. Now the athletes have moved, but the University hockey and football clubs play on the outfield in winter and the hard courts of the tennis club are in one corner, screened by some extremely gloomy evergreen trees. In the days when they would have been grass Percy Chapman enjoyed beating Cambridge's number one player before going out to bat for the University.

It was during the early days of the combined cricket and athletic clubs that Fenner's most colourful non-playing figure appeared, the Rev Arthur Ward. Non-playing is not strictly accurate, for he did captain Cam-

bridge in 1854. He was, however, chiefly renowned for his support of the club off the field. One wonders how he managed to play at all, for as an undergraduate he weighed twenty stone. Merciless teasing about his bulk from the crowd during Cambridge's match against MCC at Lord's meant that he refused to appear in the University Match and controlled operations from the safety of the pavilion.

Ward was the son of the banker William Ward, who saved Lord's from becoming building land and made the then record score of 278 on the ground. After his years as an undergraduate he returned almost immediately as a curate and remained in Cambridge until his death in 1884. He was a Victorian cleric who could have been created by Anthony Trollope: undergraduates were entertained to breakfasts of salmon and champagne before matches and he devoted himself to support of the cricket club.

It was largely thanks to Ward that, on the expiry of Fenner's original lease with Caius in 1876, the cricket and athletic clubs were able to forestall any ambitions the college may have had for development and negotiate a new lease. (Finally, in the 1890s, they were able to buy the freehold.) His other major contribution was the raising of the necessary funds for a new pavilion – the one which stood until 1972. Even Edward VII was one of 1,500 people solicited for money for the new building which, once complete, was the scene of constant distribution of Ward's hospitality.

His most celebrated move, during his years as joint President and Treasurer, was to make two dogs life-members of the CUCC. They both belonged to Dr Porter the Master of Peterhouse who, taking exception to Ward's strict ban upon dogs in the pavilion, applied for the first of the two, a Dandie Dinmont named Hugo, to be elected a life-member once the proper fee had been paid. After the demise of Hugo the privilege was extended to his successor, Rollo.

Continuity at Fenner's has been perpetuated to a remarkable degree by the groundsmen, of whom there have been only four in a period of 140 years: Walter Watts, Dan Hayward, Cyril Coote and Tony Pocock. Until shortly before Hayward's retirement the grounds-man lived in the ground floor of the pavilion.

Watts presided over the golden age of Cambridge cricket, from 1870 until the turn of the century: a period which began with A. G. Steel – possibly the University's best all-rounder – in the 1870s, and went on to see Stanley Jackson, Ranji, Frank Mitchell, and Gilbert Jessop in the 1890s. Jessop incurred Watts's wrath on one occasion by bombarding with sixes the prize asparagus in his garden next to the pavilion. Distinguished

Opposite *Fenner's, the old pavilion, which is always remembered with affection*

though this quartet became, as undergraduates they were probably overshadowed by Norman Druce who scored nearly 2,500 runs in his four years as a blue.

In between there were the brotherhoods of Lyttel-tons and Studds, the latter sharing with the Ashtons of the 1920s the distinction of providing three consecutive captains of the University side. Charles Studd was the outstanding player of the three and when, in 1882, the year of brother George's captaincy, Cambridge defeated the Australians for the last time, he scored a hundred and took five wickets in an innings. Both he and George became missionaries.

1890 was a highlight which saw S. M. J. Woods captain a side which contained five future Test players. One of the most famous Fenner's sights was Gregor MacGregor standing up to the wicket for Woods's fast bowling and during that summer the University scored 703 for nine declared against Sussex at Hove.

During Dan Hayward's period as groundsman the outstanding years for the University were the early 1920s, when the three Ashton brothers – Gilbert, Hubert and Claude – all captained the side and when Percy Chapman, Arthur Gilligan and G. O. Allen were among the players. Not long afterwards, in 1927, K. S. Duleep-sinhji broke the ground record for Fenner's by scoring 254 not out against Middlesex and at the same time became the only person to score more than 250 for Cambridge.

If Fenner's reputation as a batting wicket was well established by the time Cyril Coote became groundsman in 1936, he was to extend it to unknown heights and enable the young stars of the late 1940s and early 1950s to amass great quantities of runs. In 1949 J. G. Dewes and G. H. G. Doggart made 429 for the second wicket against Essex which remains only 36 runs short of the world record.

Dewes's prolific run-scoring was matched by his opening partner in 1950, David Sheppard and against the West Indians in that year their opening stand of 343 set Cambridge on the way to a total of 594 for four declared. When the visitors batted for the rest of the match to score 730 for three, giving a match aggregate of 1,324 runs for the loss of seven wickets, Coote's ambitions for the ideal batting wickets were well and truly vindicated. Dewes and Sheppard's scoring ability was, however, by no means limited to Fenner's and in the same year of 1950 they established a Cambridge first-wicket record of 349 against Sussex at Hove.

As far as Cyril Coote was concerned – as well as groundsman he was confidant and adviser to countless grateful undergraduate cricketers until his retirement in 1980 – Peter May was the best batsman of them all. As well as his run-scoring for the University, which included 227 not out against Hampshire at Fenner's in 1950, May's years as an undergraduate saw the launch of his future career: as a freshman in 1950 he played for Surrey at the end of the summer term and the next year, aged twenty-one, he scored 138 in his first innings for England, against South Africa at Headingley.

Batsmen have continued to dominate Cambridge sides since the early 1950s: from Ted Dexter to Tony Lewis and R. M. Prideaux and J. M. Brearley who, as well as becoming Cambridge's most prolific batsman with over 4,000 runs (partly as a result of his extended career as undergraduate and post-graduate), was giving early signs of his prowess as a captain. More recently there have been Paul Parker (who scored a double-hundred as a freshman against Essex), Peter Roebuck, Matthew Fosh and Robin Boyd-Moss, who, in 1983, became the first player to score a hundred in each innings of the University Match.

There have, however, also been a handful of first-rate bowlers, not least O. S. Wheatley who, in 1958, took 80 wickets during the University's shortened season, Robin Marlar, the all-rounders Goonesena and Derek Pringle, and Philippe Edmonds.

The return of blues to play at Fenner's for the counties is always enjoyed by regular supporters of the University's cricket and when I went in 1987 to watch Cambridge play Northamptonshire the highlight for the two old boys in deck-chairs was the appearance of Robin Boyd-Moss for the visitors. 'Just like the old days to see Robin batting again' said one to the other.

It was a day which in many ways seemed to show how the University grounds differ from those of the counties, for they lack the work-a-day atmosphere of county championship cricket. Steve Coverdale, Nor-thamptonshire's secretary-manager, who played his county cricket for Yorkshire made a welcome return to Fenner's where he had been a blue for four years, playing as a last-minute replacement and during the visitors' innings Richard Williams, their diminutive all-rounder took the opportunity to indulge in the expert art of fly-tying on one of the pavilion tables.

Outside the atmosphere was equally relaxed, hand-fuls of undergraduates wheeled in and out on bicycles, while others lay on the grass around the boundary, some – usually the men – watching the cricket, others – the girls – more often reading books. As at the Parks, stalwarts of the club sit on the tiered benches in front of the pavilion, discussing the iniquity and stupidity of admissions policies and longing for the days when young men could go up and get a blue and not bother to take a degree.

Looking across Fenner's to the flats standing behind the site of the old pavilion, with the spire of the Roman Catholic church in the background

INDEX